KT-294-402

M
Managing
Sustainable
Development

This

WITHDRAWN
FROM
UNIVERSITIES
AT
MEDWAY
LIBRARY

1566334

Managing
sustainable
development

UNIVERSITY OF GREENWICH LIBRARY

WITHDRAWN

333.
715
CAR

Michael Carley and Ian Christie

EARTHSCAN

Earthscan Publications Ltd, London

First published 1992 by
Earthscan Publications Ltd
120 Pentonville Road, London N1 9JN

Reprinted 1994

Copyright © 1992 Michael Carley and Ian Christie

All rights reserved

British Library Cataloguing-in-Publication Data:

A catalogue record for this book is available from the British Library

ISBN 1-85383-129-8

Typeset by DP Photosetting, Aylesbury, Bucks
Printed and bound by Clays Ltd, St Ives plc

Earthscan Publications Ltd is an editorially independent subsidiary of Kogan Page Ltd
publishing in association with the International Institute for Environment and
Development and the World Wide Fund for Nature (UK).

Contents

List of tables

List of figures

Acknowledgements

We would like to thank several people who provided inspiration and assistance in the preparation of this book. They are not, of course, responsible for the views advanced in this book, and any errors are entirely our own. Thanks to: Dr Mayer Hillman, London; John Davidson, Groundwork Foundation, Birmingham; Dr Martin Odei, Institute of Aquatic Biology, Ghana; Professor E E Okun and Dr W Odofin, Ministry of Science and Technology, Nigeria; Dr S Silangwa and Chris Mwasile, National Council for Scientific Research, Zambia; Dr Andrew Mathuthu, Chemistry Department, University of Zimbabwe; Professor J Manrakhan, Vice-Chancellor, and Dr Kishor Baguant, School of Engineering, University of Mauritius; Dr Abu Bakar Jaafar and Hasmah Harun, Department of Environment, Malaysia; Dr Walter Chin, Guyana Agency for Health Sciences Education, Environment and Food Policy; Dr S Varadarajan, Consultancy Development Centre, India; Dr Ray Zammit, Office of the Parliamentary Secretary for the Environment, Malta; Michaela Smith, Commonwealth Consultative Group on Technology Management, London; Dr Alexander King, past President, Club of Rome; Dr Dominique Levieil, of the fisheries management section of the European Community; Dr Joop Rodenberg, Shipping Research Bureau, Amsterdam; Professor Bill Rees, School of Community and Regional Planning, and Professor Brahm Wiesman, Centre for Human Settlements, both at the University of British Columbia; Professor Keith Banting, Queens University, Ontario; Patricia Carley, US State Department, Washington; Dr Susan Sherry, Growth Management Consensus Project, California State University; Dr Joan Wilson Anderson, Southern California Water Committee; Dr Christopher Moore, CDR Associates, Boulder, Colorado; and Michael Chapman, San Francisco.

We would also like to thank our families: Sarah, Nicholas, Thea and Judy, who are not only 'green' but also very patient.

Michael Carley and Ian Christie
London, 1992

Preface

The argument of this book is straightforward. We believe that, unwittingly, our unequivocal acceptance of industrial growth and expansion has brought us to a threshold in the earth's ability to absorb pollution and in the exploitation of its scarce resources. These resources include air, fresh water, the seas, the land, and many human cultures. There is nothing new in this observation, and we do not intend to dwell on it in the book. Following the report of the Brundtland Commission, the need for change is discussed in terms of 'sustainable' development, but there is little agreement on what it means or how to achieve it.

Our ability to affect the environment is matched by an inability to assess the consequences of our actions, as we come to realise that natural and human processes are inextricably intertwined. To what end, we no longer know. We must now develop some realistic guidelines on means of achieving genuinely sustainable development and enhancing the quality of our relationship with the planet. What is required is good environmental management on a global scale, which means on national, regional and community scales as well. The issue is complicated by the fact that environmental problems have arisen largely because of the cumulative effects of industrial development in and by the 'developed' countries. The North in general, and the West in particular, has become rich at the expense of the planet. Therefore the industrialising countries of the Third World are insisting with justification that they are owed economic and technological recompense for this unfair situation. This intensifies the North–South debate.

The situation is also complicated by rapid world population growth. By the end of the twenty-first century world population will have doubled from its present 5 billion to between 10 and 14 billion. The growth will be almost entirely in the developing countries.

All this suggests that environmental management is about far more than biophysical manipulation and control – it concerns the mutually beneficial management of the humankind–nature interaction to ensure environmental and social quality for future generations. This kind of environmental management begins with a sense of collective vision about the future, and continues with difficult decisions about the appropriate balance between industrial production, consumption and environmental quality. The nature of these decisions means that the realisation of sustainable development, however defined and on whatever scale, is an intensely political process involving continual trade-offs between economic, social and biophysical needs and objectives. It is a political process of mediation in which old Right–Left thinking is largely irrelevant. This is the human dimension in environmental management.

The challenge of sustainable development is also made more complex by three recent developments in the world's political economy. The first is the rapid demise of the socialist experiment, and the spread of what the World Bank calls 'market friendly' policies, under terms such as structural adjustment. Market friendly policies imply a reduced role for the public sector in countries of all political hues, and new freedoms from state control for entrepreneurs ranging from those in multi-national corporations to what in Malaysia are called 'backyard' industries. While such freedoms make a proven contribution to economic growth, and may help redistribute growth to the world's poorer regions, they may not be compatible with sustainable development. The question remains to be answered.

A second development is that the spread of economic liberalism is being accompanied by a Westernisation of the world, in terms of the adoption of Western science and technology, and the spread of liberal democratic ideas. Democratic notions are deeply attractive for many reasons, but it is dangerous to conflate political and economic liberalism. At the extreme, one recently popular kind of liberalism is utilitarian, laisez–faire capitalism, represented by 'Reaganomics', which is incompatible with sustainable development.

A third development is that both economic and political liberalisation are accompanied by a rapid spread of what has been called the ideology of consumerism, or 'Coca-Cola/Sony culture', spread by word of mouth and by advances in communication, such as the rapid spread of television following rural electrification, and now CNN–style satellite TV. Increase in the worldwide flow of advertising has led to a heightened awareness in developing countries of how the rich world lives, and legitimate desires to share in those lifestyles and standards of living. For example, it is likely that increased prosperity in Asia will double the number of automobiles in the world (from the current 500 million vehicles) in the next 30 years, with dramatic environmental consequences.

The result of these trends is that just when we are reaffirming the dominance and efficacy of capitalist industrialism as the means to economic growth, we also need to question the fundamental assumptions behind this dominant mode of social organisation, in terms of its implications for sustainable development. We are not implying, of course, that answers to all these grand questions are likely to emerge from this book. As we will see, the tension between individualist entrepreneurialism and the need for social control in pursuit of the greater, public good has been a focus of unresolved debate since the seventeenth century. We are no closer to a resolution. On the contrary, we suggest that there are no grand answers and that, instead, environmental managers will need to 'muddle through', but in a much more sensitive and reflective manner than has been the norm. Sustainable development will be an ongoing, cumulative process, rather than an 'end-product', based on millions of right decisions at all levels of management from the global to the local.

Constructive responses to environmental crisis are threefold. The first requirement is continuing philosophical and moral debate about the appropriate nature of sustainable development, North-South relations, and the need to empower local communities to manage their own futures. The second is for the development of human resources and organisational capacity for environmental management, linking governments, business and community groups in a sense of common purpose. The third requirement is for fundamental research and development, especially in energy, agriculture and manufacturing processes.

This book makes some contribution to the first two requirements and none to the third. Our focus is on the constraints to improved human resource management and organisational capacity, and the means to improve that capacity. We believe improvements in environmental management skills, encompassing the human dimension, are not only possible, but that they are beginning to surface in many different countries. This book is intended to help promote better practice in environmental management. We have drawn partly on recent thinking in business management, public administration and organisational development, but mostly on our knowledge of, and involvement in, some notable existing innovations in environmental management. These innovations in practice, mainly from Europe, Africa and North America, are documented in the fifth section of the book.

It is these case studies which illustrate what we call the action-centred network approach to environmental management. As we will show, such networks focus on tangible challenges of environment and development. They work at a number of levels: as growing constituencies for sustainable development, seen as an on-going political process of mediation and consensus; as new partnerships between government, business and non-governmental or community groups; and as groups of natural and social scientists and public administrators with a commitment to mutual learning to develop new management skills.

As the case studies show, the network approach works by turning constraints on environmental management into opportunities for sustainable development. It also involves a substantially revised definition of management. This replaces the idea of control by a few people with that of negotiation and organisational learning. In this model, many relevant participants, or stakeholders, attempt to arrange their mutual affairs in a manner which is in harmony with nature and with each other. In this definition, *management is teamwork* based on a continually evolving consensus on the direction towards sustainable development. This more egalitarian, participative approach to management is fundamental to the idea of an action-centred network. It also renders obsolete some common, but divisive, distinctions, such as the idea of 'developed' and 'developing' countries, for reasons set out in Chapter 2.

OUTLINE OF THE BOOK

The book consists of five parts. Part I looks at the main trends in the world over the next 50 years, and their likely environmental consequences. These include: population growth, industrialisation and urbanisation, changes in land use and ground cover, and what we call globalisation effects. Chapter 2 looks at the nature of sustainable development: whether it is compatible with economic growth, the idea of carrying capacity and the limitations of market economics. The chapter goes on to consider the relationship of world trends, particularly the momentum of industrialism, to political change on a world scale: the collapse of communism, the recent 'market revolution' embodied in such terms as 'structural adjustment', and the rise of a world culture of consumerism. The implications for the notion of sustainable development are considered.

Part II looks at patterns of thought and action deeply ingrained within the Western industrial model of development. Sources from the Enlightenment onwards are examined to help us understand the relationship of individuals with industrial societies, and that of humankind with nature and its embodiment in our economic systems. Factors considered include our perceptions of nature, our ambivalent relationship with science and technology, and emerging perceptions on humankind and nature which are likely to be influential in the next century.

This section also looks at the political assumptions of Westernisation and 'market-friendly' policies, and their implications for the management of sustainable development. We consider the possibility of 'excessive individualism', the relationship between the individual and the state, and the implications of neo–conservatism.

Part III turns to the present organisation of world business and finance, the emerging global culture of industrial consumption and consumerism, and the implications of these for sustainable development. Factors considered include: the globalisation of the industrial economy, the nature of consumerism and advertising, and North–South inequalities in trade and other resource flows.

In Chapter 6, these 'top-down' economic arrangements are contrasted with growing need for 'bottom-up' local participation, both to fulfil democratic aspirations and for effectiveness in developing and implementing policy in environmental management. The tension between centralisation and decentralisation is indentified as a major challenge to sustainable development and environmental management. Proposals that radical decentralisation could foster sustainable development are analysed.

Part IV turns to the potential of innovative management approaches to contribute to sustainable development. Chapter 7 reviews the main institutional and organisational constraints on 'integrated' environmental management. Chapter 8 considers management in conditions of endemic turbulence and uncertainty, and the potential role of networks in environmental management, including policy, issue, professional and producer networks. These are contrasted with the action-centred network, which links government, business and voluntary organisations in problem solving and mobilisation of resources. In this approach, conflict is seen as opportunity for innovation, based on 'action learning' strategies within networks. Chapter 9 describes the assumptions and methods of working in action-centred networks.

Part V comprises four case studies in environmental management, which illustrate the action–centred network approach in the industrialised and developing worlds. The projects and methods these case studies describe work at different geographic levels: local or neighbourhood (the Groundwork Trusts in Britain); regional (watershed management in Ghana, Zambia and Zimbabwe, waste management in Lagos and Kuala Lumpur, and resource management in Mauritius and Guyana); provincial or state (the California Growth Management Consensus Project); and national (the National Environmental Policy planning process in the Netherlands).

PART I
Introduction

1 The ecology of an industrial planet

. . . there is no 'natural habitat', in the sense of a terrestrial ecosystem that has evolved without the presence of a human element. There is only the choice between different methods and forms of human involvement in the habitat.

T Swanson and E Barbier, 1992[1]

In terms of the life of the earth, two hundred years is the merest flicker of time. Yet within the past two centuries the rise of industrialism has transformed the planet in ways that natural processes and previous civilisations would have taken millennia to achieve. In this short time we have wrought dramatic changes in the environment, the most far-reaching being our effect on the chemistry of the atmosphere and the genetic diversity of the planet. These changes have given rise to fear of a global environmental crisis, and to calls for a shift from exploitative industrialism to something called 'sustainable' development.

In Chapter 2 we consider what kind of development can be defined as sustainable. Here, we review global social trends and negative environmental consequences likely to lead to unsustainable development in the next half century. These constitute the first of a series of constraints on sustainable development explored in this book.

This chapter can do no more than provide a brief overview of global environmental issues: many comprehensive sources are available.[2] Our purpose is to explore the scale of major challenges to sustainable development, to give some idea of their interactions and to set the stage for discussion about how we might improve environmental management. This book is about the *processes* of environmental decision-making and implementation, the assumptions and values that underlie these processes, and how they can be improved to lead to sustainable development.

MAJOR SOCIOECONOMIC TRENDS AND SUSTAINABLE DEVELOPMENT

Figure 1.1 outlines some major world trends and their consequences. The trends are not necessarily malign in themselves, whereas the consequences we have listed always are. So for example, we do not immediately interpret as negative: population growth, industrialisation, the growth of cities, the shift of land from forestry to agriculture, or the increased mobility offered by the automobile or global air transport. Population growth can be easily accommodated in some eco-systems; many countries need industrialisation to alleviate poverty; for many people an urban life-style is preferable to the limitations of rural life; almost everybody wishes to travel; and so on. On the face of it, there is nothing intrinsically wrong with these facts and aspirations.

The key issue for sustainable development is the magnitude of the changes induced by the trends listed above. There is a 'technocentric' school of thought which suggests that the negative consequences of these trends can be overcome or managed; and that human technological prowess will allow indefinite economic growth, population

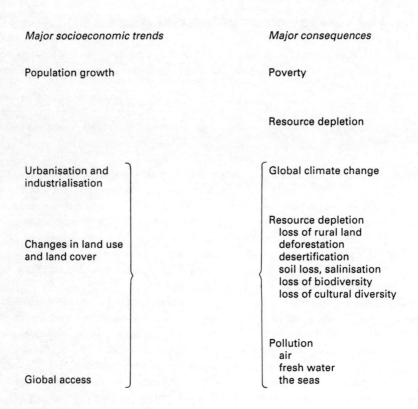

Figure 1.1 *Major world socioeconomic trends and consequences*

increase and rise in living standards.[3] However, this perspective fails to take sufficient account of the delicate balance of complex ecosystems, and the possibility of dynamic negative changes being triggered by excessive human growth. For example:

- the current world population growth of 91 million people per year virtually ensures poverty, undernourishment and resource depletion in many ecosystems;
- industrialism on the current fossil-fuel burning model is unsustainable in atmospheric terms;
- a certain amount of urbanisation is manageable, but not on the scale of the more than 22 million people predicted for 2000 in São Paulo;
- the 400 million people driving cars are precipitating local crises of congestion and

pollution, and the 800 million cars predicted for 2010 will contribute greatly to global pollution problems;[4]

- deforestation on a massive scale is eroding the earth's built-in adjustment mechanisms in many areas.

Similarly, a small number of tourists on a Greek or a Caribbean island can be a boon to local life, and even provide an economic basis for sustainable development. But when tourists outnumber local people by ten to one, and foreign travel companies package both local economy and local culture for sale, a threshold has been exceeded, and negative effects begin to pile up for all concerned. In every case, the magnitude of change is too great. Critical, if unknown, thresholds have been exceeded and the situation is no longer amenable to beneficial local management. Usually, thresholds for sustainability – carrying capacities – are substantially exceeded even before we become aware of the nature of the problem.

The situation is made more complex and intractable because the trends and their consequences are highly interactive in a manner that is difficult to identify and measure, and sometimes even difficult to imagine. So, for example, urbanisation is partly a result of, and partly a cause of, migration from countryside to city. The urbanisation process itself generates economic activities which raise income levels, draw in resources from the countryside and even from faraway savannahs and rainforests, and generate enormous amounts of waste which end up as pollution of air, water and land. The increased income generates more consumption, more industry, more pollution, more automobility, urban sprawl, endemic traffic congestion, and so on. Urban sprawl results in loss of prime farmland which, when combined with rural population growth, contributes to lowland forest loss due to agricultural expansion in the countryside well away from the city, thus completing a cycle of interaction. These processes are rapidly unfolding, but our responses to date fail to match the size of the problem.

Relationships between such trends and their consequences are not merely distinctions on a continuum of 'good' to 'bad' environmental effects: they are the very stuff of debate over the nature of sustainable development and the future of the planet. They go to the heart of our values and assumptions about how much of the earth's finite resources we are individually entitled to consume, and to our views on how much resource depletion is allowable in a sustainable framework. They are also important because there has been little public debate about the *meaning* of sustainable development. It is perhaps most important to acknowledge that, given the political and economic constraints on environmental policy, progress towards sustainability will have to be incremental rather than revolutionary. This means that the best time to start doing something, and then to learn from what we are doing, is now.

THE MAJOR TRENDS AND CONSEQUENCES

Population growth and poverty

Between 1850 and 1950 the world's population doubled from 1.25 billion to 2.5 billion. By 1987 it had doubled again, and by the year 2000 another billion will have been added. Estimates for the next hundred years range from a total population of

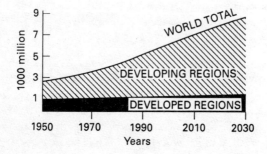

Figure 1.2 *World population growth, 1950–2030*
Source: Mannnion[2]

8 to 14 billion before a levelling off takes place. This rapidly rising rate of population growth reflects progress in the form of increased life expectancy and improved health care. It also implies a rapid increase in pressure on the earth's resources and food producing systems.[5] In 2000, 80 per cent of the world's population will live in developing countries, 37 of which have population growth rates in excess of three per cent per annum (Figure 1.2). Most of these countries are in Africa, where populations are expected to double from around 647 million to about 1500 million around 2020. By that date the population of Nigeria will have risen from 112 to 274 million, and that of Kenya from 23 to 79 million. In the same period, the population of India is predicted to grow from about 850 million to 1400 million.

Approximately one-fifth of the world's population (about a billion people) lives in absolute poverty, defined as per capita income of less than UK£206 (US$370) per year. Population growth, environmental degradation and poverty are closely related, and agricultural production is the decisive influence on the evolution of rural poverty.[6] The relationship is demonstrated clearly in Tables 1.1 and 1.2. Of particular note is the rise of the incidence of poverty and undernourishment in Africa during this period. In Asia, the situation is more complex. Significant improvements in agricultural production and technology have led to increased agricultural productivity in many nations. But this has not been sufficient to prevent a rise in the absolute number of people living in poverty, despite a fall in the proportion of people in poverty.

Population growth, combined with land and soil degradation, means that the situation is not likely to improve in the foreseeable future. According to the United Nations Food and Agriculture Organization, the amount of arable land in developing countries will fall from 0.85 to 0.6 hectares per person between 1980 and 2000. New land will be brought into production, but much of this land will be of poor quality and only briefly useful because it comes from deforestation or the cultivation of hillsides.[7] As much as seven million hectares of arable land is lost to soil erosion each year. If the effects of soil erosion, salinity, overgrazing and water shortages are added, the FAO suggests that 245 million hectares will go out of production by 2025. By then

Table 1.1 *Trends in absolute poverty in lower income countries*[1]

Country group	Incidence of poverty (%)		No. of poor (millions)	
	1970	1985	1970	1985
All developing countries[2]				
Total	52	44	944	1 156
Rural	59	49	767	850
Urban	35	32	177	306
Latin America				
Total	40	36	116	146
Rural	62	45	75	57
Urban	25	32	41	89
Africa				
Total	46	49	166	273
Rural	50	58	140	226
Urban	32	29	26	47
Asia[2]				
Total	56	43	662	737
Rural	61	47	552	567
Urban	42	34	110	170

[1] The absolute poverty line is the income level below which a nutritionally adequate diet and essential non-food items are not affordable.   [2] Excluding China.

Source: United Nations, Department of International Economic and Social Affairs, as reported in United Nations: *1989 report on the world social situation* (New York, 1989), table 24, p. 39; cited in[6].

Table 1.2 *Trends in undernutrition in lower income countries*

Country group	Incidence of undernutrition (%)			No. of undernourished (millions)		
	1969–71	1979–81	1983–85	1969–71	1979–81	1983–85
Developing market economies	27.0	21.8	21.5	460	475	512
Latin America	18.5	14.6	14.2	51	52	55
Sub-Saharan Africa	32.6	30.6	35.2	86	110	142
Near East	22.9	10.8	9.1	41	25	24
Asia	28.7	23.5	21.8	281	288	291

Note: Estimates cover a total of 89 developing countries and exclude China and other centrally planned economies in Asia. The figures reported above relate to the alternative which sets the minimum calorie requirement levels for adults and adolescents at 1.4 times the basal metabolic rate (BMR). Estimates using 1.2 times the BMR as the cut-off point result in lower figures but show similar trends.

Source: FAO: *The impact of development strategies on the rural poor* (Rome, 1988), table 8, p. 115. cited in[6].

there will be no new high quality arable land available. If existing trends in fertility and farming continue, the gap between Africa's food needs and its agricultural output will grow from 15 million tonnes of cereals in 1992 to 200 million tonnes by 2020, roughly equivalent to the USA's current annual cereal harvest.[8]

In many rural areas of the developing world, rapidly increasing populations put pressure on limited natural resources. Fuel wood demand and slash–and–burn cultivation, often alongside new roads, have resulted in deforestation, deterioration of soil quality, erosion and downstream flooding. The pressure extends out to sea, with extensive overfishing and destruction of coral reefs. To compound the problem, large farms producing export crops such as coffee, sugar, bananas, cotton and cattle, destined for industrial countries, have in many places displaced small farmers growing food for local consumption.

The implications of these trends are disturbing. Sir Crispin Tickell (former UK Ambassador to the UN) notes that the distribution of world population corresponds less and less to the distribution of the earth's resources.[9] In the industrial countries labelled 'developed', industrialisation was sustained by an agricultural revolution which greatly increased food production, and those countries had substantial natural resources. The same cannot be said for much of the industrialising world: in many cases there has been no agricultural revolution to sustain an industrial society, and urban poverty is growing.

Land degradation

Deforestation

Living forests absorb carbon dioxide from the atmosphere and store carbon, thus reducing the the build–up of greenhouse gases that contribute to global climate change. Industrial timber cutting is reported by the World Resources Institute to be a major cause of primary forest destruction in both temperate and tropical ecosystems.[10] Having expanded by more than 50 per cent since 1965, the world's annual commercial timber harvest supports a trade in forest products of US$85 billion. Logging in the tropics, for example, degrades 4.5 million hectares annually but also opens up woodlands to clearing by ranchers and farmers, which is a major direct cause of forest loss. When forests are burned, they release carbon, thus accelerating the build–up of greenhouse gases in the atmosphere.

Tropical forests account for half of the world's forested land. In their natural state, tropical forests are the most productive of the earth's ecosystems. They harbour the widest diversity of plant and animal species, and produce two or three times as much organic matter as temperate forests.[11] In an area of 10 hectares in Sarawak, Malaysia, 780 tree species have been found.[12] Tropical forests also supply many products including fruits, vegetables, bush meat, nuts, oils, spices, medicines, fibres, resins, tannins, honey, firewood and building materials.[13] The economic value of these sustainable resources is rarely considered in decisions about logging. The most rapid rates of deforestation in the tropics are in the rainforests: in Africa 72 per cent of rainforests have gone, almost entirely cut for timber exports.[14] There is also significant deforestation in savannah woodlands.

Estimates of the rates of deforestation vary, but those in Table 1.3 are said to be

Table 1.3 *Estimates of the extent and rates of tropical deforestation*

	Extent (millions of hectares)			Rates of deforestation (millions of hectares per annum)					
	Land Area[1]	Area of forest & woodland[2]	Area of forest and woodland as a % of total Land area[2]	Closed forests				Open woodlands[2]	
				All Tropical[2]		Moist Tropical[3]			
				Area	% of total	Area	% of total	Area	% of total
Africa	2190	896	40	1.33	0.61	1.20	0.59	2.34	0.48
Asia & Pacific	945	410	43	1.82	0.59	1.61	0.61	0.19	0.61
Latin America	1680	1067	64	4.12	0.61	3.30	0.54	1.27	0.59

Sources: cited in[2].

reliable by Mannion, who comments that these 'illustrate that the area already affected is immense and that average rates of deforestation in these regions are sufficiently high that there is a real danger that the forests will disappear altogether in the next 200 years'.[15] The implication of continued deforestation is that about 1.2 million species, a quarter of all those existing in the 1980s, will disappear by the year 2020. In addition to habitat loss and species extinction, the environmental effects of deforestation include soil degradation, water run-off and erosion. In the Philippines in 1991, the death and destitution of many thousands of people in flash floods was attributed to deforestation. In El Salvador, three-quarters of the country is said to suffer from erosion, and complete deforestation is imminent.[16]

The most significant reasons for deforestation, in addition to industrial logging, are: plantation agriculture, (with crops such as oil palm); large scale cattle ranching; mineral extraction; road and dam construction; and shifting small-scale agriculture and fuelwood collection. The exact contribution of each factor is debatable.

In Amazonia and Central America the establishment of large scale cattle ranches to meet North American demand for beef have made a significant contribution to deforestation. Prance suggests it is by far the largest cause of forest loss in Amazonia.[17] In Amazonia during 1965–1983, the establishment of 470 cattle ranches of an average size of 23,000 hectares accounted for 30 per cent of the total deforestation.[18] The schemes have resulted in rapid loss of soil fertility. The government subsidy regime at the time encouraged further clearance, rather than investment in land maintenance. Ranching is also linked to road building and mineral extraction, in what can amount to a subsidised industrialisation package for the rainforest. Figure 1.3 shows the relationship between road building and deforestation in Rondonia, Brazil.

Mining also plays a role. In the Grande Carajas region of Brazil, project subsidy for an iron mine from the World Bank and the European Community is resulting in the clearance of 30,000 square kilometres of forest for ranching, iron mining, road and rail construction and the establishment of heavy industry. A further 15,000 square

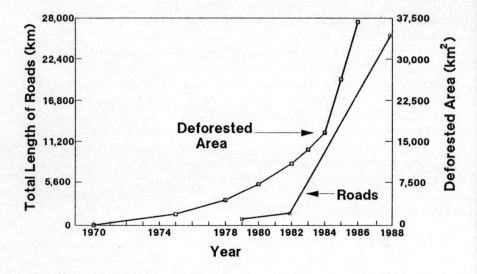

Figure 1.3 *Road development and deforestation, Rondonia, Brazil 1968–1988*
Source: Southworth et al, after Frohn et al[63].

kilometres is cleared each year to provide charcoal for pig iron smelters along 900km of new railway connected to a deep water port.

A report of a Committee of the European Parliament, prepared in 1990, expresses alarm over the possibility of the Community funding a process of 'industrial colonization' in Grande Carajas which results in a:

> massive onslaught on virgin forests in the regions through the Grande Carajas Programme, partly because charcoal is used to fuel blast furnaces for smelting and reducing Carajas ores to produce pig iron, [which] could be extended even further and result in the destruction of 100000 sq km of forest.[19]

The Committee goes on to note that in the Minas Gerais region, which had supplied pig iron to Europe for some time, the forest destruction is now so extensive that no more charcoal can be had; and that the life of the Amerindian communities in the region had been 'severely disrupted'. The report notes that it is not so much the direct environmental impacts of project funding as the indirect effects that are likely to 'trigger a disaster'.

The report of the EC Parliamentary Committee follows a resolution of concern of the Parliament, passed in 1989, which:

> held it to be unacceptable for the Community to leave supervision of the environmental impact of the projects to institutions, such as the World Bank, which did not enjoy an unblemished environmental reputation, particularly in Brazil which is racked by environmental problems and concerns.[20]

However, in spite of the obvious concern of the European Parliament, the Community has started to import from Carajas, pig iron which was produced using charcoal obtained from virgin Amazon forest. This case highlights a process of initial industrialisation, and the linkages in the world economy that give rise to the rapidity and intensity of environmental impacts. Chapter 5 considers these connections in more detail.

Although tropical deforestation is now highly controversial in the West, and has aroused public alarm, it is important to note two points. First, the tropical countries are merely emulating a process of deforestation, and conversion of land to agriculture, which the northern countries have carried nearly to completion, and which has contributed to their economic advancement. Virtually all of Europe's virgin forests have disappeared over many centuries, cleared for agriculture and/or to fuel the industrial revolution, replaced by a few species in intensive and unsightly plantations. In the continental United States, the same process began in the nineteenth century, and less than 5 per cent of primary forest is now intact. For example, 96 per cent of virgin redwoods have been logged, most in the past 40 years. In Canada, logging is a major industry and source of income, employment and 'stumpage' royalties to government. At current rates of harvesting, the last stands of Canadian old-growth temperate rainforest will disappear in 15 years, well before the last of the Amazonian rainforest vanishes.[21]

Second, the loss of forests is largely attributable to the failures of markets and governments in the industrial world to place adequate value on the goods and ecological services they provide.[22] Whether or not the near-total destruction of virgin forest in Europe and North America, and its replacement with plantation forest, is sustainable behaviour is open to debate. However, clearly a voracious appetite for wood products in the industrialised countries, increased by market signals that do not reflect environmental costs and values, is a main cause of world deforestation. Furthermore, the industrialised countries themselves are not only importing timber, but arranging, funding and profiting from deforestation. In countries such as Malaysia, Indonesia, Guyana and Honduras, major logging and plantation forest concessions have been sold to Japanese and American logging and paper firms.

Desertification

Desertification is more controversial in terms of its possible connection to man–made change. There is dispute as to whether normal cyclical drought causes land degradation, or whether drought itself is caused by reduced vegetation due to mismanagement, such as over-grazing or fuel wood collection, to the point of becoming self-perpetuating. For example, Calder argues that remote sensing shows the idea of Sahelian desertification south of the Sahara to be a 'far-fetched' assertion that can be explained by the region's normal but highly variable rates of rainfall.[23] Mannion recognises the uncertainty in the debate over the Sahel, but says that there is a significant problem in regions adjacent to many of the world's hot arid zones, and including rain-fed croplands, irrigated lands and rangelands in China, Southern Africa, Pakistan, Australia, Argentina, North America and in a number of former Soviet republics. Most available evidence, he argues, 'points to human activity as the more important catalyst' and he cites 170,000 square kilometres of man-made desertification in China since 1920.[24] As for the effects, Myers suggests that 10 per cent of the 700 million people in arid and semi-arid zones are becoming impoverished and that about 12 million hectares are degraded annually to the point that they become agriculturally unproductive.[25] Other sources put the figure much higher.

Salt intrusion

This is a process of land degradation associated with irrigation caused by the leaching of salts out of the soil in irrigated fields. In extreme cases the land has to be abandoned. Some 12 per cent of the world's cultivated land is irrigated, about 300 million hectares, and about half is reported to be affected by salination to the point of reducing crop yields. For example, in Pakistan more than 65 per cent of the country's irrigated land is affected; in Egypt, Iraq and India the figure is about 35 per cent. Salination of surface waters and soils is reported as a significant problem in the United States, where 25–35 per cent of irrigated land is said to be affected, and in Australia and Israel.[26]

A dramatic case of salt intrusion is associated with cotton production in Soviet central Asia and the shrinking of the land-locked Aral Sea. Until about 1960, when irrigation began, the Aral Sea contained about 10 billion tons of salt. But as the rivers that feed the sea were diverted for irrigation, the water inflow fell below the evaporation rate, and the sea began to shrink. It has now lost 60 per cent of its water, and 40 per cent of its surface area, and its coastline has retreated as much as 30 miles. A windblown salt/sand mix is being deposited on the surrounding farmland, villages and towns at the rate of about half a tonne per hectare per year.[27] The increased salt content in the air and water has sharply reduced the amount of available drinking water in the region. This water already contains large amounts of pesticides and fertilizer residues, which have given rise to an increased number of birth defects and other forms of ill-health.[28] The general effects of salination are that:

> Once living villages are becoming ghost towns as the Aral continues to disappear. Because of the rapid growth in the amount of salt in the sea itself, crops are being ruined . . . and livestock are starving without grass to feed on, in addition to the effects . . . on the people's health.[29]

Loss of wetlands and valleys

Wetlands are intensely important as habitats to waterfowl, fish and other species, as filters for pollution and as buffers for floodwaters. Their loss to urban sprawl or tourist development is another factor in land degradation. The loss of wetlands can be seen as largely the result of 'intersectoral policy inconsistency', leading to systemic failures of markets and economic regulators to recognise the value of the ecological services the areas perform.[30] All too often, wetlands have been regarded as areas for conversion to other uses – which may be of dubious long term value compared with the functions performed by the original ecosystems.

In the United States, 54 per cent of all wetlands have disappeared. For example, in North Carolina, developers and farmers drained more than 10,000 acres of the Great Dismal Swamp in the 1980s, despite federal laws intended to protect wetlands, and water extraction by urban areas threatens the rest. In Spain, the 77,000 hectares of the Coto Doñana, one of Europe's finest wetlands, is under grave threat from the proposed construction of hotels to accommodate 30,000 tourists.[31]

Hydroelectric projects are a controversial source of energy and land loss associated with industrial growth. In the past 40 years, the amount of water behind large dams has increased 25–fold to 5000 cubic kilometres, roughly 13 per cent of the total runoff of rivers to the ocean. Pearce suggests this is 'a substantial interruption to the planet's hydrological cycle'.[32] For example, the proposed Chisapani dam in Nepal would generate 11,000 megawatts of 'clean' power, but at a price of the flooding of 125 miles of fertile valley and the displacement of 70,000 people.[33] This is part of a grand scheme of 12 dams which would generate 90,000 megawatts of power, almost all of which would be exported to the industrial areas of India's northeast. India itself plans three dams more than 800 feet high in the valleys of the Ganges and Brahmaputra rivers.

Some scientists suggest that large dams are a case of Northern technology inappropriately exported via multi- and bilateral aid and loans to developing countries. The problems include:

- the accumulation of silt, often at 10 to 20 times the predicted rate;
- short reservoir lifespan for this reason;
- the threat of catastrophe in earthquake zones;
- the flooding of scarce fertile land, forcing resettlement of tens of thousands of people; and
- the alteration of natural flood cycles, which can have dramatic downstream effects.[34]

In Colombia, the capacity of the Anchicaya Reservoir was reduced by siltation from five million to one million cubic metres in just 12 years. The Aswan Dam resulted in the annual loss of 100 million tonnes of sediment for fertilizer, now replaced by chemicals; erosion of the Mediterranean coastline by 2km in places; and destruction of Egypt's Mediterranean fishery.[35]

Many other large dams are proposed: there is hardly a large river system left on the planet which is without its grand scheme. Among the most significant proposals is for ten dams on the major rivers in China including the largest dam in the world at Three Gorges on the Yangtze River. The project will displace up to 1.7 million people.[36]

Urbanisation

While world population has increased five-fold in the past 200 years, the number of people living in urban areas has increased five times more. Within the next decade, half the world's population will be living in cities, and during the twenty-first century a more uniform level of urbanisation will spread around the globe, tending toward the 75 per cent levels of urbanisation prevalent in industrialised countries. This implies a virtual reversal of the current ratio of urban to rural population in developing countries, where 70 per cent of people still live in rural areas.[37] Because of their sheer scale and complexity, the problems of managing big cities and urban regions will be increasingly severe in the next century. In cities, people tend to consume more resources per capita and to produce more wastes than their counterparts in rural areas. Cities as different as Lagos and Toronto are now engaged in a desperate search for somewhere to dump the daily outpouring of garbage.

It is in the developing world that the urbanisation of the twenty-first century will occur. By the turn of the century, 8 of the 10 most populous cities, and 21 of the 25 most populous cities, will be in developing countries (Figure 1.4). The number of cities in developing countries with a population of one million or more will increase from 119 in 1980 to 279 in the year 2000 and 486 in 2025.[38] The movement from the countryside this implies will constitute one of the great mass migrations in world history.

In India for example, rural poverty and caste are forcing many people, especially the unskilled and the landless, to seek employment in the larger cities. Lack of successful land reform, and improved transport, encourage this movement. Bombay grew by 2.3 million people to 10 million in the decade between 1971 and 1981, with Delhi and Calcutta experiencing similar growth rates. Nearly half of Bombay's population live in what are officially categorised as slums, in dwellings made of tin, bits of wood or old sacks, often adjoining a main road or railway track.[39] About one million of Bombay's residents live on the streets. The strains on human services and physical infrastructure are severe, and air and water pollution, waste disposal problems and health problems are endemic. Bombay's population is expected to grow to 15 million by the year 2000.

Industrialisation

Urbanisation invariably sustains industrial developments that generate economic growth and provide much-needed employment, but also contribute to air and water pollution and ill-health. The unchecked pollution and damage to public health experienced in the original wave of industrialisation in Western Europe has been repeated in every nation embarking on the path to industrialism. At the extreme are environmental catastrophes such as Bhophal, responsible for the death of more than 4000 people; and the environmental devastation centred on heavy industrial complexes throughout the ex-Communist states of Eastern Europe and the former Soviet Union. But much of the current process of industrialisation is the result of inward foreign investment, or the growth of small and medium enterprises, over which it is difficult to exert pollution control. Taiwan, for example, has more than 80,000 small factories, responsible for its rapid economic growth and equally dramatic pollution.

Bangkok provides an example of the costs and benefits of rapid industrialisation. In 1989 alone, Japan invested US$1.2 billion in Thailand, almost all of it flowing into the Bangkok region. Thirty thousand Japanese managers, representing nearly a thousand Japanese companies, provide around a third of a million industrial jobs and fuel a growth rate of 10 per cent per year. A further 600 factories are due to open in the next few years, and 82 per cent of Thailand's gross industrial output is located in the region.

In addition to phenomenal economic growth, which opens up new markets for Japanese products, the environmental costs of industrialism are also obvious. Lignite-burning power stations, and vehicles in an almost continuous traffic jam, emit clouds of pollutants which include almost a tonne of lead a day. Five hundred new cars per day, almost all Japanese cars assembled locally, are coming on to the streets of Bangkok. There are 1.25 million tonnes of liquid toxic wastes generated each year,

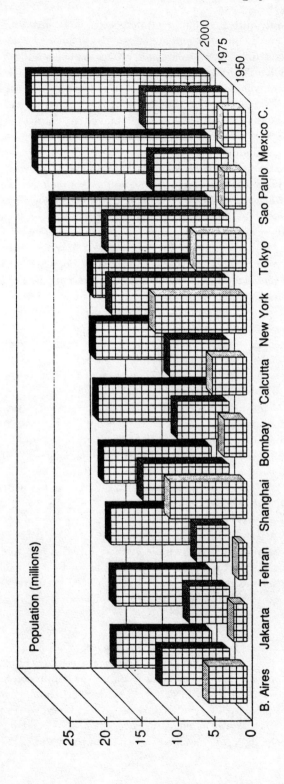

Figure 1.4 *The growth of large cities, 1950–2000*
Source: UN Population Division

which is dumped, mostly untreated, into the watercourses. The Chao Phraya River receives 1.25 million cubic metres of untreated waste daily.

Now that Bangkok is 'full', some 24 industrial estates are being built in outlying areas, including a $356 million national petrochemical complex and a $1.5 billion heavy industry and port complex. However, Bangkok's congestion and rising labour costs are causing many Japanese investors to look to Kuala Lumpur as a location for industrial plant investment. Given the almost unlimited supply of Japanese investment funds, the cycle of industrialisation represented here is likely to continue throughout most of the major cities of Asia.

The combined processes of urbanisation and industrialisation worldwide are a major cause of urban sprawl, air pollution, water contamination from human and industrial wastes, and of overuse of water resources. Many of the world's rivers have turned into open sewers. In Poland, 95 per cent of rivers are unfit for human consumption, and 50 per cent are so polluted with waste chemicals that they are unfit for industrial use. The capital city, Warsaw, does not treat its sewage but dumps it raw into the Vistula River. In Brazil, where two-thirds of the population lives in nine cities, less than 10 per cent of sewage is treated. Canada's International Development Research Centre estimates that if urban growth continues unchecked 'few, if any' rivers in the developing world will be available for drinking water without expensive treatment.[40] However such problems are hardly confined to developing countries: Canada's Great Lakes, particularly Lake Ontario, suffer from a legacy of toxic pollutants such as PCBs, which have recently been associated with learning disabilities and possibly infertility in the region.[41] Similar toxicity levels can be found in the North Sea and the Mediterranean.

Similar problems of urban management are found across Asia, Africa and the Americas, in cities such as Mexico City (24 million people by the year 2000), São Paulo (23 million) and Shanghai (14 million). In Mexico City, for example, the cloud of pollution which hangs over the city comprises five million tons of ozone, carbon monoxide, sulphur dioxide, heavy particles and faecal dust from shanty towns built on dry lake beds. In Asia, rapid urbanisation, industrialisation and growth of motor traffic endanger the health of millions.

These problems of poverty, poor infrastructure and environmental degradation are compounded by a trend to cut public expenditure and by a lack of skilled administrators in local government, who are often lured either into central government or the private sector by higher financial rewards. And while global environmental issues such as the greenhouse effect dominate Western debate, the immediate threat to many city-dwellers is local: the lack of clean water, basic services and effective pollution control.[42]

Intensification of land use due to population growth

A trend related to urbanisation is population growth in rural areas up to urban densities. On the Indonesian island of Java, for example, the population has grown from 5 to 95 million this century, with density of settlement reaching some 1000 people per square kilometre by the year 2000. Densities are also growing rapidly on the other main Indonesian islands, aided by the government-sponsored migration of Javanese, nearly three million of whom have moved to Sumatra alone. The result is intense competition for land use between industry, human settlements and agriculture, and for water and the remaining timber resources. Mannion comments:

> What remains unclear is whether this redistribution of the Indonesian people has actually reduced the environmental problems associated with high populations . . . where deforestation and soil erosion are acute. Or does it mean that the problems of environmental degradation are being magnified and transferred into hitherto uncompromised regions? Once again, the interplay between politics and environment is apparent.[43]

For Asia generally, population projections make it clear that existing urban areas cannot accommodate the overall population increases. Population growth combines with the shift of people towards urban areas to create intensively settled regions around the major cities. McGee calls these *desakotas* ('village-towns' in Indonesian), in which population densities are near urban levels.[44] These regions are characterised by:

- large populations engaged in small-scale cultivation, mainly rice, but with an increasing proportion of employment in manufacturing (such as beverage, cigarette and textile production) or small-scale trading;
- a fluid and highly mobile population dependent on cheap transport, such as two-stroke motorcycles, buses and trucks, with an intense movement of people and goods; and
- an intense mixture of land use with agriculture, cottage industry, industrial estates, suburban development and other uses existing side by side.

This new form of Asian urbanisation, McGee argues, challenges the Western paradigm of urban transition, based on the historical experience of Western Europe and North America in the nineteenth and twentieth centuries. However, it also parallels the emergence worldwide of a new form of regional urbanisation based on dispersed urban functions linked by intensive use of road transport. It may be that the *desakota* is a Asian version of this phenomenon.

The city of the future: a crisis of automobility

In spite of their wealth and resources, regional cities in the West such as New York, Tokyo and London, with populations between ten and twenty-five million, require tremendous ingenuity and resources to deal with traffic congestion, public transport, water extraction, air pollution and waste disposal. The more these regions sprawl, the more intractable the problems become. Yet a common feature of urbanisation in the industrialised world in the late twentieth century has been the radical decentralisation of employment, housing, retailing and leisure pursuits to what has hitherto been agricultural land, well away from the city centre. In many of these cities of the future the traditional city centre loses its unifying function altogether.

The new urban pattern is most obvious in the sprawling 'megacounties' of the USA, like the Los Angeles–San Diego metropolis, containing eight million vehicles, or the 7000 square miles of urban sprawl in the Baltimore–Washington Metropolitan Area. In these regions, the structure of employment and retailing location has changed dramatically: in just five years from 1982 to 1987 the proportion of office space in suburbs in the United States increased from 42 to 58 per cent.[45] The location of retailing has shifted even more decisively to the suburbs: city centre retail sales are commonly less than ten per cent of the regional total.

This decentralised lifestyle results in tremendous increases in vehicle trip generation, as many as 6000 daily car trips per hectare of office space, and 24,000 trips per day to and from a typical shopping mall of around a million square feet. In the Washington area, 78 per cent of journeys to work are now to a suburb, and the proportion is rising steadily. In spite of sustained investment in public transport in this region ($48 billion over 20 years), dependency on the automobile is growing, and public transport's share of the passenger market is down to 2 per cent and falling.[46] In effect, the economy and the lifestyle of these regions are entirely dependent on the private automobile.

Although America is in the vanguard of the trend, fuelled by both decentralisation and economic growth, the 1980s witnessed its emergence on other continents, such as in the south-east of England, in the Tokyo–Osaka belt, and around booming cities like Bombay, Kuala Lumpur and Mexico City. Similar growth can be expected whenever income levels rise sufficiently. A key element in the crisis of automobility is the complete failure of policy makers to reflect environmental and social costs in the price paid for road transport by consumers, and the consequent absence of any market pressures to restrain traffic growth and the land use patterns that promote car-dependence.[47]

In the decentralised urban region, there are fundamental alterations in the nature of the traffic problems: congestion spreads in *space*, with the worst problems no longer on radial routes leading to the city centre but far from the urban core on circumferential highways, along suburban roads, and even in rural countryside. Endemic congestion pervades the entire regional highway network. Congestion now also spreads in *time*. In some regions the rush hour lasts 14 hours a day, and leisure and shopping trips extend it through the weekend.[48] In America, the combination of sprawl and traffic has reduced much of suburbia to:

> a kind of a 'teenage wasteland' as the predominant setting for our lives: a place of strips and malls and interchanges and vast parking lots; of signs and overhead wires and dying trees in concrete pots; of toothless main streets and decaying empty areas at the center of our cities, and equally bleak new but half empty areas at their periphery . . .[49]

The world growth in car ownership will continue, and the problems of the West will spread to Asia and Eastern Europe as economies modernise. There is likely to be a near doubling of the number of vehicles in the world by 2010, with a trebling by 2030. Economic growth in Asia alone could double the number of vehicles by 2020. Worldwide motor vehicle sales are forecast to increase by more than 50 per cent in the next 20 years to 75 million vehicles per year.[50] One-third of the growth will be in Asia, excluding Japan, and strong growth in sales is also forecast for Eastern Europe. By 2010 more than a third of world vehicle sales will be in developing countries.

Air pollution

The world vehicle fleet is already the largest single source of global air pollution, accounting for an estimated 17 per cent of the main greenhouse gas, carbon dioxide. Road transport also accounts for a significant proportion of other pollutants. The contribution of road transport to environmental problems has been estimated as: climate change, 20 per cent; acidification, 20 per cent; smog, 70 per cent; lead pollution, 50–85 per cent; nuisance, 60 per cent; and waste, 5 per cent.[51] The cumulative effect of these problems has given rise to the notion of a 'crisis' of automobility; the potential growth in vehicle numbers compounds the sense of impending global crisis.[52]

Industry also makes an enormous contribution to air pollution. In the last 30 years for example, there has been a ten-fold increase in chemical production. The result of industrial expansion is not only waste gases from power stations and factories, but also thousands of new trace gases whose impacts are little understood.[53] Some effects are localised, some contribute to wide-ranging effects such as acid rain and atmospheric change. Other problems of local and regional air pollution are well documented. Acid rain is by now considered an acute problem in industrialised countries, and has led to agreements on preventive measures at the international level. A more recent realisation concerns the global impact of air pollution and fossil fuel consumption.

Global climate change

No problem more dramatically illustrates the scale of our industrial interaction with the biosphere than the possibility of global climate change. The basic situation is that:

> The atmosphere has been exploited by all without reference to the possibility of ultimate degradation, or to the access rights for the different parties. It has been treated as a free and infinite resource, and humanity is now faced with the realisation that it is neither, and indeed that a portion of the reservoir has been 'used up'.[54]

The main concerns are depletion of the stratospheric ozone layer and the enhanced greenhouse effect. The depletion of the ozone layer results from the effect of a group of pollutants called chlorofluorocarbons (CFCs) in the atmosphere. The chlorine released depletes the ozone in the upper atmosphere which filters out cancer-causing ultraviolet radiation. These chemicals are used in aerosol propellants, refrigerants, and in the production of electronic components and certain plastics.

'Greenhouse effect' is a term that describes the man-made enhanced warming of the earth's surface and lower atmosphere due to increased levels of carbon dioxide and other atmospheric gases. Acting like the glass in a greenhouse, these gases trap heat inside the atmosphere.[55] The sources of greenhouse gases are set out in Figure 1.5. Sixty-two per cent of the gases produced by human activity arise from industrial processes, energy consumption and transport, and the remaining sources are divided between carbon dioxide produced by wood burning, and methane from a variety of agricultural sources. The production of greenhouse gases is mainly a function of industrialisation and consumption; atmospheric carbon dioxide is increasing by just under half of one per cent per year. North America, with 6 per cent of the world's population, accounts for 23 per cent of carbon dioxide emissions; and the USA and Canada, the former USSR, the European Community and Japan account for 55 per

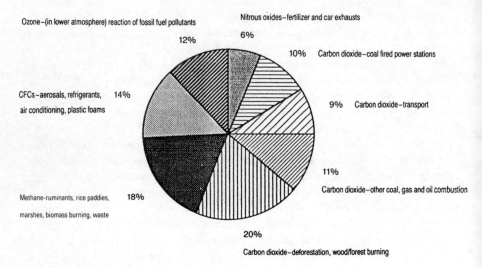

Figure 1.5 *Greenhouse gases – relative contribution to the greenhouse effect*
Source: Barton[64]

cent in total. Figure 1.6 shows the enormous disparity in cumulative and current carbon emissions.

The regional effects on the world's climate are as yet highly uncertain, but there is general agreement among climate researchers that global mean temperature will rise by 1–2°C by 2030, with the main effects in polar regions, where changes of 7–10°C are possible. There would be a shift of temperate conditions towards the poles, greater climatic instability with more storms and droughts, and a rise in mean sea level from a combination of thermal expansion and melting ice. Tickell comments on the meaning of these changes:

> Change is at present taking place at a rate of some ten times faster than the average over the last 10,000 years, and at a rate many times faster than that since the last ice age. Indeed the rate of change could be so fast that it could cause disruption to ecosystems comparable to those which caused major extinctions of species in the past.[56]

The effect of globalisation

The man-made greenhouse effect is a worldwide phenomenon, bound up with the globalisation of industrial systems. Socioeconomic interactions, and production and distribution of environmental risks, are now problematic on a global scale. In terms of climate change, for example, globalisation effects are apparent in at least three respects.[57] First, greenhouse gases, wherever released, disperse rapidly into the global inventory of gases. This is, in effect, systemic global pollution. Second, the impact of this over time may be a change in the global circulation of air and water and a change in temperature differential between tropical and polar regions. We thus face cumulative global impacts. Table 1.4 shows types of global environmental change.

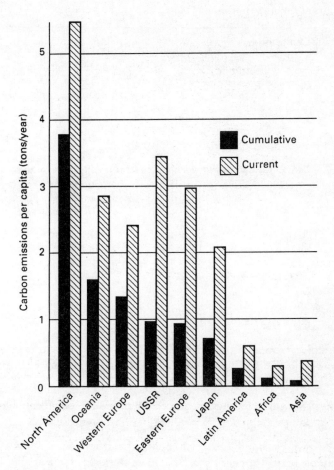

Figure 1.6 *Carbon emissions per capita by region from the burning of fossil fuels*
Source: IIASA[65]

Third, no individual country, with the arguable exception of the USA, will find it economical to reduce greenhouse gas emissions unilaterally. A realistic effort will have to involve an international regulatory regime, covering the larger fraction of world energy consumption, and lasting at least 50 years. Unprecedentedly, policies and implementation must therefore be global. Such solutions require the participation of nearly all the world's governments, and major shifts in the consumption patterns of the industrialised world in particular, which is responsible for by far the largest proportion of global carbon dioxide emissions.

The constraints on achieving such an international agreement are identified by Grubb:

Reaching such an agreement will be extraordinarily difficult. An agreement that bites would be quite unlike any previous environmental agreement. It

Table 1.4 *Types of global environmental change*

Type	Characteristic	Examples
Systemic	Direct impact on globally functioning system	(a) Industrial and land use emissions of 'greenhouse' gases (b) Industrial and consumer emissions of ozone-depleting gases (c) Land cover changes in albedo
Cumulative	Impact through worldwide distribution of change	(a) Groundwater pollution and depletion (b) Species depletion/genetic alteration (biodiversity)
	Impact through magnitude of change (share of global resource)	(a) Deforestation (b) Industrial toxic pollutants (c) Soil depletion on prime agricultural lands

Source: Turner et al[66]

would have major implications for some of the world's largest industries, and for land use policies in the developing world. It could affect international trade flows, and alter patterns of economic development.[58]

The main difficulties in negotiating any agreement to reduce the greenhouse effect are:

1   control will have profound and costly political and economic implications – necessary measures will appear to consumers as 'sacrifices' (for example, less car use) and will therefore be unpalatable for politicians to champion;
2   countries vary greatly in past and current contribution;
3   the impacts of global warming, such as sea-level rise, and the costs of control will vary greatly between countries;
4   many countries at very different stages of economic development would need to be involved in negotiating an agreement;
5   there are long time lags involved in the implementation of any programme to modify carbon emissions.[59]

Points 2 to 4 involve basic questions about international equity and the nature of sustainable development. For example, can development be less sustainable (that is, more polluting) in one region, and more so in another to redress historical imbalance?

There are other global pollutants, such as industrial PCBs which have spread among the seas worldwide and have been introduced even into the bodies of Innuit (Eskimo) peoples in the Canadian Arctic. There are also other global effects arising from the capacity for access to all corners of the Earth. For example, international tourist arrivals have increased 15-fold since 1950: tourism is now the world's largest civilian industry and of great importance to the economic development of many lower income countries.

The sheer volume of movement of people, goods and information across borders and continents has created a qualitatively new situation of global interaction which we are only beginning to understand. Because of advances in biophysical remote sensing, for example, we can begin to track the physical effects of global interactions. But we are far from understanding the social, political and cultural implications of this valuable information: there are layers and layers of human systems represented which are as yet invisible to us. The complex process of interaction between poverty in the Third World, environmental destruction and global change is a profound challenge to natural and social science, and the collection and interpretation of the data we need to understand our predicament has barely begun.

We know that the planet is now girdled by supranational economic and political systems, and that the extent of the problems we can observe requires some supranational system of stewardship for the planet. But how to exercise this responsibility? The stakes are high: we will achieve either a more balanced world or one stricken with environmental disasters and gross disparity between rich and poor. Lourdes Arizpe analyses the challenge:

> The way in which it will go will depend, partly, on how quickly and accurately science is able to cope with the challenge of thinking and analysing phenomena from a global perspective. The social sciences face a fundamental challenge in studying global change. As has been pointed out, the 'sociosphere' cannot be seen with the eye when a photograph of the planet is taken from outer space. For this and other reasons, the impression is sometimes given that the changing textures of the geosphere and biosphere are merely natural phenomena when, to a large extent, they are subject to a human-driven process, one deeply involved with the human use of the resources of the planet.[60]

It is obvious that neither natural or human systems models, on their own, will be sufficient for the task of environmental management. Figure 1.7 shows a useful conceptual framework for analysing the human/natural system relationship, developed as part of the Human Dimensions of Global Change Programme.[61] Using this diagram, we can locate our work in the rest of this book as falling mainly into the sociopolitical, human systems framework.

CONCLUSION

We have not intended a comprehensive survey of the world's environmental problems; there are many others we might have mentioned. We have not considered, for example, the possibility of serious water shortages – half of the world's population may suffer from water shortages in coming decades.[62]. We have not discussed problems of management of industrial toxic waste or nuclear waste, or pollution of the seas, which receive seven million tons of ship-borne waste a year. Longer range threats to the survival of the mega-cities are also looming because of the extreme vulnerability of the great coastal and estuarine cities to sea level rises induced by global warming.[63]

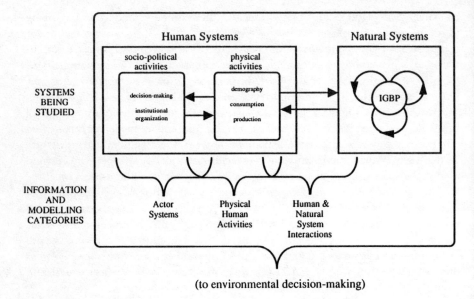

(to environmental decision-making)

Figure 1.7 *Conceptual framework for analysing the human – natural system relationship*
Source: Robinson[61]
(Note: IGBP is the International Geosphere-Biosphere Programme)

A number of general points can be made. One is that all of the issues catalogued above are very complex problems. Direct cause and effect are often far from obvious and there is bound to be some disagreement among scientists. Yet the severity of the problems suggests that doing nothing while waiting for definitive scientific judgement (which may never come) is not an option. Also the degree to which the problems exist is not universally agreed, because they involve value judgements. How much rainforest can we afford to lose, and how much of this natural capital could or should be replaced by reforestation in the United States or Europe or Australia? How much right do citizens of a deforested, wealthy industrial country, like Britain, have to challenge the resource use policies of a still heavily forested, poorer country like Brazil or Malaysia?

A number of key points are clear:

1   The resource systems of the planet are now bound up with social systems through our exploitation and management of them, and social, economic and political factors will play a highly significant role in resolving the complex environmental issues stemming from this fact. Many problems of ecological degradation arise from shortcomings of institutions, and in particular from failures in integrating environmental factors into decision-making. This is reflected in market failures to treat resource values adequately, and in the fragmentation of policy-making on the environment and its interactions with economic systems.[64] Many problems are also simultaneously both cause and effect of poverty and inequalities in international and national economic orders.[65]

2   The very complexity of the problems suggests that understanding and resolving them must depend on a very wide range of human knowledge and skills, extending over the scientific, economic, political and philosophical fields. In other words, teamwork is essential. Prediction of the effects of human interventions will be difficult, and continuous monitoring of vulnerable ecosystems is crucial.

3   The lack of apparent agreement on the existence and severity of these problems, and on responsibility for, and means of, resolving them among many peoples and nations suggests that the development of conceptions of common interest require negotiation, mediation and consensus-building as the only viable methodologies.

4   Finally, globalisation does not imply that the only viable solutions are global ones. On the contrary, all global problems have local implications and therefore offer scope for local action. The magnitude of the problems, and the need to involve local people in their resolution, suggest that co-ordinated efforts must take place on a number of levels of human endeavour: international, national, fluvial, regional, citywide, in the neighbourhood and in the home. No level of effort is likely to be more effective or superior, all efforts must be sustained and linked, and solutions will involve both centralised and decentralised action.

The next chapter turns to the concept of sustainable development, and the implications of global industrialism and recent changes in the world's political and economic systems.

2 Sustainable development and political change

The power and reach of the market system have been truly remarkable and have often been underestimated in the past. But a reliance on the market system often does not produce better results, when results are judged in terms of human lives and freedoms and not in terms of commodity productions only. The role of public action can be very important not only for equity but for efficiency in securing human freedoms and dignity. This applies not only to the Third World but to the richer economies.

Amartya Sen, 1991[1]

The environmental challenges facing humankind clearly transcend the capacities of science and technology to provide technical solutions. They have many ramifications for politics and other fields, including culture, philosophy and religion. Any programme to tackle such 'metaproblems' will therefore require many kinds of expertise.

As noted in the preface, appropriate responses fall into three broad categories:

1   Strategic and philosophical reflection: on the future course of industrialism as a form of social organisation for fulfilment of human needs; the extent to which 'market friendly' policies can result in sustainable development; whether high economic growth, no-growth or some middle option is the more viable in environmental and social terms; the need for greater equity on a world scale and for self-determination and the empowerment of local communities in the face of the globalisation of the industrial economy.
2   The development of organisational and regulatory capacity for managing sustainable development, at scales from the global to the local. This is not only about the implementation of policies for promoting sustainable development, but about encouraging debates about our visions of the future and how to realise them, and the pursuit of new knowledge and skills for both human development and environmental management.
3   Research and development to generate new knowledge and appropriate technologies, especially in sustainable energy, agriculture, transport and low-waste and low-energy manufacturing.

The three types of response each contribute to the successful realisation of the others. This book focuses on the second type of response, with particular emphasis on non-hierarchical networks for building skills in environmental management. We will set out a management approach which, we will argue, is more responsive to the nature and complexity of the problems outlined in the first chapter, and which can help us overcome many of the constraints on good environmental management which arise from our existing forms of top-down policy making and industrial development.

The emerging global problems affect the most local level, and every environmental challenge is part of a nested hierarchy of local, fluvial, regional and international problems and opportunities. Appropriate responses to global problems will include local initiatives, following Hazel Henderson's dictum 'Think globally, act locally'. The action-centred network approach to environmental management that we propose facilitates international learning and local action in a continuous reinforcing cycle.

Environmental issues are not separate from management issues and methods: the two are fundamentally intertwined. Many of the constraints on good management arise because of the nature of the issues themselves, and any efficient and effective response must address those issues. We argue that environment management is a social and political process, not a technical exercise, and therefore no one should be involved in management at any scale without some grounding in these issues.

The proposed approach to environmental problems is one in which the process of discussion and debate gradually broadens and deepens into practical action on issues of sustainable development. In short, we know what the process might look like, but where it will lead in any given context is the business of the participants. The process underpinning the action-centred networking approach to environmental management seeks to promote:

- active participation in conditions of equality, based on teamwork;
- a process of mutual, non–hierarchical learning-by-doing (action learning), intended to develop new perceptions, new skills, and confidence;
- horizontal integration between sectors of human interest such as agriculture, health, transport, housing etc, and vertical integration between policy making groups, including big business, and community levels; and
- collective self-development and self-management.

ARE SOME COUNTRIES 'DEVELOPED' ALREADY?

The approach set out here also implies that habitual distinctions between so-called developed and developing (or less developed) countries are not only meaningless in terms of sustainability, but paternalistic and destructive of the idea of mutuality. We therefore substitute the terms 'lower income' and 'higher income' countries for 'developing' and 'developed' in the rest of the book. In so doing, we agree with Rahman that this is no mere semantic distinction, but that the mistaken perceptions encouraged by the terminology have contributed to a 'most fundamental loss' for lower income countries, which is '. . . obstruction of the evolution of indigenous alternatives for societal self-expression and authentic progress.'[2]

Having dispensed with the notion that countries and their citizens fortunate enough to be wealthy are somehow more developed, we adopt a definition of development which covers all countries on earth with equal applicability:

Development is a process by which the members of a society increase their personal and institutional capacities to mobilize and manage resources to produce sustainable and justly distributed improvements in quality of life consistent with their own aspirations.[3]

This is a very good definition of the general purpose of environmental management.

t is important to note that, while the higher income, industrialised countries may have slightly more experience of formal environmental policy and management, they contribute disproportionately to the environmental crisis and face a challenge equal to, if not greater than, that of the lower income countries. Below we cite some arguments for the idea that sustainable development, as far as it exists, occurs mainly in lower income countries. Finally, as will be seen from the case studies later in the book, the action-centred networking model is equally relevant in high income regions such as California as it is in the townships and countryside of Ghana.

GROWTH OR NO GROWTH?

There are complex debates in progress about the meaning of the term sustainable development. Originally proposed in the World Conservation Strategy in 1980,[4] the term gained widespread currency as result of its promotion by the World Commission on Environment and Development, better known as the Brundtland Commission. Their definition of sustainability is '... development that meets the needs of the present without compromising the ability of future generations to meet their own needs'.[5]

Since the term came into common currency, the proponents of sustainable development have fallen into two broad groups, with many variants on the basic position. One advocates continuing economic growth, made much more environmentally sensitive, in order to raise living standards globally and break the links between poverty and environmental degradation. The other calls for radical changes in economic organisation, producing much lower rates of growth as we know it, or even zero or negative growth. The World Commission was firmly in the first camp, equating sustainable development with 'more rapid economic growth in both industrial and developing countries' which 'will help developing countries mitigate the strains on the rural environment, raise productivity, and consumption standards, and allow nations to move beyond dependence on one or two primary products for their export earnings'. The World Commission anticipated a five- to ten-fold increase in world industrial output at some point in the twenty-first century.[6] Mathews summarises this position: 'Global economic output ... must continue to grow rapidly, if only to meet basic human needs, to say nothing of beginning to lift billions out of poverty'.[7]

It should be emphasised therefore that the 'sustainable growth with redistribution' side in this debate is not looking to increased industrial production for the sake of profits alone; nor does it propose 'business as usual'. Rather, what is at issue is how to increase wealth in an environmentally sound way in order to make major redistributions of income, for example from North to South, and thereby alleviate poverty and improve quality of life worldwide. The Commission argues that high rates of ecologically responsible economic growth are essential both to reduce poverty in the low income world and for environmental improvements to be affordable worldwide.

Many others, however, believe that the sustained economic growth represented by present levels of industrial activity is the root cause of the global *problematique*. Growth as we have known it, in this view, has led to dangerous stresses on the environment resulting in a process of degradation and pollution which threatens the living conditions of generations to come. The 'no or low growth' school argues that the only viable option is to curtail economic growth, change lifestyles to reduce consumption of damaging industrial products and fossil fuel energy in the North, and redistribute resources more fairly on a global basis. The Canadian ecologist Bill Rees sees sustainable development as:

> . . . an opportunity for humanity to correct an historical error and develop a gentler, more balanced and stable relationship with the natural world. This view . . . also raises moral considerations such as the need in a limited world for more equitable sharing of the world's resources.[8]

The questions of how much economic growth is sustainable, and what kinds of growth can be sustained, are immensely complex, especially given the reasonable aspirations of lower income countries to higher levels of economic growth and the obvious material benefits which come with it. The record of economic growth in generating environmental degradation suggests that at the least what is required are sophisticated skills in *growth management*. Chapter 12 gives an example of a process designed to foster such skills and policy ideas. It is clear that the low/no growth approach can only be a very long term strategy, politically inconceivable under any other circumstances; yet 'business as usual' is not an option, as recognised by the sustainable growth camp. The gap between the schools of thought is not always as large as it seems in terms of recognition of key environmental constraints on economic activity. Both camps would agree that one critical aspect of any sustainable path seems to be adaptation of our activities to the *carrying capacity* of the planet.

Sustainable development and carrying capacity

Carrying capacity concerns the number of people who, sharing a given territory, can be supported at any time on a sustainable basis, taking into account known resources, as well as sociocultural factors.[9] This suggests two principles of sustainable development. One is that renewable resource harvest rates (including that of soil quality) should equal regeneration rates to give sustained yield. The other is that waste emission rates should not exceed the natural assimilative capacity of the ecosystem. Regenerative and assimilative capacities are treated here as 'natural capital', and failure to maintain these represents unsustainable capital consumption. Carrying capacity can thus be defined as the maximum rate of resource consumption and waste that can be sustained indefinitely in a region without impairing ecological productivity and integrity.[10]

Numerous difficult issues arise in relating this to economic activity in the market. One is that the market as we now know it has no means of determining the optimum scale of economic activity from an ecological point of view, and runs the risk therefore of exceeding carrying capacities as a matter of course. For example, people will continue to purchase and use more and more automobiles over the next two decades, even though many argue that current levels of traffic congestion and air pollution from cars have already reached crisis levels. This apparent folly arises as people commonly ignore the ecological limits to growth because no economic signals are given to indicate that they are being approached or exceeded.[11]

Arguments for new forms of economic 'signalling' – such as road pricing or environmental taxes – in order to discourage unsustainable consumption and promote new patterns of behaviour have been refined considerably in recent years.[12] There is no doubt that there is significant scope for using market-based instruments to promote sustainable development and combat global problems such as man-made global warming and loss of biodiversity.[13] The use of market mechanisms combined with corrections of institutional failures can be shown to contribute to wildlife preservation and maintenance of crucial but vulnerable and hitherto under-valued ecosystems.[14]

Advocacy of such measures tends to be associated with the view that ecological sustainability and modified forms of economic growth are compatible. Allocating monetary values to environmental assets is often rejected by environmentalists as an unacceptably instrumental approach to nature. However, advocates of market-oriented environmental economics rightly note that some form of explicit or implicit valuation is necessary to make any decisions on protecting or exploiting ecosystems or species.[15] Assigning monetary values has the potential to help correct many failures of markets and regulators in valuing ecosystems. It can be seen at least as a valuable tool in the long range task of greening the industrial economies we have to deal with.

However, implementing new forms of economic valuation to be effective in the immediate future is clearly immensely difficult. In particular, appropriate valuation calls for much-improved information on ecosystems and human interactions with them. Sustainable development requires an immense store of scientific knowledge about stresses on ecosystems and limits to carrying capacity. Our understanding of the 'services' provided by ecosystems and the critical stresses on them is subject to radical uncertainties. These arise from: the massive complexity of the interactions; the problems of data gathering; reliance on modelling due to the impossibility of experimentation in many cases (we cannot try out global warming on another planet); and the fact that the 'object of study' is dynamically changing the world over as ecosystems are affected by industrialisation and population growth. Given these constraints, and the kinds of difficult value judgements involved in such topics as deforestation, the development of clear, efficacious and timely economic signals is highly problematic.

Another difficulty is the inadequacy of Gross National Product (GNP) or Gross Domestic Product (GDP) as the general index of national well–being and measure of economic growth. There are many limitations to the GNP/GDP measures, and here we just touch on a limitation particularly relevant to environmental considerations. This is that when GDP (or GNP) shows an increase, economic growth is said to have taken place.[16] But production often has an unrecorded environmental cost. If a forest is logged for its timber, the money value of the timber is included in GDP but nothing is subtracted to reflect the loss of the forest. Much economic growth is the result of commodifying nature and turning it into goods for sale, but GDP does not record the resultant decline in environmental wealth. Similarly, if industry or agriculture pollutes a water supply, and people buy bottled water instead, as is happening in many countries, GDP goes up because bottled water costs far more than tap water. Once again GDP goes up as quality of life declines.

There is also a social dimension to this problem, which is that GDP only takes account of economic activity in the formal market-place, which is basically defined as that activity recorded quantitatively within given statistical systems. Resources not covered by the market are ignored: trees that maintain the integrity of a watershed are valued only in terms of timber, for example. GDP also does not accord any value to human activity in the informal economy, which is often the work of the poor, nor to what is called the caring or the 'love' economy, for example, women caring for children or elderly relatives. Recent calculations suggest the value of domestic production in America, Britain and France to be about 40 per cent of GDP.[17] All this essential activity is invisible in conventional assessments. Finally, there is a 'time problem', in that accounting conventions discount future values, although the future value of scarce natural resources, like a rainforest, may be far higher than now, and certainly no less.[18]

To address these issues, environmental economists are now looking at ways in which natural capital can be included in an overall indicator of national wealth, which could also include social measures such as infant mortality, male and female literacy and life expectancy. A variation of this is the argument that, for the majority of the world's population, biomass production is the basis of survival, the main source of income and the protector of the environment. Agarwal and Narain, for example, suggest that 'Gross Natural Product' would be a far more accurate indicator of welfare than the cash-based Gross National Product.[19]

A further limitation of markets in relation to carrying capacity is that in the past era of 'empty world' economics (that is, with apparently unlimited natural resources) it was assumed that man-made capital (a house) was an appropriate substitute for natural capital (a forest), and that development was limited by a lack of man-made capital. But many would argue that we have now irrevocably entered the era of 'full world' economics in which natural capital is limited and in which what Pearce terms 'critical capital' environmental assets (such as the ozone layer) cannot be substituted at all.[20] Sustainable development, on this argument, requires that the overall stock of existing natural capital should remain more or less intact, with critical resources maintained in working order for future generations.

This raises the question of the sustainable use of non-renewable resources. One important line of current thinking is that any investment in the exploitation of non-renewables should be paired with a compensating investment in a renewable substitute (a 'shadow project'). For example, in the case of coal extraction, paired tree planting can serve as a sink for the carbon dioxide which results from burning the coal, and as an alternative renewable source of energy for the future. The general principle is clear, but much debate is required about the shadow projects to be carried out as compensations, and about the accounting conventions to be used.[21]

Another major concern is the risk that relatively minor adjustments, for instance in environmental taxation or other market-based measures, are not sufficient because we may be very close to key thresholds in our abuse of carrying capacity. For example, Rees argues that while human society depends on many ecological resources and functions for survival, carrying capacity is ultimately determined by the single vital resource or function in least supply.[22] On a global scale, loss of ozone layer is a possible example, or, on a regional level, the environmental disaster of the

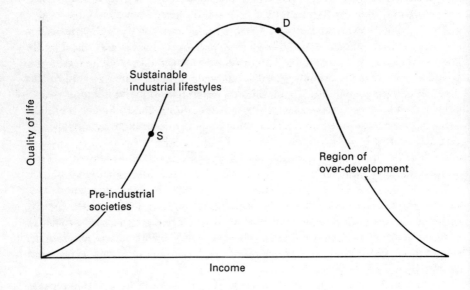

Figure 2.1 *Income and quality of life*
Source: Professor M. Thring, unpublished

shrinkage of the Aral Sea may be another.

Finally, following from these points, the environmental economist Herman Daly of the World Bank argues that there is a fundamental misunderstanding about the word 'growth', which is generally taken to be synonymous with an increase in wealth.[23] Thus it is argued that we must have growth because only if we become wealthier will we be able to afford the cost of environmental protection. Daly questions whether economic growth, at the current margin, is really making us wealthier. Rather, as economic growth pushes us beyond optimal scale relative to the biosphere, it in fact makes us poorer.

Thring calls this situation 'societal over-engineering' and explains it in a simple graph (Figure 2.1) where the upward curve describes a sustainable but non-industrial lifestyle, for example, of hunter-gatherers in the Brazilian rainforest.[24] The area at the top of the curve, between points S and D describes a sustainable, industrial lifestyle where the advantages of modern science, education and medicine generate maximum quality of life in a sound environment. The downward slope represents an unsustainable lifestyle, in which quality of life is decreasing in spite of rising incomes. Unfortunately it is never unambiguously clear when we have arrived at D and are therefore passing out of the zone SD into the realm of over-development.

The location of point D is the nub of political debate about sustainable development. Societies may pass well beyond point D before becoming painfully aware of the environmental and social consequences of overconsumption, which is itself addictive. For example, the bio-economist Georgescu-Roegen argues that humankind is now addicted to all the technological devices which enhance our physical powers and provide us with increased comfort.[25] It is this addiction which drives our endless pursuit of natural resources, and takes us out of zone SD. For the lower income countries, including Eastern Europe and the former Soviet Union, the question is whether they can design their emerging societies within zone SD while they still have the chance. Their scope for action offers both a risk and an opportunity.

Daly describes the conditions which hold in zone SD as those of the steady-state economy, which keeps within limits of population, throughput of industrial goods, and inequality.[26] The steady-state economy is ecological in orientation; physical growth is economic only as long as the marginal benefits of growth exceed the marginal costs. Daly gives an analogy: a library with a constant stock of books limited, say, by storage space or maintenance budget. For every new book acquired, an old one must be recycled, and no book would be replaced unless the new one was qualitatively better. The quality of the library would improve although the quantity of the books would remain constant. He suggests that 'a steady-state economy, far from being static, is a strategy for forcing qualitative improvement and sustainability'.

The idea of the steady-state economy, Daly notes, is not new. He cites John Stuart Mill's chapter 'On the Stationary State' in *Principles of Political Economy*. He also notes that for most of the history of mankind, near steady-state conditions held. Only in the past two centuries in the West has growth become the norm.

The steady-state economy is an attractive concept. Other authors have taken it up – for example, Alexander, who prefers the term 'steady-flow' for its dynamic implications:

> Steady-flow . . . means movement and process. Steady-flow is like a dependable river or stream. Flowing merrily along many interesting things happen, sometimes in unexpected and exciting ways. The size of the stream flow, the quantitative aspects change little. Quantitative limitations on the use of the earth's resources allow the regenerative capacity of Gaia to remain constant or increase.[27]

There are huge problems in adjusting market mechanisms and political values to such notions of sustainable development and carrying capacity, and we have reviewed just a few. The implication of Daly's 'full world economics' is that all resources, including clean air, are now under threat from continuing, unsustainable industrialism. Political mediation is the only alternative to war over these scarce resources, or to authoritarian imposition of sustainable activity. It is plain that a shift towards sustainable development within democratic systems will demand changes in behaviour that in turn will demand intense political debate and trade-offs in attempts to forge consensus.

Above all else therefore, sustainable development, however defined through economic concepts, will be the result of a process of mediation among environmental, economic and social goals. This will include political choices over methods of valuing the environment: the use of new economic valuation techniques cannot be divorced from ethical and political considerations concerning environmental protection, human development and exploitation of resources.

It is in this essentially political process that improvements in human resource capacity and new organisational concepts can make a major contribution to the realisation of sustainable development. We offer a revised, working definition of the process underpinning sustainable development:

> A continuing process of mediation among social, economic and environmental needs which results in positive socioeconomic change that does not undermine the ecological and social systems upon which communities and society are dependent. Its successful implementation requires integrated policy, planning, and social learning processes; its political viability depends on the full support of the people it affects through their governments, their social institutions, and their private activities.[28]

In the light of this, we suggest that the *process* of sustainable development must precede the *product*. We cannot yet establish what sustainability amounts to scientifically and economically; but we have an idea of what unsustainable development paths look like, and we can identify general directions towards improving policy making to avoid them. We can also experiment with new forms of policy making to promote more sustainable development.

Once the truly political nature of the sustainable development process is understood, there is great potential to build a consensus around specific problems, and to broaden that to encompass diverse approaches to sustainable development, for example in watershed management. In later chapters we will suggest ways in which mediation can become an important tool for environmental management, and give some examples. Here, having introduced the notion that environmental management is a political process, we look at some of the main socioeconomic trends in the world which are relevant to a more innovative approach to environmental management.

WORLD TRENDS AND THE POLITICS OF ENVIRONMENTAL MANAGEMENT

There are three recent major world trends which sharpen the need for understanding the politics of environmental management. These are: the spread of industrialisation or its by-products into every last nook and cranny of the planet, the failure of socialism and the reaffirmation of capitalism as the dominant economic system of the world, and the rapid spread of westernised consumerist culture to almost all the peoples of the globe.

The momentum of industrialism

Global economic output has quadrupled since 1950. The current high income countries account for only 16 per cent of the world's population and 24 per cent of its land area. But their market economies account for about 72 per cent of the world's GDP, 78 per cent of all road vehicles and 50 per cent of world energy use. They generate 76 per cent of world trade and 55 per cent of the world's carbon emissions. The newly industrialised Asian countries (NICs) are queueing up to join this elite group.

Chapter 1 documented many of the effects of industrialism and the relentless commodification of natural and even human resources for economic gain. This is the culmination of the 250 years of industrial production which began at the Iron Bridge in England, and which was spread worldwide by colonialism. The scientific–technological–industrial revolution initiated a movement which now threatens to escape our control. The amazing fact about this dynamic process is that we now seem within striking distance of its logical conclusion, Daly's full world economics, in which we have colonised, by resource exploitation or pollution, every last bit of the planet:

> We must understand that we already live in a largely, and increasingly, and irreversibly, artificial world. 'Nature' and the 'natural world' (in the sense of an environment . . . uninfluenced by human activity) scarcely exist anywhere.[29]

Walter Truet Anderson describes the implications:

> Even though the air is thick with talk of paradigm shifts and predictions of new global post-industrial civilization, we seem unable – or afraid – to grasp the truth of how the world has changed, or what it means to govern. Evolution no longer follows the Darwinian rules . . . That vision is as obsolete as its first cousin, Newton's clockwork cosmos. Today the driving force in evolution is human intelligence . . . The world has changed; and the human species, which has wrought the change, is now being required to change in response to the conditions we have created. The change calls for a massive reappraisal of basic ideas . . . we are talking about . . . a transition in the evolution of the planet itself.[30]

The situation is made yet more complex by the unequal distribution of the existing benefits of industrialisation. For example, in 1989 the richest fifth of the world's population accounted for 83 per cent of global GNP and 81 per cent of world trade; the poorest fifth accounted for 1.4 per cent of world GNP, and their incomes were at least 60 times less than those of the richest fifth.[31]

Although this inequality is glaring and morally unjustifiable, it would be a mistake to impute evil intent to the over-consumers. The lure of consumerism is powerful, and many people in lower income countries would like nothing better than to emulate lifestyles common in the advanced industrial economies. Commodification and consumption of industrial products are part of a 'modernisation' process in which most of humankind would willingly participate. At the family level, acquisition of consumer goods is an extension of the drive to satisfy basic needs. At the village level, incipient commodification is often the first step towards integration with national and world economies and money-based exchanges. For example, Vandergeest[32] documents how peasants in the rice and palm-sugar growing area of the Satingpra peninsula in southern Thailand initiate commodification in order to circumvent traditional relations of domination and control by an old elite – in other words, to modernise their situation.

However, continued global industrialisation is untenable in its current form. For example, if the lower income countries were to have the same standard of living as the industrialized countries, total global industrial output would need to rise by more than 130 times, resulting in unimaginable resource depletion and pollution. Even if we just look at the proportion of the world's population, mainly in Asia, who are likely to achieve higher income status in the next thirty years, and even if we project a continuing downward trend in energy use per unit of GDP, their industrial achievements could increase carbon dioxide emissions fivefold using current energy sources.[33] This is in addition to the constant rise of carbon dioxide from current sources. There is a potential purchasing power in Asian markets alone to double the number of cars in the world, from the current 400 million, in this thirty year period. Almost all of these cars would be produced as well as consumed in Asia, as auto production and assembly spreads beyond current centres in Japan, Korea, Malaysia, India and Thailand. In Thailand alone, one Japanese company already assembles a car every three minutes for domestic consumption.

Clearly there is no going back on industrial production and the promise of a better life it offers to the citizens of lower income countries. But the ecological limits to industrial growth as we have known it are in view, and we therefore need a new model of sustainable 'eco-industrialism', which is less energy- and resource-intensive than the traditional industrial system.

There may be a clue in areas of the world with sustainable resource use and low levels of non-renewable energy use, but also high quality of life, as measured by infant mortality, literacy and life expectancy. Sen, for example, compares GNP per capita and life expectancy at birth in five countries in 1985[34] (Table 2.1).

The difference in quality of life compared to economic achievement, and thus resource consumption, is paralleled by other indicators. Sen attributes the difference to well-coordinated government policies in health, education and social security. This idea that there can be a substantial difference between economic and human development is explored at length in the UN Development Programme's Human Development Reports, which since 1990 have presented an index of quality of life as an alternative and corrective to conventional macroeconomic indicators.

In another example, Kerala State in southern India has been proposed as a model of sustainable development by Alexander.[35] In Kerala, a per capita GNP in 1986 of

Table 2.1 *GNP per capita and life expectancy*

	GNP per capita (US$)	Life expectancy (years)
China	310	69
Sri Lanka	380	70
Brazil	1640	65
South Africa	2010	55
Oman	6730	54

$182, compared with $17,480 in the United States, indicates a very low throughput of industrial products and generation of pollution. And yet Kerala, for historical and political reasons, has a very low birth rate, low infant mortality, a life expectancy of 70 years, an adult literacy rate of 78 per cent, compared with 43 per cent for India as a whole, and a female literacy rate of 66 per cent, compared with 25 per cent for India as a whole. To find similar indices of quality of life, one needs to look to European countries such as Spain and Portugal, with ten times the industrial throughput and pollution. Alexander concludes his analysis by suggesting that Americans become eco-tourists in Kerala to learn something of the true nature of sustainable development.

The collapse of communism and the market revolution

A second trend affecting environmental management in a profound way is the spectacular collapse of the communist states in Eastern Europe and elsewhere, and the wholesale abandonment of Marxist–Leninist forms of economic and political organisation on a worldwide basis. As a result, old ideas about economic policy and the role of the state are being challenged and cast aside.

The demise of Marxist–Leninist socialism, richly deserved and commendable in itself, has given rise to much dangerous self-congratulation in the West about 'a victory for capitalism'. The danger is that the urgent need to re-examine the direction of industrial capitalism, and the implications for enviromental quality of excessive private consumption, will be deferred or made more difficult. Putting aside this risk for the moment, it is worth considering the failure of the communist experiment as a major historical event in the late twentieth century, and on a par of significance with the rise of environmental metaproblems.

The failure of communism is twofold: the moral failure of the one party state based on totalitarian oppression and social control, and the practical failure of the centralised command form of economic management. In the Eastern European countries and the former Soviet Union therefore, the new challenge is to make the shift from a command to a market economy linked into the world economy, and to shift from the one party state to pluralism. These interrelated processes constitute economic and political liberalisation.

The restructuring process involves liberalising prices, freeing trade, selling state companies, dismantling monopolies and establishing a convertible currency. Some Eastern European countries are likely to experience a fairly rapid integration with the world economy, while the countries of the former Soviet Union may take longer to transform entrenched economies and to establish new trading links with the world economy.

The market revolution is not confined to Eastern Europe and the former Soviet Union, and governments in many countries are converting from socialist to market economic policies. In countries as diverse as Brazil, Mexico, Bolivia, Venezuela, Jamaica, Malaysia, Zimbabwe, and Ghana, goverments are introducing, albeit at different rates, the now familiar package of assaults on the centralised economy: the establishment of a workable domestic price system, increases in exports to cover debt repayments and imports, opening the domestic economy to international competition, elimination of distortions in the foreign exchange market, public spending cuts, tax reforms, and privatisations. These reforms are often spurred by the insistence of the International Monetary Fund on such 'structural adjustments' as a precondition for loans. Zimbabwe, for example, has tempered years of largely unworkable import and export controls with a new trade liberalisation programme which is being received warmly by the somewhat beleaguered private sector. Given the country's long standing policies towards universal and well-funded health and education, substantial economic growth is likely to follow.

The new economic perceptions have been summarised by Indonesia's co-ordinating Economy Minister:

> We have looked at the economic performance of our neighbours and we have studied the lessons of history. We have abandoned our own earlier version of mercantilism and, instead, discovered the wisdom of the market economy. Entering the 1990s, we are genuinely convinced that a market-oriented approach will offer the most practical and speedy means of achieving our overall national economic goals.[36]

Clearly there is a new consensus worldwide that market forces must be given the dominant role in the creation of the world's wealth. The consolidation of liberal capitalism and the rise of environmental meta-problems is a convenient conjunction, for it exposes the commonality of environmental problems in East and West under markedly different, but nonetheless industrial, systems. It also provides an important opportunity for states shifting out of communism wholesale, like Poland, or incrementally out of collectivist economic policies, like Zimbabwe, to begin a necessary rethink about the balance between industrial development and environmental quality. This balance underpins the notion of sustainable development.

Evidently there is danger for the environment in a headlong rush to embrace capitalism. The recent ruinous demise of many communist regimes may have demonstrated the superior adaptability and efficiency of liberal capitalism by comparison with collectivist economies. However, while Marxist analyses of the socioeconomic 'contradictions' that would bring down capitalism have proved to be flawed, the capitalist economies have yet to overcome the emerging ecological contradictions which threaten them.

For the lower income countries, neither their own long term economic and environmental viability, nor the need to reduce global warming, can allow for unrestrained economic growth via industrialisation on the traditional Western model. Yet there will be every tendency to pursue this path to development. For example, in China, Deng Xaoping's economic reforms urged farming communities to set up rural private enterprises. The result is that, since 1984, independent rural industry has grown at a rate of 37 per cent per year, four times that of state industries. This has put severe strain on energy supplies and scarce raw materials, and 8.5 million hectares of farmland is lost to new construction every year.

The need to devise an alternative, sustainable industrial path is also pressing because industrialisation and urbanisation are transforming lower income societies and turning many of their inhabitants into wage dependent consumers of manufactured goods.[37] Today's poor countries are growing richer at a far faster rate than today's industrialised countries did at a similar stage of development. Britain and the USA, for example, required 60 and 50 years respectively to double real incomes per head at the early stages of industrialisation. Recently South Korea and China have required only 11 and 10 years to accomplish the same. Given these rates of growth, by about 2025 the total number of consumers with industrial consumption habits similar to those of the developed world could be five times that of today.[38]

Here we can return to the danger that the failure of communism will obscure the growing need for forms of community and collective action at local and international levels – allowing individual efforts to be subservient to a common cause or larger entity – such as state or even international controls to maintain the world's environmental quality. It is this characteristic tension in capitalism between individualistic, entrepreneurial action and the need for communal mechanisms that should shape political debate for the foreseeable future. This debate shapes the context for attempts at environmental management for sustainable development.

It is worth elaborating on this point. The secularisation of society since the Industrial Revolution (ie, the marginalisation of religion) has been accompanied by the recasting of spiritual debate and arguments over values into competition between political ideologies of Left and Right. The essential political conflict in industrialised societies has been over the attempt to achieve the material benefits of modernisation while maintaining or building forms of community. The dynamics of industrialisation, as noted by commentators early in the industrial era, tend to corrode traditional forms of community. So capitalist development poses problems for conservatives and liberals who wish to secure a role for 'traditional values' as well as to promote business-led prosperity. It also challenges social democrats, socialists and others of the Left, who may wish to undermine tradition but need to replace it with forms of community in order to combat atomising and fragmenting forces of industrialism. Both sides now face huge problems: for the Right, the seemingly unstoppable fragmentation of old forms of community such as the family; and for the Left, the failure of social democracy and communism to build forms of community more potent than tribalism and nationalism, as is evident in Eastern Europe and the former republics of the USSR in the aftermath of communist rule.

The end of history: a flawed thesis

An obvious danger lies in allowing the failure of communism to be taken as a vindication of capitalism as it exists. At the extreme of this tendency is the 'end of history' thesis advanced by Francis Fukuyama. He argues:

> What we may be witnessing is . . . the end of mankind's ideological evolution and the emergence of Western Liberal democracy (Capitalism) as the final form of human government . . . this phenomenon extends beyond high politics and can be seen also in the spread of consumerist Western culture in such diverse contexts as the . . . color televisions now found throughout China . . . and the rock music enjoyed in Prague, Rangoon and Tehran . . . We might summarize the content of the universal homogenous state as liberal democracy in the political sphere combined with easy access to VCRs and stereos in the economic.[39]

Fukuyama appears to have conflated capitalism (an economic system) with consumerism (a value system) and with liberal democracy (a political ideology), and then to have assumed the righteousness and inevitability of the whole package. This is by now a common misconception which makes it more difficult to think intelligently about environmental issues and how to implement change in the capitalist system. State, economy and human values are separate, although none exists by itself, and each influences the others. On the one hand, it is true that so-called 'socialist' states have been undemocratic and repressive. But on the other, it is equally true, as Robert Heilbroner points out, that capitalism has no inherent dependence on, or affinity with, political freedom.[40] Or with environmental quality, we might add. Later we consider why economic and political liberalism should not be confused.

Fukuyama recognises the vacuity of the materialist future he forecasts, although he appears to see no alternative.[41] Critics have attacked the thesis with passion. For example, Jonathan Sacks, the Chief Rabbi of Britain, responded in a BBC Reith Lecture:

> Fukuyama's analysis takes us deep into irony. Because such a brave new world suggests a massive impoverishment of what we are as human beings, its accuracy as a prediction is matched only by its narrowness as a prescription. The human being as consumer neither is, nor can be, all that we are, and a social system built on that premise will fail . . . Modernity is the transition from fate to choice. At the same time it dissolves the commitments and loyalties that once lay behind our choices. Technical reason has made us masters of matching means to ends. But it has left us inarticulate as to why we should choose one end rather than another.[42]

Fukuyama's identification of economic liberalism with liberal has also been attacked:

> Mr Fukuyama writes from an American perspective, which takes the success of economic liberalism for granted as a natural concomitant of liberal democracy. Yet economic liberalism poses a serious threat to greater democracy; the free market gives increasing power not to the ordinary worker or trader but to the big and essentially unaccountable corporations that are allowed to grow unchecked.[43]

Fukuyama is right, however, that the demise of communism, global trends to economic integration, and improved communication mean that hitherto collectivist economies, such as Mozambique, are opening up to the West. This is partly because, as the Soviet Union withdraws support from the economies of its former clients among the lower income countries, states are forced to open up to Western capital and to allow greater economic flexibility. Following from this is external and internal pressure for multi-party democracy and for increased consumption. The resultant lessening of state control, and the burgeoning private sector (both multinational and backyard industries), raise significant challenges to environmental monitoring and control. Again there is no guarantee that the resultant development will be any more sustainable than the previous collectivist industrial effort.

The culture of consumerism

Another risk of postulating the end of ideology is that it obscures the fact that the demise of communism is less a victory for capitalism *per se* than the culmination of decades of ruinous misrule in the countries concerned, and a demand for access to the rapidly spreading culture of consumerism. Rabbi Sacks summarises the situation for the Soviet Union:

> In the end, the colour television had proved a more seductive prospect than The Communist Manifesto. Politics had moved beyond ideology. As Eduard Shevardnadze, the Soviet foreign minister, put it, 'the struggle between two opposing systems had been superseded by the desire to build up wealth at an accelerated rate'. Dialectical materialism was over; mail order materialism had taken its place. Eastern Europe had discovered the discreet charm of the bourgeoisie . . .[44]

Consumerism exerts a powerful hold, nowhere more so than in the United States, and like the industrial system itself, it is spreading worldwide to become one of the most powerful ideologies of the twenty-first century. Yet it is entirely possible that consumerism is an inferior and grossly inappropriate value system for a world facing mounting environmental crisis. Already there have been some rebellions against consumerism, for example, the anti-materialist, anti-Western Islamic Revolution in Iran. In the West itself, many environmentalists are questioning excessive material-ism. For example, William Leiss argues that in:

> . . . a lifestyle that is dependent upon an endlessly rising level of consumption of material goods . . . individuals are led to misinterpret the nature of their needs and to misunderstand the relationship between their needs and the ways in which they may be satisfied . . .[45]

These concerns, which parallel those of the social indicators movement of the 1970s, are generally 'post-materialist' insofar as they tend to arise after wants and needs are well met, or where consumption is already at a level which many people feel is excessive. And at present, only a tiny and electorally insignificant minority of Westerners are questioning the consumerist ideology.

The problem for the world's environment is that only a small minority of the world's population is in any position to adopt such a post-materialistic perspective, and only a very small minority of these choose to do so. Conversely the billions not yet anywhere near the materialistic standards of the developed world feel, with justification, that they have every right to fulfil their material needs and desires through industrialism, just as the rich world has done.

Among these people, 70 per cent will be concentrated in just eight countries: China, India, Indonesia, Brazil, Pakistan, Bangladesh, Nigeria and Mexico. The Chinese and Indians together are two billion people: 1.2 billion Chinese and 800 million Indians. The approach to sustainable development of these eight countries will be a major factor in the world environment. But the developed world can hardly have expectations unless they themselves are prepared to make radical changes in their own lifestyles.

The spread of western-style consumerism across the globe is serving to erode core values in many traditional cultures, and great cultural traditions, such as of China, India and Africa, are now facing fundamental changes because of the criss-crossing encounters of individuals, institutions, societies and cultures on an unknown scale.[46] Although new possibilities for synthesis and co-operation are opening up, this trend may also result in a severe loss of cultural diversity just at the point when we are questioning the dominant paradigm. The Swedish sociologist Bertil Egero summarises the situation:

> The post-industrial countries are facing the challenge of an ultimately necessary transition to ecologically sustainable economies. Today, however when history is said to have come to an end, there is not even a theory to guide our way to a realisation of such a transition. A similar uncertainty . . . concerns the way forward for many poor countries in the South. I believe I am justified in interpreting the crisis in these countries as in no small part a 'cultural crisis', a result of West-supported development strategies aimed to 'bypass history' and carry the country in a swift change to a modern industrial society.[47]

ENVIRONMENT AND POLITICAL CULTURE

A basic assumption of this book is that environmental issues are quintessentially political, for they involve trade-offs between different, sometimes mutually exclusive, options in society and choices which extend over long time scales with far reaching consequences. These trade-offs, for example between more, cheaper goods and environmental quality, cannot be addressed within the market economy alone: they involve more than monetary values and are bound up with competing ethical and political viewpoints. The trade-off process invariably involves some level of social organisation which can mediate among competing interests and objectives. This often involves the state, with the lead of its government, but may also increasingly involve other major social formations which bring interests together: for example, the United Nations at the international level; and, as described later, networks of organisations at lower levels from the public, private and community sectors. Finally, because of the long lead time for major industrial or infrastructural investments, like highways or dams, and the need to anticipate environmental impacts, it is not enough to mediate, states must also *plan* for the future. In the modern capitalist economy, however, many forms of planning by the state are contentious.

It is worth considering why the market economy does what it does so much better than the command economy. First, the profit-oriented objectives of the private firm are clear, simple, and unhindered by conflicting claims. This means that the cost of inputs can be related to outputs in a direct manner impossible in government, and that incentives can be linked to the achievement of certain outputs, say for example, market share. Second, the use of information and reaction are the key to success: the private firm responds to new information (feedback) in the society (the market-place) with a rapidity impossible in government, and engages in self-correction. The penalty for not self-correcting is failure – customers will vote with their feet, which they cannot do in a command economy, except by resorting to the black market.

Increased complexity in the world economy, and increased information and choice, reinforce the advantage of the market which, although far from perfect, has this critical feature of self-correction. In short, the successful firm in the market is adaptive and responsive. Successful environmental management emulates these traits.

Given the efficiency of the market economy in delivering goods, but also the absolute need for mediation at the interface of humankind and nature, one major challenge to sustainable development is to understand the history and alternatives for the relationship of the state to the private sector, and of both to the voluntary (NGO) sector. In particular, given the basic tension between the need for communal action to maintain our environment and the need to preserve and enhance individual freedom and the opportunity for initiative, we must begin to establish an understanding of the relationship of what we call political culture to market operation. Daniel Bell calls this question of state–society relationships, '. . . of the public interest and the private appetite . . . the salient problem for the polity in the coming decades'.[48]

The first step is to understand that modern capitalist societies work on two levels (Figure 2.2). The first is the level of the market economy, that is, the level of the individual and the firm. At this level, in economic terms, market arrangements are the best approach to the realisation of goals and objectives for the reasons given above. Activities at this level are important to material well-being. They also tend to be efficient and basically irrepressible: it usually requires the full power of the state to repress market transactions, which spring up as black markets when forbidden. However, the market is not a political or moral philosophy, but only a mechanism of economic transaction, and one which is not likely to generate sustainable development. This is for the many reasons described earlier, but also because market transactions must be profit-maximising, or utilitarian, or they are nonsensical.

Market operations are necessary therefore, but not sufficient, for a sustainable, healthy society, environmentally or socially. As Sen puts it, '. . . the market mechanism is an essentially incomplete specification of a social arrangement', which can be adjusted by political will to work in different ways.[49] A second, higher order of human activity is necessary. This can be termed the level of political culture, which can derive and attain higher order social goals, define and address environmental problems, and promote human development. Some of these higher order goals (state supported R & D or vocational training, for example) can be important in attaining efficiency at the level of the market; others promote quality of life in areas where social benefits cannot be quantified and economic efficiency is not paramount. Higher order goals cannot be derived from considerations of economic efficiency alone.

In this conception, politics is not about the enforcement of commands or the exchange of political favours, but rather '. . . a process by which citizens come to see the world and themselves in a different way'.[50] A society operating in this manner would be '. . . like a classroom, a debating chamber, a Quaker meeting or a Jewish *Yeshiva*.' Only in such a mode can the members of society redefine their common purposes so that the public realm denied by individualism can be recreated and sustained.[51]

The development of such a political culture can be nurtured by the state, but need not be a function solely of the state. Now that command economies have lost

LEVEL	FOCUS	OBJECTIVES	CHANGE AGENTS	BEST APPROACH
• Level of *political culture*: International community, nation state, the region, the municipality	• Political relationships • Ethical systems • Longer-term, strategic, holistic and cumulative aspects of human existence; The broader externalities of market arrangements • Meta-organisation	• Societal effectiveness in terms of quality of life for this and future generations	• Cultural consensus • The state • Other important social or voluntary organisations • Political leaders	• Dialogue • Co-operation • Reference to to ethical frameworks • Pluralism
• Level of the *market economy*: the firm and the economic individual	• Economic structures • Market operation • Market enhancement • Individual and family well-being	• Economic efficiency for material well-being in this generation • Individual freedom	• The economic entrepreneur • Global and other corporations	• Competition in a market economy

Figure 2.2 *Two levels of social organisation*

credibility, and welfare state bureaucracies have been too often revealed as inefficient, the idea that 'civil society' should be the primary arena of political activities has become a major theme of debate, especially now that old ideologies in the industrial world are fading. In many societies, political culture reflects a measure of societal consensus which can be traced to long standing traditions and organisations quite apart from the state. Religion, the tribe, the trade union, the educational system, the voluntary association – these can all be agents for the development of consensus. This is of course no guarantee that consensus is socially progressive (for example, societies may be consensually racist) or environmentally sustainable. This suggests that the process by which consensually held values and social goals are derived must have reference to moral considerations.

For environmental management, we need to understand the role of consensus, which is a sharing of views and values by a broad constituency within a society. In participating in any public policy debate, an objective should be to assist the development of a sufficient degree of consensus for action. At best, consensus reflects a transcendent societal view which goes beyond the individualism of the market, but is complementary to it, reflecting a marriage between market economics and social responsibility. This involves trade-offs between individual freedoms in the market-place and the quality of public life, for example, in a recognition that taxation to fund public services can raise the quality of life for the whole community, and that a low rate of contribution by the well-off towards public goods will in the long run diminish their welfare as well as that of the less affluent.

It is also important to note that we use the term 'political culture' here rather than talk about the state or government *per se* because the mediation process between economy and biophysical environment is far more complicated than the bipolar state–market distinction suggests. Clearly the state has an important and increasing role in maintaining environmental quality. But the state's direct role should not be dominant: in order for policy to be based on the fullest possible understanding of the tasks and problems in hand, the activity of the state should be complemented by that of other structures and organisations contributing to the maintenance of environmental quality.

State action can be complemented by other organisations in civil society able to take on a role in mediation between the demands of human development and protection of natural environments, and to foster the necessary drive towards consensus on sustainable development. This idea takes us to the heart of the action-centred networking approach. These networks can include voluntary organisations or NGOs (non-government organisations), citizens' groups, representatives of the education system, firms and business groups, trade unions, the church or any combination of groups working together.

In the ideal networking concept, government, business and community organisations of many kinds become equal players in a broad partnership. This kind of coalition can either buttress the weak state apparatus, as is the situation in many lower income countries, or it can temper the power of the state or of business where that is a problem. This notion that civil society can play an important role in environmental management is also in tune with calls for more attention to local and regional autonomy, particularly in light of the globalisation of economic activity and consumer culture, and the resultant erosion of cultural diversity and identity at the local level.

In this regard, Daniel Bell makes the crucial point that many of our problems – especially environmental ones – are now *too small and too big* for the nation state to handle adequately. Thus local/regional groupings and international structures come to the fore and, indeed, are mutually reinforcing.[52] Following chapters describe a concept of mutually reinforcing 'nested networks' which can realise these ideas.

CONCLUSION

There is no consensus on what sustainable development will look like as a 'product': whether it is reconcilable with continuing, albeit modified forms of economic growth, or whether it ultimately demands a 'steady state' economy. It is clear, however, that the process of making development sustainable is about more than devising new economic tools and methods of valuing the environment, urgent and important though this is. Movement to a sustainable development path in industrial and industrialising countries will be a political, not just a technical process. It can be seen as a continuing process of mediation and trade-offs between different goals and aspirations; it cannot be divorced from wider issues of political culture, values and social tensions.

We have argued that the demise of communism, the emergence of the worldwide trend towards market economies and western consumer culture, the lessening of control by the state, and the possibility of rapid economic growth in some of the world's lower income countries, pose major challenges to the realisation of sustainable development. In particular there is a tension between the entrepreneurial individualism of capitalism and the need for societies to develop a sophisticated political culture which can derive and implement higher order social goals, like sustainable development. New skills for developing social consensus around issues of sustainable development could play an increasingly important role in environmental management.

In other chapters we will explain how the development of 'environmental constituencies' around specific issues or tasks can be broadened into action on sustainable development. The action-centred network approach, described in Chapters 8 to 13, is emerging as a methodology for accomplishing this. Chapters 3 and 4 consider in more detail the question of values and political culture in relation to environmental management.

PART II

The Western view of humankind and nature

Part II   The Western view of humankind and nature

The two chapters in this section explore the historical background to the relationship between humankind and nature in Western society. The understanding of this relationship was transformed by philosophers of the sixteenth to nineteenth centuries, reacting against a broad view of nature which held sway for centuries. This enormous philosophical programme helped give rise to, and was nurtured by, the Reformation and the Renaissance. It was at the core of the Enlightenment, which provided the foundation for liberal political values in the West.

This creative period of intellectual, political and scientific activity has shaped structures and beliefs in Western society, and in the modern state. Further, the broad value system it developed, which at the beginning of the twentieth century was mainly confined to the West, is spreading rapidly, as states as diverse as Malaysia and Mexico aspire to, or achieve, industrialised status. Now, not only is the capitalist basis for economic life accepted worldwide, but Western liberal political procedures and values are spreading into Eastern Europe and the former Soviet Union and to hitherto quasi-socialist states such as Ghana, Tanzania, Zambia and Zimbabwe. The acceptance of Western political values and institutional structures is increasingly a condition of aid to lower income countries.

The industrial revolution, and subsequent dramatic population and economic growth, gave rise to many of the serious environmental problems described in Chapter 1. But the opportunity for their development, the fertile ground of beliefs and values, can be traced further back to the philosophy of the Enlightenment. European philosophy created a powerful secular world, with religion progressively shifted to the margins of society, and in which debate over values increasingly took the form of competition between secular political ideologies of Left and Right.

As part of this revolution in thought, Newtonian science saw the rational human observer as separate from nature, which enabled nature to be studied in a detached, analytic fashion. This approach has generated a vast amount of scientific knowledge, but it also marginalised a spiritual, emotional or holistic perception of the relationship of humankind to nature, as had been common in earlier civilisations. Nature now became a realm of impersonal objects, to be studied, then 'conquered' or exploited by man. This worldview separated facts from values. The need to analyse nature in a systematic fashion also gave rise to the compartmentalisation of knowledge in academic disciplines.

In the sphere of production, both the capitalist, and later Marxist, industrial systems, while bringing many unprecedented material benefits, encouraged the packaging of nature into discrete commodities to be bought and sold. The Newtonian view of nature, as separate and inert, helped validate this process. Much of industrial growth over the past two hundred years has consisted of this commodification of nature and life's experiences into new products for the market-place, and into numbers for entry on corporate balance sheets. To compound the problem, the pollution generated by the industrial process has been put back into the natural environment. In economists' terms, the costs of these pollutants, either for nature or future generations, have been 'externalised', that is, not included in the prices charged for the products. Neither the producer-polluter, nor the consumer, has paid.

Finally, out of the Enlightenment arose the modern, secular state, which institutionalised a separation between the economics of business, the 'private' sector, and the realm of joint social organisation, the public or state sector. In liberal capitalism, fundamental importance has come to be attached to individual freedom in private or civil life. This private society is perceived as the area of life where individuals develop the strength of their creative forces in order to promote knowledge, wealth and progress. Conversely, it smacks of a now discredited socialism to insist that a collective, or public, interest exists outside the market-place, and that either the state or 'civil society' (voluntary organisations, the press, interest lobbies, etc) have an important role in maintaining or enlarging that public interest, often at the expense of individual freedoms. Yet environmental quality is just such a public interest, and it is hard to conceive of a political system maximising individual economic freedom, and also resulting in a sustainable environment.

Now the rise of environmental problems, and concern about the ultimate communal good, the air itself, highlights the debate between the laissez faire approach and one favouring government intervention in private life for environmental maintenance. As we shall see, the debate has run for at least three hundred years, with no sign of a resolution.

There are two basic questions involved:

1 Is the provision of a high level of environmental quality compatible with maximising individual freedom?
2 What balance between public or state action and private activity will maximise quality of life, and what trade-offs are involved?

Chapter 3 takes up the issue of the influence of the scientific worldview on management of the environment. Chapter 4 looks at the evolution of political thought in the West on the question of the relationship of the individual to the state and society, and the implications for environmental management.

Finally, it may seem odd to some readers that we have reached back to sources centuries old to understand the modern world and prospects for the twenty-first century. The reason we believe this is helpful is that our present ways of thinking are 'short-termist' and culture-bound. We need to see how the original reasoning and insights of thinkers have given rise to larger doctrines, been reinforced in the process, and explicitly shape how we think and act today. And how we are likely to think and act in the twenty-first century, unless we consciously do otherwise.

3   Science and technology and the natural world

Traditional science or positivistic science has attempted to place science and thereby knowledge outside of history, culture and language. In this view, the goal of good research is to remove the subjectivities situated in the person. This type of research has led critics to argue that science (and its brainchild, legitimate or bastard, technology) is amoral, without conscience.

Sohail Inayatullah, 1991[1]

. . . natural science as a form of thought exists and has always existed in a context of history, and depends on historical thought for its existence. From this I venture to infer that no one can understand natural science unless he understands history: and that no one can answer the question of what nature is unless he knows what history is.

R G Collingwood, 1949[2]

The environmental movement has an ambivalent relationship with science. On the one hand, scientific research has alerted the world to many serious environmental problems, such as global climate change, the threat to the ozone layer, and the degradation of water supplies. Objective testing and reasoning about environmental problems from a scientific perspective debunks modern myths and provides sound information about the severity of those problems, and their trends, and allows participants in the debate to speak with some authority.

For example, leading scientists from Britain's Nature Conservancy Council (NCC) were able to establish that organochlorine insecticides used by farmers were accumulating in the food chain and were a threat to health. This was not a question of opinion, but of authoritative scientific fact. Speaking about attempts to persuade the agrochemicals industry to assist in changing these farming practices, the former Director-General of the NCC states '. . . had not the scientific base of ecology and conservation been already so sound, the successful agreement with the industry could not have been concluded'.[3] Government, NGOs and environmental pressure groups all rely on scientific authority and method to a great extent.

Turning to the field of environmental management, we find that some of the world's most innovative thinkers, policy advisers, managers and administrators are scientists by training, and often eminent in their fields. They are a tremendous human resource to address environmental problems, in part because of their perceptive analysis of areas of life invisible to the non-scientist.

On the other hand, and in spite of the obvious contribution of science to our understanding of environment, many people are also deeply concerned about the role science and technology have played in bringing about environmental problems:

After all, scientists invented the CFCs which are threatening the ozone layer. Technological advance allowed humans to develop nuclear power, which in turn has brought us persistent environmental problems. It was scientists who developed the pesticides which in the past three decades have contaminated our food and our wildlife ... Some (environmentalists) see scientists as active collaborators in our society's ecological destructiveness.[4]

Part of the reason for this ambivalent view of science is that in the last 50 years in the West we have allowed the authority attributed to science to become exaggerated. This should not necessarily be laid at the door of scientists. Rather it arises from the obvious contribution of science to industrial advancement through technology, which has steadily improved standards of living over time. This has fostered a strong belief in the value of continuous scientific advance, and supported what has been called 'a fixation with technology'.[5]

Another difficulty is that in overestimating the authority of science, we have became blind to the inherent limitations of the scientific method, particularly when dealing with complex humankind–nature interactions. Many scientists would agree. Factors which affect the accuracy and validity of any scientific conclusion are the size of the sample in relation to the whole population, and the representativeness of the sample. Biologists, for example, if they are studying whole plants or animals, and the simpler cells of which they are composed, can seldom study those units in large numbers.[6] The range of difficulties increases as we move into the realm of humankind–nature interaction, which requires joint natural and social scientific research to begin to untangle a myriad web of influences. Here sufficient sample sizes are often impossible, and intervening and dynamic variables of culture and social organisation make scientific assessment more of an art than the kind of science we have traditionally relied on. It is worth noting here that ecology, as a science, is a departure from the traditional model. It concerns itself with complex networks of organisms and habitats and with dynamic relationships (eg feedback loops, and 'chaotic' indeterminacy in the behaviour of physical and biological systems) rather than with mechanistic cause-and-effect chains.

Increasingly there are calls for such inter-disciplinary analysis, for example, in tackling global climate change, but such approaches are also relevant for almost any environmental problem. Take for example, a problem of water pollution in the Weija Reservoir in Ghana. Once scientists working at the Institute of Aquatic Biology in Accra understood the scientific aspects of the problem, they used the action-network approach, through the IDEA programme described in Chapter 11, to build a team to analyse its broader dimensions. They found that the underlying causes of pollution in the watershed arise from rapid urbanisation; intensification of agriculture, including monoculture, deeper ploughing and inputs of fertilisers and pesticides; fuelwood collection along the length of the river; and logging activities in the upper reaches. Problems are compounded as modernisation erodes traditional, sustainable methods of river management evolved within the tribal framework.

FRONTIER SCIENCE AND THE HUMAN-ECOSYSTEM INTERACTION

This kind of complex environmental management situation precludes straightforward, cause-and-effect scientific analysis of the problems, and also precludes simple solutions. Science has an important contribution to make, but complementary kinds of expertise are required to analyse a problem correctly, including the knowledge of local people, such as fishermen and farmers.

In fact, all 'frontier' science, whether astrophysics or ecology, must depend on elements of judgement and interpretive skill. This accounts for the common situation where opposing scientific opinions are brought into play to substantiate both sides of an argument. In well established fields, there may be little or no controversy. However, there are many 'frontier' areas in human–ecosystem interactions – which is why ecology, nutrition, and so on are marked by deep disagreements among experts. These are to be expected, but they can subvert public confidence in the image fostered of 'science' as a clear-cut, logical path to the cause-and-effect understanding of events. Myriad influences can only be understood through intensive data gathering – often very hard – and lengthy analysis. Replication of conditions, for example toxic spills or nuclear accidents, may be impossible. The links between, say, health, food and the wider environment are inherently complex; and the 'object' of study is always changing as new technologies are introduced, and these interact with other variables to produce new forms of risk.

The debate over the 900 foot high Tehri Dam in the Himalayan mountains of Uttar Pradesh provides a good example of expert disagreement. The project is intended to provide power to the industrial cities of northeast India. Scientists, environmentalists and local people are furiously debating the location of the dam, the soil stability, the effects of weather on run-off, the effects of the reservoir on the weather, the seismology and geology of the region, the effect of the dam on seismic activity, and the likely rate of siltation in the reservoir. The soundness of the research upon which the engineering is based is being questioned.[7]

These scientific arguments are part of the larger debate over whether the dam needs to be built at all, that is, will it contribute to development, and if so, to whose development: local people who will be displaced, or urban residents and industry who will make use of the power provided? If development benefits are likely, the next question is: will they outweigh the social and environmental costs, and by whose criteria is a decision to be made? Some scientists question whether the impondment of the reservoir itself will not trigger geological instability sufficient to cause damage to the dam and widespread flooding and death downstream. Good hard science is only one factor in the complex mediation processes over such a project, and in such a tense political atmosphere is it any wonder that scientific authority is invoked on both sides of the debate?

Such examples also serve to raise more fundamental issues about the role of science and technology in modern development, particularly about:

- the uncertainty of control in industrial societies; and
- the assumption in the Western view that it is appropriate for mankind to 'dominate' nature.

UNCERTAINTY OF CONTROL IN INDUSTRIAL SOCIETIES

Our inability to anticipate negative environmental and social impacts and to control our apparently sophisticated technology raises questions that extend to many areas of life. The continued risk of nuclear holocaust is an extreme example. In the field of nuclear energy, the nature of the technology itself magnifies the effect of human error in accidents such as those at Chernobyl or Three Mile Island.[8] At Chernobyl a fire in the reactor sent graphite rods exploding through the cement roof. A cloud containing more than 200 types of radionucleides spread across the Ukraine and Byelorussia, and the effects of radioactive fallout were found in sheep as far away as England and Wales.

The implementation of new technology often takes place in such a subtle and incremental fashion, that we are unable to understand its cumulative effects. This is the case in such fields as agrochemicals, toxic wastes, nuclear power and the massive commitments to fossil fuel consumption by power stations, industry, and the world's 400–500 million motor vehicles.

To understand the influence of established scientific worldviews on the environment it is helpful to consider the processes of scientific and technological development, as well as its products, paying particular attention to the interaction of technical, socio-political and cultural factors. To get at these more basic concerns about the assumptions of Western science, it is helpful to distinguish what has been called the 'orthodox representation' of environmental issues from what has been called an 'alternative environmental agenda'. Grove-White describes the orthodox view:

> On this representation, the problems of the environment are seen as a set of objectively existing physical problems, discovered in nature, through the methods of natural sciences – a group of physical problems arising from specific human interventions in natural systems ... In all these cases we can detect important assumptions about human behaviour. These are dominated by the assumptions of rational choice theory – by the view of the human subject as rationalist-individualist calculator. The paradigm of human behaviour is economistic. Human beings, whether individuals or nation states, overwhelmingly seek to maximise their utilities. In political language, they pursue their interests.[9]

There is nothing inevitable about this conception of humanity. Rather it is an historical and cultural artefact, derived from a positivistic view of scientific knowledge and the assumption that detached, objective observation of nature is unproblematic. But there is an alternative view, which questions some of the fundamental assumptions of Western societies:

> In industrial societies we have become more and more locked into a range of deep structural commitments – industrial, infrastructural, technological. These mean that, socially, more and more, we are running to stand still. Our social systems are ever more perilously interdependent and enclosed, because of the encompassing and increasingly complex nature of technologies ... Most of these structural commitments ... are propelled by technological change, which is almost always producer–led. Most of the choices on these matters have been made blind, in the absence of any significant assessment of potential wider social consequences.[10]

In this view, rational choice and objective assessment of physical problems are severely limited by the structures of industrial modernity and by the effects of successive technological innovations. The spread of the car is a good example: almost unwittingly and within the space of about 65 years, industrialised countries have reorganised their societies around the car. The result is that we now face a crisis of congestion, pollution and car-dependence. In the United States this is said to have '. . . eliminated town and country simultaneously, replaced by a vast suburban wasteland'.[11] In Britain, the dangers of road traffic mean that most British children are no longer allowed out of the house without an adult escort: in the two decades between 1970 and 1990, the proportion of British seven and eight year olds allowed to walk to school unaccompanied has fallen dramatically from 80 per cent to just 9 per cent.[12] Nor is there any likelihood of abatement, as the number of vehicles in the world is predicted to treble by 2030. This trend is unsustainable, and a clear case of technology out of control, with choices about its exploitation made blind.

THE WESTERN VIEW OF NATURE

The Western view of the world, in which nature is 'out there', separate from man, and in which human progress involves increasing domination over the natural world, has its origins in the revolution of thought from the Renaissance and Reformation which also gave rise to liberal capitalism. But this in turn was part of the larger redefinition of humankind and its relation to the world, which had its culmination in the Enlightenment. One aspect of this rethinking of the human condition and potential was a wholesale change in the means of knowing the world, based on the development of scientific method.

With the work of Copernicus, whose model of the solar system displaced the earth from the centre of the universe, humankind was for the first time able to formulate 'laws' which appeared to hold good in the furthest reaches of the heavens, and this transferred to scientists new powers of knowledge previously reserved for scholars of the Church. The Renaissance view of nature is also based, according to Collingwood, on the emerging human experience of designing and constructing machines:

> . . . by the sixteenth century the Industrial Revolution was well on the way. The printing press and the windmill, the lever, the pump, and the pulley, the clock and the wheelbarrow, and a host of machines were established features of daily life. Everyone understood the nature of a machine, and the experience of making and using such things has become part of the general consciousness of European man. It was an easy step to the proposition: as a clockmaker or a millwright is to a clock or a mill, so is God to Nature.[13]

It is at this time that modern science begins to diverge from philosophy and theology. Galileo writes of the language of the 'vast book' of Philosophy: 'It is written in mathematical language, and the letters are triangles, circles and other geometrical figures, without which means it is humanly impossible to comprehend a single word'.[14] The implication is that the truth of nature consists in mathematical facts; what is real is that which is measurable and quantitative.

Francis Bacon took the proposition one step further. Knowledge acquired by scientific analysis could be put to work to give the human race mastery over nature:

> From this perspective, knowledge is regarded not as an end but as a means, expressed and applied in technology, by which humans assume power over the

material world. A high premium is thus attached to the growth of knowledge because it is on this that the enhancement of human powers through the development of technology depends.[15]

The Scientific Revolution, which presaged the Enlightenment and the Industrial Revolution, was most dramatically marked by the work of Newton, who developed both a world model and the scientific method upon which modern natural science is based:[16]

> Newtonian physics, the crowning achievement of the seventeenth century, provided a consistent mathematical theory of the world that remained the solid foundation of scientific thought well into the twentieth century.[17]

In the Newtonian conception, reality is likened to a continuously operating machine composed of isolated parts, which relate mechanistically together to make the whole.[18] By the use of the scientific method these relationships can be discovered, understood and ultimately manipulated for man's purposes. At the core of the scientific method is the principle of analysis, in which the scientist, emotionally detached and neutral, through making empirical observations of selected parts of nature, seeks to uncover causal connections between them, within a framework of universally applicable theories.[19] Priority is thus given to the parts, studied in distinct disciplines, over the whole.

The Newtonian legacy

Modern science is associated, then, with a view of nature as something separate and value-free; and Enlightenment ideas about science and progress encouraged the notion that nature should be dominated by humanity in the name of material and social progress. It is important to note, however, that such conceptions also found support in the Judeo-Christian tradition, which preached the dominion of man over nature. In the words of *Genesis*: '... replenish the earth and subdue it: and have dominion over the fish of the sea and over the fowl of the air and over every living thing that moveth upon the earth'. And, of course, pre-Enlightenment societies in Europe, and many elsewhere, were marked by many unsustainable practices, and a lack of ethical restraint in dealing with nature: their key constraint was the level of technology.

It would thus be quite wrong to see the rise of Western science and industrialism as a radical break with a pre-Enlightenment world in which mankind and nature existed in sustainable harmony. However, it is clear that industrialisation and the rise of modern scientific research provided both the means and an ideology of progress with which Western societies could exploit nature as never before.

As a result of the intellectual revolution of the Enlightenment, Western science and scientific method assumed an ascendancy over all other forms of knowledge in industrial societies; so much so, that knowledge which is labelled 'unscientific' is taken to be wrong. Scientific method provided the technology by which European industrial man set out to conquer both nature and the peoples of the earth in the eighteenth and nineteenth centuries. Moreover, the unequivocal attachment to economic growth in industrial society depends on continual advances in scientific knowledge, which is the basic prerequisite for the development of the technology upon which industrial society depends for the 'subjugation' of nature.

What are the implications of the legacy of Newtonian scientific method over our ways of thinking? There are two problems: fragmentation of knowledge, and the effects of interaction. Under the Newtonian model, because each of the parts of the great machine were in some fixed relationship, small fragments of reality could profitably be studied in detail; all such studies, it was assumed, could gradually build up a picture of the universe. But the more this mode of analysis became adopted, the more perspective on the bigger picture was lost, until the point arrived when fragmentary analysis became the objective, and holism was increasingly viewed with suspicion as unscientific. The physicist David Bohm calls this 'the habit of fragmentary thought'.[20]

The problem is compounded by disciplinary reductionism in which highly specialised disciplines in the natural and social sciences, isolated from each other, have sought '. . . to explain the whole through the construction of theories specific to their respective perspectives'. Jones calls this the searchlight effect in which an intense beam of light gives detailed knowledge of a part of reality, leaving the rest obscure.[21]

This syndrome of knowledge fragmentation, or reductionism, has today become:

> the principal handicap in knowing and solving the global problems that confront mankind. More than that, numerous pressing problems for the evolution of civilisation, which cover several different and specialised areas, cannot be understood and explained.[22]

Such an emphasis of the parts of the system at the expense of the whole is not only typical of the natural and social sciences however, but has become a general characteristic of Western culture. Specialisation, division of labour, individualism – all are expressions of the modernisation process.[23]

Another problem has to do with the nature of causality in the highly interactive humankind–nature relationship, and a fundamental limitation of the scientific method. Causal explanation in the natural sciences rests on a basic assumption that an event to be explained can be isolated or insulated from the effects of its surroundings. In other words we must be able to demonstrate that A is directly affected by B, and not by C, D or E; that acid rain causes certain effects, and that certain industrial processes have caused acid rain. But when science works with complex metaproblems there is no way of observing cause and effect, where every action causes multiple interactive effects. There is no way of bounding the problem in a rigorous fashion because the number of actors and independent actions creating what are called 'intervening' variables is indeterminate.

This indeterminacy defines what we call a 'turbulent' environment – turbulent because the interactive effects are inherently unpredictable. This is the uncertainty of control discussed earlier. Rather than scientific prediction, the best that can be hoped for might be called 'realistic expectation', and our expectations must be tempered by our knowledge of the reality of the turbulent environment. Instead of prediction, the intellectual and emotional basis on which we appraise our increasingly uncertain future must rest on wisdom derived from understanding the implications of past actions – wisdom being the very fusion of knowledge and ethical values, which overemphasis on the scientific method has done much to separate. We return to the concept of the turbulent environment in Chapter 8.

In relation to the resolution of complex environmental problems, our existing capacity for generating new wisdom is poor and our chosen socioeconomic and cultural system conditions us against so doing. Unfortunately too our commonplace vision of progress in terms of ever-increasing production and consumption may also condition us against the backward reflection necessary to understand our environmental predicament. Worse still, excessive consumption is itself a form of conditioning – it is an addiction from which withdrawal becomes increasingly difficult.

In summary, the evolution of detached scientific method, by providing a justification for the utilitarian commodification of nature, presents us with four problems:

1   Our knowledge of the world has become fragmented by the compartmentalisation of experience, making it difficult to understand complex socio-environmental interactions. One response has been to develop more 'holistic' approaches, although there is much debate about what this means.
2   Conventional scientific method is predicated on the functional separation of humankind from nature: this colours our perceptions and may lead to overemphasis on technical solutions to solve human problems.
3   Scientific method has been extended to the study of humankind itself, in the social sciences, through positivism, but this has been largely unfruitful. The response most relevant to environmental management has been participative action research, described in later chapters.
4   Western science has encouraged us to detach knowledge from values. This has reinforced a utilitarian approach to life. But wisdom is the conjuction of knowledge with ethics – we have therefore not increased our wisdom at the rate of our material progress or destruction of nature. One response has been to rekindle discussion about the moral dimension of the humankind–nature relationship in environmental debate. This is part of a broader movement to shift political debate to a moral ground which Giddens calls 'life politics'.[24]

THE STUDY OF HUMANKIND IN RELATION TO NATURE

Before going on to say how these new responses contribute to innovative approaches to environmental management, it is helpful to look at the social sciences, which have developed in parallel with the natural sciences, often apeing the scientific method, albeit not very successfully. These are important because, as the complexity of environmental problems becomes obvious, so does the need for multi-disciplinary approaches that combine the natural and social sciences.

The fusion of Enlightenment thinking in political philosophy, examined in Chapter 4, with the scientific worldview, gave rise to a literature concerned with methodological issues in the study of social life. These issues continue to engage social scientists to this day. Having established a powerful rationale for the mastery of nature, Western philosophers looked for some similar means of analysing man himself. In particular this was stimulated by the prospect of finding in social processes the analogues of Newton's laws of physical processes.

Thomas Hobbes for example, set out in *Leviathan* to build a 'civil science' made up of clear principles and closely reasoned deductions based on postulates derived from observations about human nature.[25] Based on the idea that all knowledge was derived from sensory perception, he set out to study first the nature of the individual human being, and then to apply the principles of human nature to economic and political problems, guided by the belief that there were laws governing human society similar to those governing the physical universe.

The scientific approach to social knowledge also impressed the nineteenth century utilitarians Jeremy Bentham and John Stuart Mill. They argued that the concepts of social contracts and natural rights, put forward by John Locke and others, were misleading, and that it was more productive to use *observation* to uncover the basic, definable elements of actual human behaviour and to use this information for *rational* decision making.

Two profound developments of the early industrial period served to reinforce this social scientific approach. First, the French Revolution demonstrated that fundamental and age-old institutions, hitherto invested with a degree of permanence and inevitability, could be transformed or overthrown. This meant that new structures were possible and encouraged the view that their nature could be derived from rational, scientific analysis – logical, empirical and quantified.[26] Second, large scale production associated with the industrial era was based on the use of rational calculation of the potential demographic and spatial spread of markets for new goods.

The fundamental propositions of the rationalist tradition stemming from the Enlightenment are:

1   that human nature is essentially the same at all times and places;
2   that universal human goals, true ends and effective means, are discoverable in principle; and
3   that methods akin to Newtonian science may be discovered and applied in morals, politics, economics, and human behaviour, toward the elimination of social ills.[27]

The relevance of the social sciences

Other philosophers, particularly Comte, worked to fuse the notion of rationalism with the methodology of the natural sciences and to extend this to the fledgling social sciences. In *Cours de Philosophie Positive*, Comte argued that the true philosophic spirit would henceforth explore reality with a certainty and precision previously unknown in intellectual life. In Comte's scheme of positive philosophy (positivism), the natural and social sciences taken together formed a hierarchy of decreasing generality, and increasing complexity, beginning with mathematics, then physics, chemistry and biology, and then moving into sociology, the science of human conduct. As with natural phenomena, it was argued that social phenomena are subject to general laws, which will become apparent through scientific study. Benton suggests the search for such general laws is at the heart of the rationalist conception of both natural and social life, and: '. . . the implication is clear: an extension of scientific thought to social

phenomena will generate systematic knowledge of society to which all must assent'.[28]
The underpinnings of positivistic philosophy are described by Giddens:

> . . . reality consists of sense impressions; an aversion to metaphysics, the latter
> being condemned as sophistry or illusion; the representation of philosophy as a
> method of analysis, clearly separable from, yet at the same time parasitic upon,
> the findings of science; the duality of fact and value – the thesis that empirical
> knowledge is logically discrepant from the pursuit of moral aims and the
> implementation of ethical standards; and the notion of the unity of science: the
> idea that the natural and social sciences share a common logical and perhaps
> even methodological foundation.[29]

The notion of a positivistic social science gained currency, particularly in America
after the second world war, based on the success of the 'science' of economics in the
Keynesian post-war reconstruction. Other disciplines, such as sociology and
psychology, attempted to emulate economics and emerge as sciences. The attraction
of the positivist approach lay in its apparent advantages in assisting social
engineering, just as such manipulation was possible in the natural world.

Quantitative social science took hold. An emphasis on quantification is closely
allied to the overall positivist approach in which an assumption of rationality is
fundamental to any explanation or prediction of human behaviour. In this approach
large samples of people, whom social scientists have empirically observed and wish to
generalise about, must be assumed to be acting rationally. The only other alternative
is that observations are of random behaviour and no explanation or prediction is
possible. Equally, rationality must be assumed if social scientists are to substantiate
statistically what are, at first instance, abstractions or generalisations.

There are two areas of concern here. First, abstractions will be simplified pictures
of a complex reality, and no quantitative models can encapsulate the multi-
dimensionality of human existence. Reductive attempts at modelling invariably lead
to criticism:

> Empirical methods such as simulation, optimisation, and multivariate statistical
> modelling all represent very considerable . . . abstractions from, the normal
> reality most of us would agree upon. Our discontinuous, nonlinear, stochastic,
> uncertain, and ill-defined world is stretched, shortened, trimmed, compressed,
> and moulded until it fits into the procrustean bed of the analytical methods at
> hand.[30]

Problems of quantitative modelling have been discussed at length and are familiar to
most social scientists.[31] The main objection is not that tools such as statistical
modelling are not useful, but that they can be misused or over-valued, in that their
simplification of reality is conveniently taken for reality itself. Although such tools can
be important when they contribute additional dimensions to an understanding of
complex social problems, they are not surrogates for reality, nor can they be
comprehensive, and so they are not in themselves a very useful guide to action. But
they are often taken to be sufficient for action: as, for example, in the use of cost-
benefit analysis in assessing development projects, like the large dams traditionally
funded by the World Bank. Finally, quantitative techniques are often predicated on

simplistic methodological assumptions (for example, the choice of a discount rate in cost-benefit analysis), which often cannot withstand either methodological or political scrutiny, and which themselves represent value judgements.

A second concern arises when social science or rationalist decision techniques are purported to be politically neutral or value-free. But all such techniques are value-laden in themselves, in that they may reflect the priorities of some dominant social group and exclude consideration of the values of groups less powerful, but often highly affected.

Quantitative analysis can also undervalue social, environmental, spiritual and other intangible dimensions of political problems – many dimensions are not amenable to quantification. In particular a focus on 'dollars and cents', as discussed with regard to GDP, means that we tend to ignore other dimensions of life which do not fit into these equations. There is also a more profound concern that decision processes, many apparently value-free, are invariably rooted in ideological assumptions and can represent a form of technocratic domination which precludes ethical considerations and opposing views in fundamental decisions affecting societies.

The result of the development of positivistic social science and rationalism as a mode of decision making was that:

> ... the whole problem of values remained unsolved, especially so far as its practical manifestation in policy formation was concerned, no secure links were forged between philosophy, particularly moral and political, and sociology. This was disastrous.[32]

EMERGING PERCEPTIONS OF HUMANKIND AND NATURE

Although the legacy of the Newtonian view is strong in everyday life, there are a number of emerging paradigms: in science itself, and in two perspectives which might be called 'local traditionalist' and 'holistic'.

Developments in physics beyond the Newtonian model

In science, the Newtonian conception has been drastically revised since the mid-nineteenth century. Since the 1920s advances in the field of sub-atomic physics known as quantum theory have provided the main basis for progress beyond the Newtonian model of the world as a mechanism. Developments in quantum theory are resulting in a fundamental rethink of not only the Newtonian world model with its notions of linear causality, but also of the epistemological presuppositions upon which all previous scientific thought has been based:

> Unless modern quantum theory is in error, the world simply does not exist in definite state without our observing it. Before matter can peep forth, even as a pebble or a snowflake, it has to be observed by a consciousness. Something must sustain it in and above the void of non-being . . . That something, it seems, is the mind.[33]

The result may be a constant interaction between mind and matter, and a definition of reality conditioned by the observer. In short, the world 'out there' is *not* wholly independent of our observation, which in turn affects that world. According to many physicists the idea of material reality without consciousness is impossible. The concept begins to emerge of reality as a field of interacting networks of complex systems at many levels of organisation.

Care is needed here. Quantum theory can lend support to all kinds of views and there is no definitive interpretation of the field. There is obviously much to be uncovered; however, it is true that any interpretation of quantum theory undermines the old Newtonian conception of the cosmos. The fundamental uncertainty affecting the observation of the sub-atomic world limits us to prediction of the probabilities of events.

Elsewhere in new fields of scientific research there is a growing interest in the behaviour of complex dynamic systems, whether inorganic or biological, which defy traditional reductionist analysis. Insights into the 'chaotic' properties of complex systems such as the atmosphere, and even of apparently simple, predictable ones such as a pendulum or an orbiting body, suggest that there are inherent limits to the predictability of events on the large scale just as there are on the quantum level.[34] This indicates that some convergence may be in prospect between interpretations and research interests in 'mainstream' science and the 'holistic' approaches to natural philosophy outlined below.[35]

The relevance of local knowledge

A second emerging paradigm is quite different. This perspective argues the case for local knowledge: a mode of understanding in which science is not dominated by Western assumptions and methods and is relevant to the local culture. For example, priests play an important role in maintaining water quality in Ghana – a cultural form of sustainable development evolved over many centuries. There are many such examples of indigenous knowledge which is often eroded by Western science and modernisation: traditional agricultural irrigation in Rajasthan or Bali; sustainable rainforestry in Brazil and Borneo; hunter-gatherer lifestyles in the Canadian Arctic, the Australian outback or the Kalahari desert. This represents a vast repository of knowledge of sustainable development refined over millennia, and under desperate threat from insensitive modernisation.

However, it is important to note that a 'local' emphasis may not always be wholly conducive to development. For example, Pakistan has attempted to develop Islamic science and economics. Inayatullah notes an advantage in local enablement and self-esteem, but warns that this emphasis may also lead to situations where old power structures – such as those of the mullahs and the landlords – are renewed:

Here, while science has been placed in an alternative cultural site, it has lost its openness to critique and debate – an openness necessary for any creative development. While freed from modernity, this indigenization of knowledge perspective has become frozen in historical-ideational religious traditions.[36]

This limitation indicates the need for local knowledge and Western approaches to be integrated – used selectively where appropriate and with both open to modification in the light of experience. A simplistic rejection of Western science is as flawed as a simplistic imposition of the Western approach.

The human ecological perspective

A third emerging paradigm is the holistic or human ecological one. The term 'holistic' was coined by Jan Smuts in 1926 in his book *Holism and Evolution* as meaning 'the whole is greater than the sum of the parts', but also embracing a hierarchy of explanation, the lowest rung of which is Newtonian mechanism. This view has re-emerged as what has been termed the new holistic paradigm. In the writings of Fritjof Capra for example, science, religion and values are reconciled through a reinterpretation of modern physics. The aim is:

> . . . not towards a local science but a new universal science that is not reductionist, but holistic, with truth simultaneously having many levels and at the same time grounded in a consciousness that exists ontologically prior to the intellectual mind.[37]

The holistic paradigm is characterised by: '. . . an emphasis on totality, the replacement of the observer by the participant, thinking in terms of processes, an affinity with systems theory, and by ecologism as distinct from anthropocentrism'.[38] There are three important aspects here for environmental management.

First, holism takes exception to the Newtonian view that the dynamics of complex systems can be understood by aggregating knowledge about the components of the system. This does not deny the importance of directed scientific research, but suggests that a higher level of integration is necessary that can bring quantitative scientific knowledge together with qualitative sociocultural knowledge and ethical values.

The point is clear with respect to the modelling of global environmental change and the contribution of science to remedial or adaptive policies. Climate modelling is constrained by limits not only on computing power but also on our comprehension of the chaotic nature of atmospheric processes and their interactions with other complex systems such as ocean currents. The uncertainties in the science underlying the modelling, and the charged political context of research into, for example, global warming,[39] have led to the description of the analysis of global environmental change as 'second order science', distinct from the 'consensual' science of better understood research with no direct impacts on human life.[40] Second order science cannot be insulated from political issues and values concerning our relationship with the natural environment.

Second, the notion that the scientist can be a detached observer is rejected along with the notion of a wholly objective universe. Rather participants define their reality interactively with nature and each other. Third, holism looks at human society and nature as an integrated system or network which is non-hierarchical – all elements are linked together but there is neither top nor bottom, centre nor periphery. A characteristic of the network is an intricate linkage of cause, effect and feedback.

The holistic approach recognises the inescapability of integrating an ethical dimension into the science of global environmental change. There is not the space here to discuss environmental ethics in any detail, but a simplified categorisation of viewpoints is possible:[41]

A   Technocentric: resource-exploitative, growth-oriented;
B   Managerial: resource-conservationist, oriented to sustainable growth;
C   Communalist: resource-preservationist, oriented to limited or zero growth;
D   Bioethicist or deep ecological: extreme preservationist, anti-growth.

The technocentric view (A) tends to take a wholly instrumental approach to nature. It is resolutely anthropocentric and places faith in the capacity of technology to harness nature and substitute man-made capital for natural resources where required. As noted in Chapter 1, this approach tends to ignore the implications of our ignorance of the dynamics and potential for collapse of ecosystems stressed by over-exploitation or pollution. It also neglects the value that many find intrinsic in wildlife and landscapes.

At the opposite extreme is the bioethicist view (D), in which moral rights are conferred on other species and humans are required to respect intrinsic value in all nature and live in harmony with it. This broad approach is highly unlikely ever to appeal to enough people to form the basis for a realisable economic programme. It also provides little or no guidance on deciding between human development and nature preservation in cases where human and non-human interests – in theory equal – are in conflict.[42]

Neither of these positions is compatible with sustainable development as we have defined it: seeking to enhance diverse forms of human development while maintaining the natural capital stock for future generations.[43] The technocentric position risks unsustainable disruption of ecosystems; and the bioethicist view is politically unacceptable and impracticable in the face of the industrialisation of the planet and the aspirations of most of the world to better quality of life and chances for human development.

The intermediate positions B and C are those associated with human 'stewardship' of nature, with differing emphases on the extent to which development should be constrained and modified by environmental considerations. Our perspective here combines elements of both the 'managerial' and 'communalist' approaches, recognising the need for sustainable growth to improve human development and environmental protection in the poor world, and the need for radical policy change and movement towards steady-state or steady-flow economic development in many aspects of the industrial world's consumption and production patterns.

What must be stressed is that implicit or explicit adherence to a general set of values concerning our impact on the natural environment is inescapable. We cannot develop our understanding of global environmental change and sustainable development paths without reference to guiding values; and disputes over the meaning of sustainable development are essentially about the values that underpin the decision-making processes we use in assessing our impacts on the environment.

CONCLUSION

Probably the greatest failing of positivistic philosophy and science has been the attempt to separate fact from value, by the argument that the basis of scientific knowledge can always be separated from ethical considerations. This gave rise to the mistaken notion that science could be in all circumstances value-free, or neutral and objective. It is now clear is that scientific and technological development for industrialisation hitherto focused mainly on one goal – growth – and on the means of achieving it, can no longer be divorced wholly from social goals or ethical and ecological considerations.

As to the broader debate over the role of rationality in public policy, the assumption that behaviour is rational or irrational is a false dichotomy. It is better to realise that behaviour in an uncertain world will often be based upon 'situational' reasoning, and that to be rational means to attempt to be efficacious and judicious in a context of uncertainty, vested interest, and inevitable ignorance of the overall long-term impact of decisions.

4   Political ideas and sustainable development

The 1990s are likely to become the 'decade of democracy': more and more nations are contemplating the establishment of democratic systems . . . this trend encourages us to reflect on the meaning of democracy and its various forms.

A Lijphart, 1991[1]

It is in their role as citizens, not consumers, that individual people will create a sustainable economy . . . it is through collective political choices that sustainability will be achieved.

Michael Jacobs, 1991[2]

The Western, post-Enlightenment view of humankind is founded on a wholly new perception of the relation of individuals to society. In medieval and many non-Western social systems, the individual is considered a minute part of a greater fixed system. In the liberal society of the West, human beings are often imagined to be self-sufficient cells, from which society is constructed.[3] In this conception, people need not accept the social order as given, but may refashion it to suit their needs. The crucial issue for political philosophy then becomes the nature of the relationship between the self-sufficient individual and the larger social organisation.

Political debate relates directly to the framework of ordered relationships which enable us to live together and satisfy our communal wants and needs.[4] Political philosophy, in addressing the problems and prospects of social organisation, is both explanatory and normative. That is, it asks how a political society does or could work, and passes judgement on whether it works well or badly. The history of political philosophy provides some key insights into constraints on resolving the environmental crisis, particularly the tension between legitimate desires for individual freedom and the need for social control, often by the state, to realise the 'common good'.

By the sixteenth century, political writers began to elaborate a distinction between public and private interests, and the domain of the 'contract' between citizens and the state, which is to provide the basis for modern political theory. From the seventeenth to nineteenth centuries, the philosophy of liberalism emerged, nurtured by the creative thinking of many of the same Enlightenment philosophers who developed the Western scientific method. Utilitarian liberalism became the philosophy of capitalism, with science and technology providing the means for the commodification of nature and industrialism on a world scale. At the same time, emerging notions of liberal democracy gave rise to ideas of individual freedom outside the confines of Church and state.

The thrust of much political thought and action towards freedom and individuality was paralleled by moves towards more rationalised organisation and constraints on individualism to meet communal needs, such as public order and the security of the state, and later, problems of poverty and environmental degradation. The vexing question of the trade-off between individual freedom and government authority has been a central point of concern in the Western political tradition. A resolution has yet to be worked out of this fundamental tension between reasonable desires for freedom and the need to restrain this freedom in the interests of the common good.

DEMOCRACY AND SUSTAINABLE DEVELOPMENT

It is unlikely that this tension between freedom and control is resolvable in that the sense that a once and for all balance can be derived based on philosophic or economic criteria for any country. Rather, following from conclusions in the last chapter, we argue that the appropriate balance is situational and derived from debate or democratic mediation.

We believe this is a fundamental aspect of sustainable development. However, we use the word 'democratic' in the sense of an equality of power among environmental stakeholders and in people taking control of their own environments, and thus 'owning' both problem and solution, rather than from any notion of imposing Western institutional structures, many of which have never worked in formerly colonised countries. This commitment to dialogue also rules out simplistic ideological viewpoints from right or left and, of course, the authoritarianism that has been so prevalent and damaging in many non-Western countries. Rather the requirement is for intelligent debate, fully aware of the intellectual reasoning and tensions which underpin the Western democratic ideas being exported worldwide. Whether non-Western leaders agree that such ideas are appropriate or not is for themselves and their people to decide. But knowledge of the origins of the debate is surely useful.

A related problem is that sustainable development, reflecting a concern for the future even to unborn generations, must imply some planning for that future. Many of our problems arise from a failure to plan. Such planning at the societal level could only be initiated or undertaken by an agency with a societal overview, and however sophisticated civil society may become, it is difficult to imagine the state not playing a crucial role. But planning by the state is currently tarnished by the collapse of communism in the East and the problems of the overloaded welfare states in the West, and the unreliability of most long term planning processes.

The imperative of sustainable development suggests some new role in planning for the state, but one substantially different from past experiences of state planning. In later chapters we will argue that this new role for the state is to provide strategic guidance and to create the conditions to unlock innovation in the private and community sectors, often by devolving responsibility within a broader framework which encourages information flow about societal options. People often use the term 'enabling state', and we apply that to the concept of sustainable development.

In this chapter we look at the gradual emergence of the concept of the liberal, democratic state, developed through the philosophies of Hobbes, Locke, Bentham, Mill and others. Although we have argued that the state, acting alone, cannot guarantee environmental quality, the state is first and foremost the provider, or guarantor, of public goods, by direct provision or by regulation, which is a form of coercive social control. Consideration of the tension between individual freedoms and the social control required for sustainable development can profitably begin with a brief history of changing views of the role of the state.

THE INDIVIDUAL AND THE STATE

The two most influential concepts in the development of the theory of the state have been the idea of the state as a structure of power, clearly distinguishable from civil society in general; and the endemic problem of reconciling the authority of the state to intervene in society by law, with the liberty of the individual. Most modern democratic theory:

> . . . has constantly sought to justify the sovereign power of the state while at the same time justifying limits upon that power. The history of this attempt since Machiavelli and Hobbes is the history of arguments to balance might and right, power and law, duties and rights. On the one hand, the state must have a monopoly of coercive power in order to provide a secure basis upon which trade, commerce and family life can prosper. On the other hand, by granting the state a regulatory and coercive capability, liberal political theorists were aware that they had accepted a force which could (and frequently did) deprive citizens of political and social freedoms.[5]

Questions of whether the state has the right to impose constraints on the freedom of individuals in pursuit of a common good are thus always on the agenda of societies which subscribe to Western notions of democracy. Unfortunately, this is not a question that allows a clear-cut answer, except in relation to extreme cases. At one extreme, if all relationships and all expectations end up being governed by the state, the result is totalitarianism. Conversely, sustainable development is probably impossible under conditions of excessive individualism. Extreme state control is throughly discredited; the excesses of individualism represent a more subtle danger.

Can individualism be excessive?

An analysis by Lane of individualism in the United States of America is instructive, for the US in many ways epitomises the successful liberal democratic state.[6] It is the most privatised, market-oriented major economic power, with the highest proportion of the ownership of the means of production in private hands.[7] Its approach to capitalism and its culture are massively powerful influences in the rest of the world.

In his examination of the nature of individualism in the US, Lane makes a distinction between two types of individualism: utilitarian, that is maximisation of economic self-interest, and expressive, that is self-actualisation in feeling, intuition and experience. He identifies the source of a serious problem in American society as excessive and aggressive utilitarian individualism, which results in a fundamental decline of a sense of community, a degradation of the quality of public life, and a retardation of opportunities for expressive individualism to be realised. This problem, that is the fear that competitive individuals would preclude achievement of the public good, is the 'most important unresolved problem in American history'.

The problem of excessive individualism in American society was also identified by de Tocqueville 150 years earlier in *Democracy in America*. The rise of neo-conservatism and 'yuppyism' in the 1980s served to sharpen a concern over this problem, as does the continued reluctance of the US Government to make binding commitments to reduce its contribution to greenhouse gas emissions, in spite of having by far the highest per capita consumption of fossil fuel energy in the world. In America 'the self has become the main form of reality' with the result that:

> . . . the yearning for community, while real and strong, is being overwhelmed by the self-seeking of individualism and self-interest that is exacerbated by the current political and economic emphasis on privatisation . . . as a result the last 20 years . . . have seen a pronounced trend toward the dismantling of public administration . . . and an overt rejection of the idea of the public interest.[8]

This strong, but ultimately debilitating, strain of American individualism, Lane argues, 'flows directly out of the political theories of John Locke' and is enshrined in the Constitution of the United States. The framing of this Constitution may be viewed:

> . . . as an exercise in compromise and expediency marked by young, ambitious men setting out to create a vigorous, large commercial empire. Notions of freedom, equality of opportunity, and the sanctity of property all contribute to the model of American economic man, contending for gain and individual aggrandizement, and defining the public interest in terms of a system that maximizes opportunity for self-interest.[9]

The catalogue of environmental ills presented in Chapter 1 indicates the ecological consequences of industrial policies in which expressive individualism is constrained, whether by utilitarian individualism or by what might be called utilitarian collectivism. The extreme cases of these latter approaches to politics in modern societies are, respectively, the US and the communist states. The ruin of communism has been caused by ecological as well as economic and ideological disaster: communism is now a proven case of unsustainable industrial development. However, as we noted in Chapter 3, there is a serious risk that many will see the failure of communist models for industrial society as evidence of the desirability of the utilitarian individualist model of liberal capitalism. While American-style (and now Japanese) capitalism has proved itself more efficient by far, it also runs grave ecological risks through favouring minimal restraint on individual choices in the market.

In order to increase understanding of the problems for environmental management posed by this style of economic development and political thinking, it is useful to look back at the origins of present ideas about the relationship between state and individual. Key themes in Western political thought on this issue are:

- the idea of the secular state, divorced from other institutions such as the Church, in the writings of Machiavelli;
- the need for the state to regulate individual behaviour, and the possibility for what Thomas Hobbes calls the 'achievements of civilization' to arise out of this control;

- the importance of individual freedom, and the right to refashion the state to serve new ends, based on the voluntary consent of the governed, from John Locke;
- a distinction between the individual, acting in self-interest, and the citizen, who sees his interests served by pursuit of the common good, that is the civilising effect of civil society, from Jean-Jacques Rousseau;
- the importance of the use of information by private entrepreneurs, which is the 'guiding hand' of capitalism as first perceived by Adam Smith;
- the use of the utilitarian principle as the sole ethical element in social and economic policy, as expounded by Jeremy Bentham;
- the important perception that liberal democratic capitalism needs to be continuously reformed on an incremental basis, as argued by John Stuart Mill;
- the neo-conservative arguments of Fredrich Hayek and others, which restate the key ideas of classic liberalism; and
- a critique of those arguments based on the need for sustainable development.

These themes are expanded below.

The emergence of the secular state

The long drawn-out transformation of the feudal order in Europe gave rise to the development of secular politics and modern sciences as autonomous bodies of doctrine and research, no longer dominated by either religious beliefs and church power or the norms of traditional hierarchies. The first important exponent of secular politics was Machiavelli, writing in the early sixteenth century. The emergence of the concept of the state in Western political philosophy can be traced back to Machiavelli's *il stato* in *The Prince*.

Machiavelli's stress on the importance of the stability of the secular state is a recurring theme, and still of major interest in political science. It arose from his concern to escape the conditions of uncertainty which characterised the feudal period in Italy. Machiavelli was also the first political philosopher to argue raison d'etat as an explanation and defence of political action, in which the common good ceased to be linked to God, but became associated instead with the interests of the state. Only after Machiavelli did the concept of the state become a central object of political philosophy. It is important to note here also, that in escaping from the confines of Church dogma, Machiavelli down-graded notions of morality in state affairs: the self-interest of the state becomes the sole criterion for decision making.

Conceptions of state control

In the century after Machiavelli, England was also confronted by instability and civil strife, both religious, between Roman Catholics and the new Protestants, and between the landed aristocracy and a rising middle class. The result was civil war. This situation drove Hobbes, in *Leviathan*, to examine the failure of sovereign authority in England. The war, in his view, represented a regression to the natural condition of man outside of the bounds of civil society.[10]

In Hobbes' writing can be found an emphasis on a secular, stable state, a

Leviathan, governed by a sovereign power as inevitably better than the anarchic condition of natural, individualistic, man. The actions of individuals created the state, and subsequent law and justice were created by the sovereign who secured the state, and who was implicitly obeyed by the individual members. The motive of this, as Hobbes put it, '. . . is the foresight of their own preservation, and of a more contented life thereby, that is to say, of getting out of the miserable condition of war, which is necessarily consequent to the natural passions of men'.

The state, in Hobbes' view, made possible the achievements of civilisation, and was constituted by social contract, which once entered into voluntarily by individuals, becomes a compulsory association wherein:

> Every man should say to every man, 'I authorise and give up my right to govern myself to this man, or this assembly of men, on this condition, that you give up thy right to him' . . . and this done, the multitude so united in one person is called a Commonwealth.[11]

Here Hobbes recognises and institutionalises the state's right to regulate individual behaviour for the general good. In this way a political power is created in the form of a strong secular state, pre-eminent in political and social life, and absolutely necessary because of the deleterious, self-seeking nature of individuals' behaviour and patterns of interaction.[12] Civilisation is impossible without this regulation, and the option to do away with it is not available once the contract is made.

In Hobbes' work we find the first conception of the state as the willing amalgamation of the interest of individuals. It may be ruled subsequently in a top-down manner but it arises from the consent of the governed. Hobbes also provides a rationale for state intervention from a conception of a greater good to be had from regulation of individual behaviour. Hobbes' views, in other words, both substantiate environmental control by government and the pursuit, by state action, of what he called 'the achievements of civilisation', one of which now would certainly have to be sustainable development.

Voluntary consent

John Locke's reaction to the English civil war was different. In *Second Treatise*, a reply to Hobbes, he stressed the role of consent as the basis of all political power, in the form of a voluntary, rather than a compulsory, contract between governor and governed. In Locke's view, men are free, equal and rational in nature, and need not submit to any arbitrary or absolute power. The instability of England was due to the exercise of arbitrary power by the monarchy, which engendered a natural rebellious reaction. The rulers of England, the embodiment of the state, had damaged their contractual relationship with the governed by taxing without consent, by creating armies, and by limiting the religious liberties of the citizenry.[13] Man had natural rights, including life, liberty, and property and these could not be abrogated by the state. A state of nature, which was a state of liberty rather than Hobbes' state of license, was preferable to bad government, and good government was created by a social contract to assist peaceful living and protect property.

In Locke's work government is seen as a contract based on the consent of the governed, to be dissolved or altered when it no longer served its purpose of safeguarding the right to life, liberty and property. This state was not only temporary but limited, and had to be prevented from suppressing natural rights by constitutional limits on the extent of its authority. Government was by consent, and consent could be revoked by individuals and the government thereby changed. In Locke's view the creation of government is a burden individuals have to bear to secure their ends. While the state exists to safeguard the rights and liberties of citizens, it must generally be restricted in scope and constrained in practice to ensure individual freedom.[14]

Locke's views on the danger of arbitrary or absolute power of the state were reinforced by his view, set out in *Essay Concerning Human Understanding*, that the acquisition of human knowledge was constrained by the inherent limitations in our ability to perceive reality. In the face of our limited knowledge, tolerance and a degree of scepticism about the ability of the state to govern were called for.

In Hobbes and Locke we find two important themes in modern thinking on the state: conservatism in its original conception, and the beginning of liberalism. In Lockean ideas, which have considerable influence today, we find the origins of liberal thought which was taken to America, and which emphasised the right to liberty and the right to revolt against arbitrary authority. Here are the intellectual roots of the revolutions to come in France and America, in support of varieties of secular liberalism, and against conservatism in the form of monarchy. With Locke we see the origin of the main philosophical arguments for the liberal democratic state, not based on any beliefs about the intrinsic nature of the state, but because of a modern conception of a man's rights.

This raises a basic question about the idea of sustainable development: can private rights, inviolable by the state, include environmentally damaging actions or actions with environmentally damaging by-products? The former presents us with little difficulty but the latter case encompasses many areas of human action that may need to be brought under government control in future. For example, many people the world over consider the use of a car as the *sine qua non* of a modern lifestyle. In America one worker in seven owes his or her job to the car industry. In many lower income countries, the car is held to be a symbol of modernity, so much so that alternative, cleaner but 'old fashioned' forms of transport are abandoned: bicycle rickshaws in New Delhi and Jakarta, or donkey carts in Cairo, for example. But given the energy consumption and environmental and social damage caused by the car, how do we balance conflicting rights? What does it mean to say that rights are inviolable? And who decides? A polluting majority or an environmentally conscious minority? Such issues must increasingly come to the fore as we move towards environmental control policies which are intended to have a more than marginal effect.

The idea of self-government

The already evolving tension between the idea of a common good promoted by the state, versus the need for individual freedom from state control, was approached from a new direction by the French philosopher Jean–Jacques Rousseau. He provides a counterpoint to evolving notions of Lockean liberal democracy by contrasting the natural man, who is whole but concerned solely with himself, with the citizen, who understands his good to be identical to the common good.

In his book, *Emile* Rousseau attempts to reconcile man's selfish nature with the demands of civil society. He emphasises that the passion of selfishness is changed by the very experience of living in a stable society. Man is not virtuous in a state of nature; virtue only comes about in a society based on law, and the unselfish virtues can increase with time. In *The Social Contract*, Rousseau argues that such civic virtue is ensured by the development of what he calls a 'civil religion' inculcated by the sovereign. The dogma of Rousseau's civil religion includes tolerance, sanctity of the social contract, and respect for law. We can think of Rousseau's civil religion as an appropriate value system, nurtured by government.

However, Rousseau was unhappy with the existing ideas of social contract and he therefore proposed a more utopian arrangement: a system of self–government in a direct democracy in which all citizens would be actively involved in the process of government, rather than simply voting periodically for a representative to take decisions. Here the idea of self-government is posited as an end in itself and a political order is proposed in which the affairs of the state are integrated into the affairs of ordinary citizens.[15] There are many proposals in current environmentalist writing for such 'direct democracy'.

The legitimate authority of the state in Rousseau's conception is based on 'the common good embodied in the general will', which takes precedence over individual will. The general will cannot be developed by a divisive, selfish, class structured society, but only by a one-class society of working proprietors, and such a society was to be achieved by government action:

> It is therefore one of the most important functions of government to prevent extreme inequality of fortunes; not by taking away wealth . . ., but by depriving all men of the right to accumulate it; not by building hospitals for the poor, but by securing citizens from becoming poor.[16]

Rousseau also begins to consider the difference between simple majority rule and the desirability of working towards consensus on difficult issues. He argues that two rules are applicable:

> One, that the more important and serious the deliberations, the closer the winning opinion should be to unanimity. The other, that the more speed the business at hand requires, the smaller the prescribed difference in the division of opinion should be. In deliberations that must be finished on the spot, a majority of a single vote should suffice.[17]

In Rousseau we find the origins of important ideas in modern political thinking, particularly in the areas of participation and equality. Rousseau has been claimed as an antecedent by many utopian thinkers for his emphasis on direct citizen participation. This foreshadows an important theme in modern thinking on community development and planning, namely the focus on the value of 'bottom-up' efforts by citizens to take control of their own lives. It is not surprising therefore to find aspects of Rousseau's philosophy in many contemporary Western ideologies, for he went well beyond the visible manifestations of the state, to consider psychological and moral aspects of human endeavour and organisation. For example, the idea of a civil religion that encourages an unselfish civic virtue, which can increase over time, is close in many ways to the idea of an evolving, less materialistic value system which can encourage an ecological ethic in our time. Rousseau sees a role here for the state in inculcating such civic virtue, just as many environmentalists may argue that the state has a role, through education, to promote a more sustainable society.

Liberalism: the philosophy of capitalism

Adam Smith was the economic philosopher of the emerging liberalism of the eighteenth century, and his theory of entrepreneurial decision making set out in *The Wealth of Nations* (1776) is at the heart of classical economics. Smith's main argument was that the free, decentralised action of economic agents in a system of competition and private property brings individual advantage and a common good, which is defined as the aggregation of individual wealth. The result of these thousands of decisions is not chaos but an underlying, orderly process – the 'invisible hand' of capitalism – and maximum efficency in allocation of societal resources.

At the time, Smith's economics were radical, insofar as they proposed limitations on sovereign power in deference to market operations, with the benefits accruing to the emerging bourgeoisie, rather than solely to the mercantilist class. Smith emphasised the importance of the production of wealth and the abolition of special privilege. Beyond this, the hidden hand of laissez faire economics would bring maximum utility to the most people, and national wealth in the aggregation of individual wealth. In *The Wealth of Nations*, Smith compiled examples of government mismanagement under the mercantilist system, and then argued that markets alone could assemble and convey essential information about scarcity and value, and therefore must be left alone to allocate resources.[18]

The essential problem of liberalism, as Smith saw it, was to develop a political system that would produce governments that would nurture a free market society and protect citizens from the natural tendency of the self-same government to exert social control. Freedom in both political *and* economic spheres was essential. In the economic sphere, all must be free to engage in business, and those who benefit themselves are taken to benefit the nation as a whole. The government was not to interfere in the workings of this natural economic system. But Smith also spelled out a positive, if strictly limited, role for governments which included the protection of the rights of private property.

In summary, the essential ideas of liberalism are that:

- all economic phenomena are linked together and interdependent;
- free competition is what makes production and exchange most advantageous for everyone;
- economic freedom is the condition of prosperity and growth; and
- intervention by the state generally produces effects opposite to those it intends to pursue.

Smith's invisible hand would probably have continued to work well had the economic conditions of the eighteenth century continued to hold. But the burgeoning Industrial Revolution had three effects which substantially altered the ability of the market to allocate resources effectively: the emergence of a growing industrial proletariat; accelerating scientific and technological development, which continually increased the dominance of humankind over nature; and growing functional interdependence between private and public sectors.[19] The growth of the urban proletariat instigated a necessary shift from the limited variety of liberalism known in the eighteenth century to the kind of liberal democracy which exists in the West today. This is discussed immediately below, while the other two effects of the Industrial Revolution are discussed in the conclusion of the chapter.

Utilitarianism and the rise of liberal democracy

The evolution from liberalism to liberal democracy initiates an important theme in Western political ideas. This democratising of liberalism began with the rise of utilitarian philosophy, in the early nineteenth century, and particularly in the work of Jeremy Bentham (1742–1832). Bentham's conception of the functions of utilitarian government were even more limited than Smith's, not extending beyond the maintenance of security and property and the promotion of a free market economy in which utilitarian principles could promote the greatest good for the most people.

The significance of Bentham's utilitarian philosophy lay in his rejection of a moral dimension in the social calculus of capitalist, industrial society. Utilitarianism, in arguing that the good of all could only be achieved by self-regarding individualism and the pursuit of wealth, removed the need for lingering doubt about the consequences of exploitation. The utilitarian framework provided moral exemption from consideration of the negative effects of industrialism by asserting that whatever served the individual served society.

Although obviously harmful social and environmental consequences of industrialism quickly tempered utilitarian thought in the late nineteenth century in Western countries, it returned in the 1980s in the guise of 'yuppyism' by which unbridled pursuit of wealth and ostentatious consumption were sanctioned by neo-liberal politics in much of the West.

Socially responsible capitalism

The issue of how to deal with environmental and social problems, within the confines of liberal capitalism, was addressed by the Victorian philosopher–economist John Stuart Mill. With his idea of a reformist, socially responsible, yet essentially liberal, capitalism, Mill provided a rationale for the modern state, of a type which governs in most Western countries. It is this tradition, of incremental adjustment and reform within liberal capitalism, which is the emerging model the world over.

Unlike the nineteenth century Utopians or the Marxists, utilitarians such as Bentham had no vision of a future society because for them, liberal, nineteenth century capitalism was the correct model of society.

All that was required was democratic government with periodic elections, a free market, and minimal state interference beyond ensuring the security of property. But two facts about life in the mid-nineteenth century demanded new thinking. One was that the working class was acquiring new political power and might therefore be dangerous to property-holders. The other was that the environmental and social conditions of the working class were so self-evidently bad that some liberals felt the situation was morally unjustifiable and that action must be taken.

Mill saw the liberal democratic state as a means to improve mankind (without having to change the nature of the state), and that democratic politics could be a mechanism of moral development.[20] Mill felt that the income inequality of capitalism was unjustifiable, but that the fault lay, not with capitalism itself, but in its lingering feudal origins. Mill and others therefore inspired a series of incremental social reforms, which had the effect of greatly reducing class conflict in Britain and other industrial countries.[21] At this time the Western state assumed its first overtly environmental role in social legislation and in public health. As a result, real incomes, along with housing and environmental conditions, improved dramatically in the late nineteenth century. Mill's enduring legacy is not in his economic analysis, but in his advocacy of reforming liberal democracy within the capitalist system. As we will see in Chapter 6, Mill also put forward powerful arguments for the decentralisation of decision making in the modern state.

The twentieth century state: a condition of conflict

Mill's liberal vision was extended and challenged by social democratic and socialist ideas on the control of market forces. Proponents of a strong regulatory role for the state argued that the evils of society are due primarily to the unregulated working of the institutions of private property and that unjustifiable inequalities of wealth and opportunity should be removed, and industry organised to promote social ends, by nationalisation where necessary.[22] This conception of the state usually resulted in a commitment to guarantee a minimum standard of living for the poor, a Keynesian macroeconomic role for the state in fiscal policy, and a considerable measure of state intervention in industry. Social democracy provided a constructive and useful outlet for radical social ideas and advanced social reforms, without commitment to a revolutionary party or to a dogmatic ideology.[23] Liberal capitalism was thus transformed in the twentieth century in many Western countries into welfare capitalism, in which government is expected to secure employment, stabilise income, and provide social, housing, and medical benefits for those at the margins of the capitalist system. Following Mill, the role of participation in democracy, particularly concern about the nature of pluralism, became a focus of political philosophy. Centralised, professional administration may be inescapable in the modern state due to the complexity of the administrative task, and the power of the bureaucracy is best countered by strong political institutions such as Parliament and the party system. In the absence of these representative political institutions, or in socialist states, the bureaucracy would elevate itself into a unitary state bureaucracy and replace pluralist public and private bureaucracies, and the checks and balances, of the liberal state.

More recent thinking on pluralism is characterised by the view that power is distributed among a range of competing interest groups, and that these groups attempt to influence political decisions by exacting whatever leverage they may have over the working of the system in a continuing process of bargaining. In this way the democratic nature of the liberal state is ensured by the working of this pluralist system of conflict and negotiation over values.

In Chapter 8 we argue:

1   that new networks involving civil society not only counter the power of the state, but can contribute very substantially to the goals of environmental management – this is the 'teamwork' referred to in Chapter 2; and
2   that the typical situation of conflict over social objectives in the democratic state can be 'managed' in a positive manner to contribute to sustainable development.

However, the parallel institutionalisation of pluralist and competitive civic life, which is presupposed in Western democracy, may be more difficult beyond the West, as the idea of beneficial conflict is not readily translated to many non-Western cultures. The religions of Asia, for example, are imbued with a more holistic conception of human society in which harmony and solidarity is set above competition.[24]

Modern neo-conservatism

In the West, the post-war consensus on the usefulness of state intervention lasted in America through Kennedy and Johnson's Great Society programme in the late 1960s, and in a slightly more entrenched fashion in Canada, New Zealand, Australia and Europe to the 1970s and early 1980s. The consensus, based as it was on expanding economies, low inflation and full employment, was broken by the post-1973 oil crisis and recession. By the late 1970s there was growing discord and confusion about the appropriate role of the state and its relation to economic well-being.

The economic and political developments of the 1970s and 1980s provided an opportunity for neo-conservative theorists to mount this 'market friendly' critique of the state:

Social welfare derives from individual satisfaction. Most individuals, most of the time, understand their own preferences and how to choose in their own interest. The state should allow individuals to advance their own welfare according to their own lights rather than enforcing on them some vision of the good life.[25]

This argument is a restatement of the views of Smith and Bentham. There are many variations on the neo-conservative position. However, Hayek has probably had the most longstanding influence on thinking about the state's role in management of national economies and the working of government. Since the publication of *The Road to Serfdom* in 1944, Hayek was a foe of 'planning' in its various guises, and is therefore worthy of some attention.[26]

Hayek's arguments restate the Smithian proposition that the impossibility of adequate information for planning in an uncertain world provides a central argument for the market against the state. In *The Road to Serfdom* he argues that planners working for the state, however well intentioned, are bound to lessen total welfare in society. This is because the socioeconomic world is marked by extreme complexity, and planners can never hope to understand it in its totality. When they try to form policy options based on what must be incomplete information and lack of relevant facts, the result will be costly economically, freedom will be limited, and overall welfare will decline. Conversely, the market, made up as it is of numerous small decision makers, does not pretend to have complete knowledge, and because it need only be concerned with market specific information it can engage in self-correction. The predisposition towards the overburdening of government in the welfare state underlines the benefits of the minimal state, in which individuals are the best judge of their own welfare.

However, in Hayek's argument, tendencies towards anarchy also must be resisted by a framework for law and order that defends property rights. So the state cannot be extinguished: liberty and economic freedom require the state as 'nightwatchman' to guarantee the ability to enjoy property and to exercise consumer choice. Although property rights must be protected by law, the minimal principle of state interference extends to taxation (except for law and order, and defence of the sovereign state), which is the primary instrument for redistribution of income or wealth. Minimalness, that is liberty, is incompatible in this conception with income redistribution.

In particular, a target for neo-conservative criticism was provided by the many obvious problems associated with an interventionist state after the recession of the mid-1970s. These included the growing cost of welfare provision, and a concern that this cost is a drag on economic growth, usually accorded highest priority in domestic affairs of state. Another problem, given the tendency for interventionist states to centralise services and to redistribute income between socioeconomic groups and between regions, was that large administrative bureaucracies had been created. These, so the argument goes, lack market discipline and accountability and are therefore inefficient. A related argument is that the administrative system of the welfare state simply does not work very well because of turbulence in national and world economic systems. In other words, government is unable to predict the unforeseen changes and unintended consequences of policy intervention on individuals, famililes or institutions. Government, with unresponsive bureaucracies, lacks the market's quick feedback mechanisms and responses and wastes funds in pursuing its aims.

In general the neo-conservative view of the conjecture of politics and economics represents a fusion of libertarian value judgements and an analysis of the market as an instrument of policy. The market is taken to be the best means for attaining libertarian, individualistic, or utilitarian objectives, and the role of the state in society is severely curtailed.

Whatever the merits of past forms of state intervention, what is important for our purposes is that there has been a substantial change in attitude towards the state. This neo-conservative ideology is unsympathetic to traditional notions of state planning that appear to infringe on economic liberty, and an expanded role for the state is no longer viewed as an objective in any country. Unfortunately, just when sustainable development clearly requires sophisticated inter-sectoral planning, the baby of planning is being thrown out with the bathwater of state control of the economy. In

Chapter 8 we demonstrate why the needs of a consensus-building approach to sustainable development suggest neither a minimal or maximal role for the state, but an enabling role.

Sustainable development and social relations

Since the time of Adam Smith, the liberal and recent neo-conservative arguments remained remarkably consistent and rather simplistic: the market provides a socially optimal allocation of resources and therefore maximises social benefit. While this is a powerful argument at what we have called, in Chapter 2, the social level of the market, there are aspects of modern industrial societies that undermine this dogma. One is the accelerating scientific and technical development that has enabled humankind to dominate nature and which has broadened the scope of human manipulation of natural resources. This presents two problems.

First, the market-is-optimal situation only held when population and pressure on resources were much smaller. The social costs involved in the private use of collective unpriced resources, such as air, water, the highways etc, were much less when their unused portions were substantial relative to those used in production, but they constitute an inherently rising proportion of conventionally measured GDP as they cease to be 'free' goods.[27] Pricing is then called for to regulate their use, but such pricing will not spring up naturally under laissez faire systems.

Second, the increasing domination of nature by humankind has opened up an increasing range of feasible options in any given situation, and this means more and more decisions are likely to be controversial, or in other words, political. The very success of the capitalist system, working at the level of the market, reinforces the need for a higher order body to mediate among feasible options. This has invariably reinforced the role of the state, and widened the range of political argument.[28]

Another effect of industrialism is increasing specialisation in social functions. This has a double effect. It creates a higher degree of efficiency in pursuing objectives, but also increases the degree of interdependence among individuals and organisations. This means that the likelihood and range of unanticipated disturbances also increases. The binary model of regulating social regulations by individual contracts is no longer complex enough for the degree of social interdependence in the system.

In Chapter 8, drawing on the literature of organisation theory, we will define the situation created by interdependencies as 'turbulence', and we will define the characteristics of the turbulent environment. The appropriate response to turbulence, we will argue, is interactive and flexible management by participatory networks. Here, for the purposes of this chapter, the interaction is between the state and the society, and what is important is neither the state alone, nor individuals alone or in groups (civil society), but the productive relations between them – that is, the quality of the overall society itself.

What are some of the characteristics of a high quality society? One is a sense of society as more than either a collection of individuals or an impersonal structure:

> Society is . . . an instrument for transacting business, an insensitive bureaucratic beast that frustrates our quest for meaning. But ultimately it must be viewed as

... mode of man's spiritual being. The social contract by which we are bound is cooperative by its very nature; it is only an acknowledgement of our belonging to a larger scheme of things called the cosmos.[29]

A second factor is the need for some new relationship between state and society in the economic sphere, neither centralised planning nor laissez-faire. This approach recognises the importance of the market for microeconomic decisions, but also the necessity of government intervention to assist in the process of deriving goals and objectives for a sustainable society, and for controlling externalities by incentive or regulation. It would not deny the necessity for societies to act as a whole through their political processes to realise aspirations beyond the capabilities of market economics.

A third factor is a need for what Daniel Bell calls 'a return to civil society', defined as 'a return to a manageable scale of social life, particularly where the national economy has become embedded in an international frame and the national polity has lost some of its independence'.[30] This emphasises NGOs and voluntary associations working at the community and regional levels, to balance the increasing centralisation of power in the international economy, and the draining of initiative and control away from localities. A counterbalancing force is required, not only to fulfil reasonable ideals of democratic participation, but as the only course open for the realisation of sustainable development. What is required are genuine, workable mechanisms for 'thinking globally and acting locally'.

In addition to generating local, knowledgeable and committed action, civil society plays at least two important roles. The first is that participation can nurture civic spirit, which is defined as 'the presence and authority of a moral conscientiousness, which binds a man to his contractual and other obligations, without needing to be underwritten by a torrid network of ritually reinforced social links'.[31] The self-regulating actions of civil society, buttressed by civic spirit, can *reduce* the need for state action in environmental management, without lessening the quality of the society.

It is also the case that democratic procedures, combined with knowledge about environmental issues provided by uncensored and conscientious media, are well suited to the task of monitoring and controlling high risk, complex technologies. Democratic procedures invite dispute, create dissatisfactions, and stir citizens to anger. Democratic procedures, with public service media, are:

> ... essential correctives to the wishful (Hayekian) belief in the decentralized anonymity of the market as a superior self-correcting mechanism in a world of complex pressures and interconnections. They are also important correctives to the mistaken trust in the therapeutic powers of unbridled technical expertise.[32]

CONCLUSION

This chapter began by looking at a classic and long-standing dichotomy in Western politics between individual freedom and the idea of social control by the state for the common good. This notion has proved to be too simplistic to account for complex relationships in an industrialised, Westernised world. Re-emerging notions of civil society, not simply defined as non-government, but a more potent interaction of individuals, government, NGOs and business, offer a clue to new directions for the state and any other organisation involved in sustainable development and environmental management. Before moving on in the new direction, we need to understand more about the complex economic world that has developed in the post-war period, and its environmental dimension. This is the subject of Part III.

PART III

Global integration and local democracy

Part III Global integration and local democracy

This part of the book turns to the present organisation of world business and finance, the emerging global culture of industrial consumption and consumerism, and the implications of these for sustainable development.

Chapter 5 examines the main elements of the international economic system as it has developed since 1945, and its environmental dimension. The post-war years have seen unprecedented growth in production and world trade, growing integration of economies and the development of a culture of consumerism in the West. The process of 'globalisation' is now taking industrialism, in a 'top-down' process, to all corners of the world, and Western consumption patterns are being emulated in the Third World and the ex-Communist countries wherever possible.

Despite the material success of the capitalist industrial model, however, the global economic order has severe impacts on the environment: the great inequalities between the high and low income countries, as exemplified in the Third World debt crisis, contribute massively to environmental degradation. The culture of consumerism in the West also degrades the environment, and we consider how it may be reaching social as well as ecological limits to growth. Chapter 5 examines the lack of integration of environmental management in the key areas of the global economy: the trade framework, development aid, Third World debt, technology transfer and the role of the transnational corporations.

In chapter 6, these 'top-down' global economic arrangements and trends to international integration are contrasted with growing demands for 'bottom-up' local participation, both to fulfil democratic aspirations, and for effectiveness in policy and implementation. This endemic tension between the powerful trend toward specialisation and integration, which characterises the modern industrial system, and aspirations for local control of social, economic and environmental forces is likely to be increasingly relevant to concerns about sustainable development. Chapter 6 examines the main forces behind the demand for centralisation and international integration on the one hand, and that for decentralisation on the other. In many cases, the very nature of environmental problems requires action on a local or regional basis, albeit within national and international contexts. Unfortunately, the trend to centralisation is powerful, and it is difficult to turn to the real world for examples of genuine political decentralisation in pursuit of sustainable development at the scale of the region, often the appropriate level for carrying out environmental management tasks. The chapter analyses a 'new decentralist' approach to regional control for sustainable development, and the powerful obstacles to its realisation.

5   The global economy: interdependence, inequality and the environment

I meant no harm. I most truly did not.
But I had to grow bigger. So bigger I got.
I biggered my factory. I biggered my roads.
I biggered my wagons. I biggered the loads
Of the Thneeds I shipped out. I was shipping them forth
To the South! To the East! To the West! To the North!
I went right on biggering . . . selling more Thneeds.
And I biggered my money, which everyone needs.

Dr Seuss, 1972[1]

This chapter considers features of the global industrial economy that contribute to environmental degradation. In particular we examine the trend described as 'globalisation' or 'integration' in the international economic system. This encompasses a number of developments of the post-1945 period that have accelerated and intensified in recent years: the global spread of industrial production; the development of intricate linkages between national economies through growth in trade and developments in communications and transport; and the global reach, through mass media, of images of Western consumer culture.

Integration has so far largely been a feature of the development of the 'higher income' countries (defined as those with membership of the OECD), whose interdependence through trade, technology transfer and communications has increased steadily. Massive inequalities in the world economy persist between the higher and lower income countries, and there are considerable divergences between and within the lower income countries themselves. It seems that neither the spread of the industrial system as we have known it in the OECD countries, nor the structural inequalities between rich and poor in the international economy, can be reconciled with sustainable development. Thus it is important to examine the global economic order and consider the changes in its design and direction that will be needed to realise sustainable development.

TOWARDS THE GLOBAL INDUSTRIAL ECONOMY

The nature of 'globalisation'

It is by now a commonplace to note that national economies are becoming more interdependent and that there has been a 'globalisation' of markets and of industrial production. The process is far from new: we are in the midst of an intensification of trends originating in the Western colonisation of much of the globe and in the Industrial Revolution, whereby more and more countries have been brought into trading networks as producers and consumers of goods on an industrial scale. The global spread of industrial systems means that there is no prospect for any nation-state of 'insulating' itself from changes in the economic climate, from major pollution flows and from the policies of international actors such as the transnational corporations (TNCs).[2] As TNCs develop there is an increasing flow of managerial and specialist personnel across frontiers; as more and more countries industrialise, so international pollution flows increase; and the development of computerised communications networks has created global flows of information and capital that ignore frontiers.

The 1980s saw a spectacular increase in international economic activity. According to the Worldwatch Institute, gross world output of goods and services amounted to some US$20 trillion in 1990, up by $4.5 trillion from 1980; and international trade in products grew by 4 per cent a year on average in the 1980s. The Institute claims that '. . . growth in global economic output during the eighties was greater than that during the several thousand years from the beginning of civilisation until 1950'.[3]

The process of globalisation is not complete. The great expansion in world trade in the 1980s was largely an increase in trade within the industrialised world, and hundreds of millions of people still live on the margin of the international industrial system. The Western lifestyles made possible by industrial development are available to only a minority of the world's population. Moreover, the evolution of the economic system has outstripped that of international political integration. Nonetheless, it is true that the industrialisation of the lower income countries is proceeding apace; and that for nation-states and individuals alike it is becoming impossible to 'opt out' of the global process of industrialisation – modernity is a near-universal condition.[4]

Actors in the global economy

The growing integration of the international economy has been assisted and promoted by numerous international institutions and structures. The main actors are described briefly below.

The International Monetary Fund (IMF)

The IMF, along with the World Bank and GATT (see below), was created in the aftermath of World War II as a result of the wartime allies' conference at Bretton Woods in 1944 on the post-war restructuring of the international economic system. The IMF is an agency endowed by subscriptions from member countries. The IMF has become a lender to member states, and through this role it has become increasingly involved in efforts to re-structure the economies of lower income countries. It now faces a critical task in helping the ex-communist states of Eastern Europe and the Soviet Union adjust to a market-based system.

The World Bank

Originally the International Bank for Reconstruction and Development (IBRD), the World Bank was established to finance post-war reconstruction in Europe. This role was diminished by the implementation of the Marshall Plan, and the Bank's focus shifted to Third World development. The Bank is a major lender to lower income countries. In mid-1991, outstanding loans totalled some $136 billion.[5] The roles of the

World Bank and the IMF have become increasingly blurred in recent years: the agencies co-operate closely, and hold a joint annual conference. Both have begun to modify their policies in the face of criticism from environmentalists (see below).

The General Agreement on Tariffs and Trade (GATT)

The GATT is the third element of the post-war international economic order. It is an inter-governmental forum for periodic rounds of negotiation aimed at reducing barriers to free international trade. The latest round has been in progress since 1986 and did not conclude as scheduled in late 1990, as a result of disagreements on agricultural subsidies.

Transnational corporations (TNCs)

Also known as multi-nationals, the TNCs are a massively powerful force in the globalisation of industrial production and consumption and in the growth of world trade and manufacturing. They are also a key source of technological innovation.

International trading blocs

In the 1980s, as competition mounted between companies in the advanced industrial countries, and as competition increased in manufacturing sectors from newly industrialising countries (NICs), there was a move towards the development of regional trading blocs in the North. The aim is to provide larger markets for producers in member countries, promote economies of scale and stimulate growth. The most developed of these blocs is the European Community, which will complete its 'single market' for goods and services free of national trade barriers by 1993. The Community will also form a 'common economic space' with the countries of the European Free Trade Association from 1993, establishing a free trade zone of some 400 million people, the world's largest. In 1992 the USA, Canada and Mexico concluded a free trade agreement, establishing the basis for what could develop into a trade zone covering the Americas. The rapid growth of the Asian NICs has encouraged speculation that a Far Eastern bloc could emerge, led by Japan.[6] Fears have been expressed that the development of blocs may promote protectionism and further disadvantage lower income countries in the world economic system.[7]

Trends in the international economy

The developing role of the actors described above has been crucial in recent years in the main structural trends of the international economy. **The spread of industrial development** throughout the world means that broad secular trends observed in the evolution of the advanced industrial countries begin to emerge also in some lower income countries as they industrialise. These include a diminishing contribution to GDP of agriculture as the importance of manufacturing grows, and the rising share in GDP of the service sector, as manufacturing industry matures and income levels rise among the population.[8]

There is **increasing competition** for the advanced industrial economies in agricultural products and mature manufacturing sectors from a number of newly industrialising countries. This demands a shift in the higher income economies towards areas in which they can achieve comparative advantage, such as high technology manufacturing, technology-based services, and other high value-added activities. In turn, the NICs of the 'first generation' such as Taiwan and South Korea, are likely to face growing competition in low-tech manufacturing as more countries build up their manufacturing capacity. Increasing competition generates pressure for protectionist policies to safeguard jobs and key companies as countries attempt to restructure sectors in which they have lost comparative advantage.

National economies become increasingly **interdependent through trade** between and within corporations. In the period 1960-1980 international trade grew faster than output, with the result that imports rose as a proportion of GDP in the advanced industrial countries.[9] Thus far, integration through trade has been largely confined to the industrialised world: lower income countries' share in world trade is only 17 per cent.[10] However, on past trends, the NICs will gradually enter more fully into the world of the advanced industrial economies.[11]

The development of a massive **international currency market** following the end of the post-war system of fixed exchange rates has brought further integration of the higher income countries' economies and investing institutions. 'The pool of savings today is worldwide, and intermediaries that mobilise those savings for use by investors know no national boundaries ... Transactions in foreign exchange currently amount to over $200 billion a day'.[12] The new world of international capital flowing through computer systems and telecommunications networks is the most striking example of global economic integration. The interdependence it produces was demonstrated by the near-simultaneous crash of securities markets around the world on 19 October 1987.

The **diffusion of technology and advances in transport technology and telecommunications** have played a fundamental role in spreading industrial development and in increasing the pace of industrialisation. The World Bank has underlined the impact of technological advance on the time taken for economic growth to double per capita output for various countries. The time needed to achieve this has progressively fallen: from 60 years in Britain after 1780, to 34 for Japan after 1885, to 20 years in Turkey after 1957, to only 10 years in China after 1977.[13]

Rapid growth has, however, not been experienced by all lower income countries, and there has been a notable **fragmentation of the Third World** in the last twenty years. Countries once lumped together under the heading of 'Third World' states have diverged radically in income levels, growth rates and industrial structures, and accordingly have very different current prospects for development in the 1990s.

Table 5.1 *Average annual growth in GDP per capita in developing regions, 1950–1989*

Region	Growth (%)
Asia	3.6
Latin America	1.2
Sub-Saharan Africa	0.8

Source: World Development Report, World Bank, 1991

Growth in GDP per head, for instance, has varied enormously among regions over the past 40 years (Table 5.1).

These indicators conceal great regional variations over time, as shown by World Bank figures. In Asia, GDP growth in the NICs from 1965 to 1989 far outstripped that in countries such as India. In Latin America, there were large gaps between the performance of Brazil and poor countries such as Bolivia. In sub-Saharan Africa real incomes per head actually declined in the 1970s and 1980s.

Such disparities indicate a shift in economic fortunes among a number of NICs in the direction of the advanced industrial economies in terms of growth rates, income levels and industrial capacity, and on the other hand the prospect of many lower income countries making minimal progress at the periphery of the international economy. Projections of economic performance to 2000 by the United Nations Secretariat[14] indicate that, on current trends, the disparities between higher and lower income countries, and between income groups within the latter, will be little different by 2000. For sub-Saharan Africa, growth in GDP per capita is likely to continue to decline in the 1990s while it rises elsewhere.[15] The massive population growth that is certain in many lower income countries will effectively wipe out gains in export performance and output. The number of people living without enough food and shelter – the absolute poor – was some 1.2 billion, one-fifth of the world's population, in 1989; this proportion seems unlikely to change much by the end of the century.[16]

What do these trends in the international economy mean? Are the gross inequalities between rich and poor countries likely to be overcome? For some analysts of the world economic system, the disparities between developed 'core' economies and the diverse low income countries of the global economic 'periphery' reflect deep structural relations crucial to capitalism as a world system. On this analysis, there are profound forces in the operation of the core economies that will maintain unequal development to the advantage of Western capital.[17]

An alternative view, increasingly popular among international economic agencies and Western governments, is that uneven patterns of development are not inevitable. Rather, they reflect the results of different approaches to economic policy. On this analysis, it is possible for low income countries to break out of the poverty trap if they adopt proven 'market-friendly' policies. According to the World Bank, studies of the recent history of economic development suggest that success or failure is largely a result of developing countries' own policy choices, although the Bank stresses the need for the high income countries to help by lifting trade restrictions and providing financial support. As noted earlier, the market-friendly approach involves minimal state intervention in markets, clear systems for market regulation, free trade, careful fiscal and monetary policy to contain inflation, concentration of public spending on education, health and the environment, and cuts in military budgets.[18] In the early 1990s, there are many signs that this consensus is promoting a major development in the world economy towards a widespread adoption of 'market-friendly' policies. This trend is considered in the next section.

The ascendancy of capitalism in the 1990s

The movement in the international economy towards a liberal market version of capitalism began in the mid-1970s in the West. By the start of the 1990s there was a rush among former communist countries to embrace the liberal capitalist model of industrial development. In reality, there is not yet so much a complete embrace of liberal capitalism, much less democracy, by developing and ex-communist countries, as a general disenchantment with collectivist models of industrial development and a move to copy policies that have brought material prosperity to the West. Nonetheless, capitalist models of development now have vast attraction for millions of people in the ex-communist countries and the South. What are the factors behind this new ascendancy for liberal capitalism, which may reinforce the trend towards global integration?

First, market-based approaches have been seen to deliver the goods, literally, to millions of people, despite the inequalities of income and opportunity that persist in the West. The trend towards more laissez-faire economic policies in the West in the late 1970s and early 1980s was associated with the massive boom of the mid- and late eighties. Western governments engaged in deregulation of industrial sectors: focused on controlling inflation regardless of consequences for unemployment; privatised state-owned industries; and promoted free enterprise. The approach was most radical in the USA and the UK, but variations on the strategy were pursued throughout the industrialised world. The industrial and financial interdependence of the higher income countries meant that avowedly socialist and social democratic governments were obliged to adopt many free-market policies and swim with the tide.

Second, there was a steady process of disillusionment in the communist world, and in many lower income countries, with collectivist economic policies. This was fuelled by observation of Western growth since the oil shocks of the 1970s, which had a severe effect on many Communist countries as well as on low income oil-importing countries, and by rising awareness of the inability of communist economies to compete technologically with the West. Already by the mid-1980s, some communist countries (such as Hungary and China), and many lower income countries with large state-run industrial sectors, had joined in the move towards deregulation and privatisation.

Third, this tendency was promoted by the activity of the World Bank and the IMF in the wake of the 'debt crisis' that erupted in 1982 (see below). As the two agencies were called upon to assist more lower income countries with debt repayment crises, they linked the provision of loans to conditions about structural adjustment in the economies in question. This meant that financial support and advice was linked to the implementation of programmes for market-friendly structural reform in the economy.

Fourth, the collapse of communist regimes in Eastern Europe and the Soviet Union in 1989–91 effectively eliminated communism as a model for industrial development. This economic failure, and the environmental calamities associated with it,[19] have been so great that there has been a dramatic reaction in the post-communist states in favour of rapid transition to a market economy. The mood in the former communist world of the early 1990s was often 'ultra-capitalist'. The new spirit of enthusiasm for the market was summed up by the former Soviet Republic of Kyrgyzstan's invitation to Western companies in October 1991 to invest in what was promised to be an 'El Dorado' for entrepreneurs.[20]

The general shift towards free market economic polices conceals some wide variations in policy, and even more in the extent to which liberal democracy accompanies liberal economics. There remain also important areas in which the market is not allowed to reign supreme. The NICs have pursued a strategy with strong elements of state intervention and selective protectionism in order to build up capacity in key sectors;[21] and the agricultural sector has continued to be heavily subsidised in the West, especially in the European Community. As discussed below, there remain many barriers to free trade between nation-states, and in particular between the higher and lower income countries. There is, moreover, no guarantee that the liberalisation of the ex-communist world in Europe, the most striking case of conversion to market principles, will meet with general success. The political turmoil, environmental degradation and infrastructural backwardness of many of the countries in question are likely to deter much hoped-for foreign investment. In the absence of long term aid and technical support on a large scale from the West, it is unlikely that private investors will move in on the scale required to achieve the progress hoped for in living standards.

The policy urged by the World Bank, IMF and Western governments for the ex-communist countries is one of rapid deregulation of prices, privatisation of state enterprises and trade liberalisation. The strategy is similar to the structural adjustment austerity programmes urged upon lower income countries in the 1980s. However, two key issues arise. First, the lower income countries of the Third World and the ex-communist countries have very different industrial structures and political backgrounds, and there is in any case no consensus about the efficacy of the World Bank/IMF structural adjustment programmes over the last decade.[22] Second, as there is no precedent for the momentous transition from communism to capitalism, there is no evidence to indicate that a full-blooded adoption of liberal market economics will produce greater industrial success, increased living standards and improved environmental quality. in the short to medium term. On the contrary, there seems to be a strong possibility that undue austerity and prolonged transition pains will produce immense social strains that could lead to authoritarian rule again, this time of a nationalist-populist kind.[23]

For all the pains of the transition towards liberal capitalism, however, it is likely that ex-communist and Third World governments will want to persist with the move to the market and join the NICs in their pursuit of Western levels of prosperity. While the outcome of the 'market-friendly' revolutions is much in doubt, there is a possibility that some of the countries in question will achieve greatly-increased levels of economic growth and per capita income, and aspire to approach western living standards. Ironically, the drive for economic growth and hunger for Western styles of consumption in the NICs and the ex-Communist world are developing precisely at the point at which consumerism in the West is beginning to appear socially self-defeating and ecologically unsustainable. This is the subject of the next section.

THE LIMITS TO CONSUMPTION

Given the wretched condition of the 20 per cent of the world's population classified as absolutely poor, and the inadequate standards of health, sanitation, education and housing endured by hundreds of millions of others, no one can scorn the aspirations of Third World and ex-communist countries to higher living standards. But critical questions are gradually making their way on to Western political agendas:

1   Can the rest of the world attain Western levels of affluence without causing fundamental ecological degradation and global warming through increased energy use and exhaustion of resources? If not, what paths to higher living standards are sustainable?
2   How much consumption is *enough* in the industrialised world?

The issues are intertwined. The industrialised nations, increasingly aware of the threats of global warming and loss of biodiversity, and the threat of mass migrations from poor countries to the rich world, cannot deny other countries the right to improve living standards. On the other hand, it is evident that the planet could not sustain the globalisation of the American consumer lifestyle as we now know it. Even a moderate rise in living standards for the mass of the world's population would seem to imply radical changes in the consumption habits of the world's most voracious consumers, namely the citizens and corporations of the West, and Western acceptance of a steady state in energy consumption. The acceptance of limits to consumption would be a fundamental turning point in the evolution of industrial societies: for decades, politics has been geared to the assumptions that economic growth is a prime aim of government policy and that individuals must be able to look forward to steady improvements in living standards. The question, 'How much consumption is enough?', has not been asked. However, the problems of global environmental change have begun to put it on the agenda; and there is a growing awareness in the industrial world of the social and ecological limits to consumption.

The culture of consumerism

While the benefits of increased availability of good food, labour-saving devices and home comforts are obvious, there has been a persistent current of criticism and unease in the West about the cultural consequences of growth in consumption. The target of this criticism (also levelled by many in the ex-communist world and in the lower income countries) is the rise of a culture of 'consumerism'. This is a term much used but rarely defined. It might be summed up as a cluster of attitudes and habits that associate success, happiness, status and self-esteem primarily with the acquisition of a steadily rising income and access to high quality goods and services. It is brutally expressed in the message of a Californian car bumper sticker: *The guy with the most toys when he dies wins.*[24]

Laments about acquisitiveness are hardly new: Alan Durning of the Worldwatch Institute cites examples of criticisms of 'consumerism' from the first century BC onwards.[25] He argues, however, that the acquisitiveness of modern Western societies is of a special kind. First, it involves consumption on an unprecedentedly colossal scale by a minority of the world's population. Second, it is promoted by forces specific to modernity, which have become more powerful with each phase of industrial development in the West and now reach out to affect the entire world.

The consumer boom of the post-war period

The post-war decades have seen an explosive growth in consumption of raw materials by industry and of goods and services by individual citizens. The trend has been propelled by advances in technology and productivity, rising per capita incomes and the falling real cost of many goods and services. The statistics of GDP growth and increases in world trade cited above translate into phenomenal changes in personal and corporate consumption over the last four decades:

> In the United States . . . on average people today own twice as many cars, drive two-and-a-half times as far, use 21 times as much plastic, and travel 25 times as far by air as did their parents in 1950 . . . Microwave ovens and video cassette recorders found their way into almost two-thirds of American homes during the eighties alone.[26]

The scale of Western consumption is made all the more astonishing when compared to levels elsewhere.[27] The 1.25 billion people in the advanced industrial countries consume vastly more, on all key indicators, than the 3.4 billion who are adequately fed and clothed and the billion or more who live in absolute poverty. The 5 per cent of the world's population in the USA consume around one-third of the world's resources.

Forces behind the culture of consumerism

The scale of current Western consumption is thus of a different order to anything known in pre-industrial times and the earlier periods of modernity. What drives the development, other than technical change, population growth and rising income? Durning identifies 'distinctively modern features' that contribute to over-consumption and consumerist attitudes in the West:[28]

1   The influence of competitive social pressures in industrial societies, in which money becomes a dominant indicator of success, status and self-worth as modernisation increasingly marginalises traditional cultural forces, such as religious belief, that could provide a strong countervailing influence.
2   The expansion of the world of commodities into the household and the sphere of 'local self-reliance' during the industrial era: goods and services provided at home or locally have been increasingly replaced by goods and services provided by the industrial market.
3   Governments have: encouraged patterns of land use leading to the 'need' for increased consumption of cars and fuel; failed to require producers to reflect environmental costs in the prices charged to consumers; and devised national economic policies on the assumption that 'more is better'.
4   The ever increasing volume and sophistication of advertising has turned shopping into a leisure pursuit.

The globalisation of advertising

These forces have been present since the early phases of industrialism. They now have global reach, principally through the spread of communications networks that bring advertising to billions of people, including a growing number in the ex-communist and lower income countries. The 1980s saw a qualitative shift in the impact of advertising and in its promotion of a link between well-being, status and consumption. The resources devoted to advertising worldwide increased enormously in the 1980s, in the NICs as well as in the advanced industrial countries, reaching $237 billion in 1988.[29] Economic growth in the NICs provided large new markets for consumer goods and for advertising.

The spread of 'market-friendly' governments means that previous restrictions on popular access to advertising outside the West are falling away rapidly. The vast majority of the new audience for Western advertising is in no position to afford the goods and services paraded in advertisements and television shows, but naturally appetites are aroused, just as ours have been for decades. Keen popular awareness of the material well-being of the West was undoubtedly a major factor in the collapse of the communist regimes of Eastern Europe, alongside profound disillusion with the political and economic systems.

The 1980s also saw a large increase in the reach and capacity of global telecommunications networks, for example through satellite broadcasting. The progressive globalisation of television means that the imagery of Western affluence is available to hundreds of millions of people in the former communist world and in the lower income countries. It is also available through the development of global travel. Migrant workers from low-income countries see for themselves the standards of living enjoyed in the West; and in the developing world, as tourism reaches ever more countries and ever more remote regions, Western affluence is advertised in the form of tourists and the facilities built to cater for them.

The limits to consumerism

The weight of transnational corporations is backed by the pervasiveness of advertising, the global reach of images, familiar products and sales messages, the incessant association of new and better goods with well-being, and the difficulty of opting out of modernity in any meaningful way.

The globalisation of the industrial system is producing a gradual erosion of local cultural distinctiveness in production and consumption, and a spread in desire in low-income countries for the products most associated with Western affluence – cars, televisions, denim jeans, fast food.

But while the factors behind consumerism may appear almost irresistible, there is a growing awareness in the advanced industrial countries that further development of many aspects of the culture of consumption will prove to be unsustainable. We are increasingly aware of limits to growth, though not in the sense of physical exhaustion of many key resources as feared by the Club of Rome in 1972.[30] These limits are social and ecological, relating to environmental degradation and the ultimately self-defeating nature of key forms of consumption.

Research indicates that there is little correlation between high levels of consumption and personal happiness.[31] The achievement of high levels of income and consumption often comes to seem 'hollow', and the erosion of religious belief in industrial societies means that for many this feeling can develop into a sense of personal meaninglessness.[32] In Western societies, the super-abundance of consumer choices and information media threaten the individual with information 'overload': many people in the West would admit to feeling confused and oppressed by what the American novelist Don DeLillo calls the 'blur and glut' of consumer culture, the disorienting sense of 'too much everything'.[33]

We can go beyond the intimations of sensory overload and spiritual emptiness that crowd modern novels and cultural critiques. The idea that there is something fundamentally self-defeating in modern consumption patterns was given more rigorous economic expression by the late Fred Hirsch in his seminal analysis of the *Social Limits to Growth*.[34] Hirsch noted the widespread dissatisfaction that accompanies the pursuit of affluence, and related it to the inevitable degradation in quality of key goods in industrial societies. Certain goods that confer status and special well-being – what Hirsch terms 'positional goods' – are only of value and can only bring satisfaction if they remain relatively scarce. As they become widely available, their quality diminishes and the satisfactions they offer are sharply reduced. Since positional goods are precisely those to which many citizens most aspire, this is a crucial limitation on the development of consumerism. As Hirsch puts it, 'The life depicted in the glossy magazines clearly is attractive to many of us . . . The snag is that much of it is unavailable to very many of us at once, and its diffusion may then change its own content and characteristics'.[35] The process can be illustrated by reference to two of the goods most desired in industrial society: cars and holidays.

The car is a potent symbol of consumer culture. However, ownership of a car in itself is not usually the prime source of satisfaction. The benefits of car driving depend upon access to road space and the free and rapid progress to one's destination. But as more and more people acquire cars, so the benefits of access to road space diminish, and disbenefits, such as congestion, pollution, frustration and noise begin to mount up. In Hirsch's terms, the positional good of free access to the road is diminished in quality as car ownership rises. Moreover, the process of rising car ownership itself promotes the acquisition of more cars, if only because there is diminishing demand for, and thus less provision of, public transport: those without a car are forced to become drivers. In this sense, the competition for positional goods becomes a self-defeating process, with ever-decreasing quality of experience of the goods for all concerned.

Access to cars allows access to beautiful places, and the rise in incomes in the West has led to a huge increase in tourism at home and abroad. Holidays and access to desirable places are also positional goods, and their value to the consumer is diminished once they become widely available. Exotic locations fill up with Western tourists, and native cultures become more and more like the ones back home. 'Unspoilt' landscapes attract more and more visitors, whose presence requires the construction of more roads, car parks and other facilities, thus rapidly 'spoiling' the scenery and atmosphere; spectacular views are gradually blocked by the numbers of people wanting to take pictures of them. The syndrome is increasingly familiar: the devaluation and destruction by tourism of the very thing which the tourist comes to see.

The awareness of social limits to the satisfactions that positional goods can bring is accompanied by the realisation that there are also key ecological constraints on certain forms of consumption. As noted earlier, the worldwide fleet of cars is forecast to grow spectacularly on present trends, with increased ownership in the lower income countries and ex-communist states as well as in the West.[36] The spread of market-oriented economies is likely to accentuate the trend, in the absence of radical policy changes, since reliance on private transport, and development of land use patterns that promote it at the expense of public transport systems, have been distinctive features of capitalist societies.[37] Yet, as noted in Chapter 1, a massive increase in car use worldwide will exacerbate the problem of global warming and air pollution: no technical advances in engine design and emission controls will help us to avoid this outcome at the global level.

Similarly, there is an ecological dimension to the growth in tourism, which shows few signs of abating in the West and which is likely to become increasingly popular in the NICs as incomes rise. There is relentless pressure on the human ecology of tourist destinations: on local cultures, buildings and settlements. And there is parallel pressure on natural ecosystems, even in the remotest corners of the Earth: the Everest base camp area is littered with the refuse of trekkers and climbers, and cruise ships now tour the Antarctic coast. The numbers of people involved in tourist travel are unprecedented:

> Now, after three decades of frantic growth, there are more than 400 million a year, plus another billion and a half domestic travellers. By 2000, there could be up to 650 million international trippers, and four or five times as many travelling in their own countries: 3 billion or more in transit. These are mass movements without parallel in history.[38]

CONSUMPTION AND SUSTAINABILITY

We are at a very early stage in our understanding of social and ecological limits to growth in consumption. It is evident, however, that indefinite increases in certain forms of consumption are incompatible with sustainable development. How this awareness can be translated into practical measures in environmental management and economic policy is much less clear. It will require above all measures that reflect the full cost of environmental damage in prices paid by corporate and individual consumers, and no doubt policies for rationing access to roads and vulnerable tourist attractions. However, major political problems arise in considering limits to economic growth and consumption. These relate to equity within the Western industrial countries, and between them and the rest of the world.

First, the experience of near-continuous economic growth over decades has accustomed politicians and electors in the West to expect future increases in incomes, production and consumption. Despite growing, though still limited, awareness of social and ecological constraints on indefinite expansion, the idea of limits to consumption is unfamiliar in Western politics and to Western consumers. Raising the question, 'How much is enough?' inevitably leads to consideration of equity and distribution of income and opportunity. If there is to be rationing of road space and access to fragile tourist destinations, how can it be made fair? Will the rich be unaffected, while the less well-off lose out? Issues of equity and distribution are diminished in political potency and are less threatening when most groups in society can feel that their standards of living are increasing, but they would come to the fore in any discussion of a 'steady state' in key areas of consumption.

Second, there is the relationship between high and low income countries in a world in which ecological limits to growth as we have known it are in sight. Many lower income countries have been following a broadly Western model of industrialisation as a proven route to progress and prosperity. In recapitulating many of the phases of development experienced by industrialised countries they have also repeated many environmental mistakes, frequently with the enthusiastic co-operation of Western corporations and governments, and are often impatient of Western criticism of environmentally destructive policies. If the industrialising countries are to avoid the unsustainable evolution of production and consumption patterns, then the high income world will need to set a positive example of sustainable development and provide the financial and technical support necessary to raise living standards in the South and protect the environment effectively.

Much the same applies in the case of the ex-communist states of Eastern Europe and the former USSR, where the end of the old regimes and the rush towards market-oriented modernisation of manufacturing and commerce has been accompanied by an impatient popular desire to achieve Western standards of living. In this case the countries in question are poised on the threshold of new industrial development. If they simply follow the 'traditional' Western model of modernisation, and are encouraged to do so, then a huge opportunity for environmentally-sound modernisation will have been missed and major new pressures on local ecosystems will emerge.[39]

Any move towards sustainable development demands policy change in four key areas of the international economic system, such that environmental management becomes an integral part of economic decision-making and relationships between the high and low income countries become more equitable. In all four areas, referred to as 'pillars of neo-colonialism' in a speech in 1991 by the Indian politician Manekha Gandhi, the inequitable relations between rich and poor countries have contributed massively to unsustainable environmental change:

1   terms of trade between high and low income countries;
2   debt and development aid;
3   technology transfer; and
4   the role of transnational corporations.

These four areas are discussed in the remainder of this chapter.

THE TERMS OF INTERNATIONAL TRADE

The enormous expansion of international trade has been a fundamental element in the globalisation of industrialism and in the spreading influence of capitalism. The key institution in this field is the General Agreement on Tariffs and Trade (GATT), whose rules cover some 90 per cent of world trade in goods. The latest phase (the 'Uruguay Round') of GATT negotiations on removing trade barriers began in 1986 and was due to finish in late 1990, but was stalled by disagreements over cutting subsidies to agriculture. The Uruguay Round saw the rise of concern that the impacts of GATT agreements on the environment were largely ignored by the organisation.

Tensions in trade policy

Negotiations over the terms of international trade highlight numerous tensions not only between the high and low income countries but also within the industrialised world. These concern the legitimacy of protectionist policies and the extent to which free trade is desirable and politically feasible in relation to particular sectors and countries. The main area of conflict in trade policy among high income countries is agriculture. There is major disagreement between the United States (backed by other industrial countries and also by developing countries in the so-called 'Cairns Group') on the one hand, and the European Community on the other. The US seeks drastic cuts in farm subsidies within the European Community, which spends some 75 per cent of its budget on its Common Agricultural Policy (CAP), which provides subsidies to farmers and has helped generate enormous surpluses of dairy products, beef, grain and wine. Surpluses have been 'dumped' at low cost on Third World markets, to the detriment of local producers, and low income countries' access to European food markets has been restricted through tariff systems designed to protect European farmers.

The alliance between high and low income countries pressing for cuts in farm subsidies within the European Community is a rare instance of North–South agreement in trade policy. Usually, the lines of conflict are clearly drawn up between the high and low income countries. There is strong pressure from each side on the other for the removal of tariff barriers and other measures designed to protect domestic agriculture and industry. Lower income countries demand access to Western markets in which they face tariff barriers. Such tariffs are set in politically sensitive areas such as agricultural sectors in which some poorer countries would have an advantage if free trade was in force.

Distortions of international trade result from non-tariff barriers as well as from tariffs, and the former do not come under the control of GATT. GATT's progress in reducing tariffs in recent years has been balanced by increased protectionism in other forms. This is a result of growing competition and reflects the increased vulnerability of domestic producers in all sectors. The Third World has been especially disadvantaged by these changes:

> By 1986, 21 per cent of imports from developing countries to the OECD were covered by so-called hard-core nontariff barriers: quotas, voluntary export restraints, the Multifibre Arrangement [which limits textile imports by developed countries from developing ones] and other highly restrictive measures. This number does not even include other restrictions such as price restraints or health and safety regulations ... Since the mid-1980s, industrial countries have done almost nothing to roll back the accumulated protection.[40]

Critics of the overall stance of the industrial countries argue that they are guilty of applying double standards in trade policy. Protectionism in lower income countries is opposed and the virtues of market-friendly policies are loudly proclaimed, yet selective trade barriers are maintained against developing countries' exports, at major cost to them. The World Bank notes that the value to the Third World of exports foregone due to industrial countries' trade barriers is comparable to the total value of development aid.[41] It is also argued that selective protection has played a key role in the development of the industrial economies, and has been crucial to the success of the NICs in building up manufacturing expertise.[42] In the light of this, critics of the Western position argue, the lower income countries should be allowed a higher degree of protection until their needs are better met in the international system.

The disputes that have marked the GATT Uruguay round have also highlighted the contribution of inequitable trade policies and inappropriate free trade measures to unsustainable development. We discuss below two key areas in which the international terms of trade have played a part in ecological degradation: the lower income countries' reliance on commodities in an unfair trading system; and the failure to integrate environmental issues into the policy making of the GATT and other trade policy fora.

Commodity prices and lower income countries

A major problem in trade policy for many of the lower income countries is their reliance on exports of basic agricultural and mineral commodities in order to earn foreign exchange. This is particularly marked among countries in sub-Saharan Africa and the poorer Asian states:

> 86 per cent of sub-Saharan Africa's export earnings are from primary commodities, virtually the same proportion for some countries as when they won independence in the mid-1960s . . . Taking the poorest countries of the Third World (other than India and China) as a whole, primary commodities account for three-quarters of all their exports.[43]

The critical factor in dependence on particular commodities is the extreme vulnerability of the economy when commodity prices fall. For lower income countries without indigenous fuel reserves, the years since the mid-1970s have seen the worst of all worlds: falls in non-fuel commodity prices and, in the 1970s, large rises in oil prices. Declines in non-fuel commodity prices are related to three key developments:

1 Recessions in importing countries and consequent decline in demand.
2 Sectoral restructuring in the industrialised world, leading to a shift away from heavy manufacturing towards light industry and services, and reduction of demand for raw materials in manufacturing. New technological developments have allowed reduction in use of materials through miniaturisation, and substitution of synthetic materials for natural ones.
3 Increased output of commodities by lower income countries in an attempt to boost earnings, with resultant gluts and depression in prices.

Dependence on commodities in a world economy in which demand is falling or static has led to general economic and environmental decline in the affected lower income countries. Falling earnings from commodity exports led to a drop in living standards and pressure to maximise production in order to try to keep up earnings. In many cases food production and peasant agriculture have been neglected in the interests of maximising cash crop exports, and poor countries have had to import food on a large scale.[44] As economic pressure mounts, cropping of agricultural commodities and extraction of raw materials may be increased beyond sustainable levels, thus undermining economic and environmental security. Countries in this situation find it extremely hard to afford domestic investment or to attract Western investment in order to diversify agriculture and industry and reduce dependence on commodity exports. Attempts at diversification are also made more difficult by trade barriers in export markets and by pressure from the West to remove domestic restrictions on trade. Finally, dependence is worsened for countries with large foreign debt burdens, since a major proportion of export earnings is not invested at home but instead disappears to creditors in the West to service the debt.

There are two further dimensions to commodity dependence that serve to reinforce the vulnerable position of lower income countries in terms of trade and environmental security. First, the inappropriateness of much agricultural commodity production given the needs of the mass of the population. This relates to the emphasis in many low income countries on earning foreign exchange – largely to service debt – from the export of cash crops at the expense of local food production.

Second, the pricing of commodities has also played a part: as we have seen, non-fuel primary commodities have declined in price in recent years, putting low-income producers at extreme disadvantage. Commodity pricing has not, in most cases, been subject to international commodity agreements that compensate low-income countries by promoting price stabilisation and assisting them to diversify. To achieve this, the industrialised countries would need to agree to commodity prices that reflected the full environmental costs of production, and would need to provide technical and financial support and reduce trade barriers to Third World exports in order to assist diversification.[45] The pricing issue also relates to other 'commodities' in the Third World, such as tropical forests and tourist attractions, resources that have not been priced in such a way as to reflect their full environmental value. In areas such as the timber trade, lower income countries receive a return for the tropical forests' resources that fails to reflect the full environmental value and encourages over-exploitation. Yet economic studies which integrate environmental valuation suggest that low income countries are losing out by degrading ecosystems in pursuit of cash cropping, and that the West ought to pay much more for forest products and conservation of biodiversity.[46]

International trade and environmental management: the need for integration

The problem of inappropriate commodity pricing raises a wider issue, that of the failure of the key agencies in the international economic system to develop policies on the terms of trade that take environmental quality into account. This lack of integration of environmental considerations in international trade policy emerged as a major issue for the first time during the Uruguay round of GATT talks.[47] While the World Bank and the IMF had been for years on the receiving end of criticism from environmentalists over debt and aid policies, international trade was relatively neglected by the campaigning NGOs. It became clear in 1990 to many environmen-

talists that the GATT negotiations were proceeding with virtually no consideration
of the effects of trade liberalisation measures on the global environment:

> . . . environmentalists have had no opportunity to learn of, assess and respond to
> present trade initiatives. Trade negotiations proceed, and agreements are
> concluded without even the most perfunctory consideration of the enormous
> environmental consequences that flow from them.[48]

Governments and agencies such as the World Bank made declarations in the 1980s
in support of sustainable development, yet the nations involved in the GATT talks
were making decisions that could undermine any progress towards sustainability in
the global economic system. The key problem is the potential conflict between
liberalisation of trade and the need for regulation of exports and imports in order to
conserve natural resources and safeguard ecosystems. The thrust of the Uruguay
round has been towards the removal of restrictions placed by countries on activities
such as logging within their borders and the export of rainforest products, and the
rejection by GATT of import bans on products deemed to be environmentally
unsound. In 1991 the GATT overruled a US ban on imports of Mexican tuna fish
(claimed to be fished in a way that killed dolphins in unsustainable numbers) on the
grounds that the restriction violated free trade. Critics of the GATT argue that a
blanket rejection of such restrictions will simply lead to unsustainable cropping of
resources.

International free trade agreements are also regarded with suspicion by environmentalists on the grounds that they promote 'harmonisation' of national standards
by reducing to the lowest common denominator, rather than seeking a general
increase in quality thresholds. The Uruguay round's agenda includes proposals from
the US for the global harmonisation of food safety standards, including controls on
pesticide use, which have led critics to argue that environmental and social standards
in individual countries would be seriously diluted, benefiting only TNCs in general
and US exporters in particular.[49] Free trade bloc regimes have also been criticised for
producing downward harmonisation: the US–Canada free trade agreement has
obliged Canada to weaken its regulations on pesticides and resource development;[50]
and warnings have been made that the development of the European Community's
integrated market could see a harmonisation of regulations at a low level of
environmental protection.[51]

The problem of the balance between trade liberalisation and restrictions based on
the need for sustainability is immensely complex. It is clear, as argued by GATT, that
restrictions on trade could be claimed on environmental grounds as a convenient
excuse for protectionism by industrial countries against one another and against
lower income countries. Thus there is a need for sensitive rulings in the GATT regime
that do justice to environmental concerns, maximise free trade where possible, and
ensure that lower income countries are fairly treated.

The debate within the GATT framework has always revolved around the polar
concepts of 'free trade' and 'protectionism', and has ignored questions of environmental sustainability. The debate should rather be one between sustainable and fair
trade on the one hand, and unsustainable and inequitable trade on the other. For this
to happen, there will have to be a re-orientation of the GATT system to allow

integration of environmental policy considerations. Shrybman proposes an amendment to the GATT agreement that would make explicit 'the priority of environmental protection and resource conservation' in any conflict with free trade, with the onus on the free trader to prove that environmental restrictions are unreasonable and not imposed in good faith.[52]

The lack of integration of environmental management in the GATT regime is indicated by the fact that GATT's working group on trade and the environment never met in the two decades after its establishment in 1971. However, following the mounting protests from NGOs and some Western governments over the failure to consider environmental issues in the Uruguay round, the GATT decided in October 1991 to activate the working party in order to investigate the conflicts between trade policy and sustainable development. This may be seen as the GATT's first step in the process of policy integration, on which the other international actors in the global economy (such as the World Bank) have already embarked, largely as a result of pressure from environmental NGOs.

DEVELOPMENT AND DEPENDENCY: PROBLEMS OF DEBT AND AID

The popular perception of low income countries in the West is dominated by images of hunger, appeals for aid, and grim statistics on the monumental debts owed to Western banks and governments. The 1980s saw crises of indebtedness in the developing world and wide recognition of the adverse environmental, economic and social effects of the aid policies pursued by Western governments and the World Bank. The problems of debt and aid are linked, and point to deeper issues of environmental management and the need for integration of environmental policy with development aid strategies.

Scale and origins of the debt crisis

The level of external debt accumulated by Third World countries and by former communist states in Eastern Europe is huge: over $1.3 trillion in 1991, with 46 countries classified as 'severely indebted'.[53] In 1988, Brazil and Mexico owed more than $100 billion; and Guyana's foreign debt amounted to an astonishing 522 per cent of its GDP.[54] The numbers are colossal, yet the total of around $1 trillion is itself relatively small compared to the total value of world output – some $20 trillion in 1990 – or the annual turnover of the 200 biggest transnational corporations, or to the public debt of the US.[55] The problem of debt is not that it is so large that it threatens the entire global economy: the crisis is effectively over for the Western banks, which have made large provisions against potential losses and reduced their exposure by selling debt on secondary markets. The problem is that the scale of debt is large enough for individual countries to suffer massive deprivation as they attempt to service their debts.

The crisis began in 1982 with Mexico's threat to default on its repayments, triggering panic among Western banks and governments and drawing attention to the mounting debt burden on low income countries. How did this burden become so crushing? The origins of the debt crisis can be traced to the oil price shock of 1974. The massive rise in oil prices placed a severe strain on the economies of low income countries needing to import oil, and also generated vast reserves of currency for the oil producers, which had to be 'recycled' by the international financial system. Much of the money was lent to lower income countries to help them cope with the oil shock, and much was borrowed by oil exporters such as Mexico on the assumption that oil prices would stay high and that export earnings and investment returns would enable easy repayment.

The lending and spending spree of the 1970s came to an abrupt end for several reasons. First, there was a second large oil price rise in 1979, putting yet more pressure on oil importing countries. Second, recession in the West spurred the sharp decline in commodity prices discussed above, leading to falls in export income for many low income countries. Third, interest rates in the West rose rapidly in the early 1980s as a result of US economic policies: tax cuts and increased military spending by the Reagan administration led to a budget deficit, which was financed by raising interest rates to draw in foreign investment. Capital flowed into the US and interest rates elsewhere rose in response, massively increasing the interest bill to be paid by the indebted low income countries at the same time as they faced a crisis of falling export earnings.

The crisis was not only precipitated by this grim conjunction of events. Short-sighted and reckless lending policies on the part of Western bankers played a key part. Vast sums never reached the people and projects most in need, but went into the pockets of corrupt officials and politicians in dictatorial regimes, or were squandered on costly and inappropriate projects. Fortunes have been taken out of low income countries in the form of 'capital flight' – the movement of funds into safe deposits in the West by rich individuals and by companies, and sometimes by corrupt officials. Corruption and grossly unproductive investments have thus reduced the value of loans to low income countries and contributed to their travails in servicing debts.[56]

Defaults on external debt have been avoided, and the international financial system has succeeded in confining the debt crisis to the debtor countries. But while creditors in the West have bought themselves time to make provisions against defaults and to grant reductions in debt to selected countries, the burden of repayment has barely been lightened for the low income debtors. The 1980s saw the net flow of wealth from rich to poor countries come to an end:

Developing nations paid $77 billion in interest on their debts [in 1989]. . . and repaid $85 billion worth of principal. Since 1983, the traditional flow of capital from North to South has been reversed: the poor countries pay more to the rich than they receive in return, a net hemorrhage that now stands at more than $50 billion a year.[57]

The growth of the debt burden has imposed heavy costs on the natural environments of the low income countries. The desperate need for foreign exchange with which to service debt has been a factor in over-exploitation of land, and destruction of forests in order to boost cash crop earnings. The misuse of loans on corrupt dealings, military expenditure, and 'prestige' projects with no productive returns have involved gigantic opportunity costs in terms of sustainable development and environmental protection. And the diversion of resources towards debt repayment has meant that there is little or no capital for environmentally sustainable development projects.

Debt management has involved an increase in low income countries' dependence on Western governments, TNCs and international agencies such as the World Bank and the IMF. The process of rescheduling debt, allowing selective write-offs and providing additional loans to tide countries over has largely been carried out by the IMF and World Bank. The management of debt relief has been based to a large extent on setting strict conditions on debtor countries' economic policies in the hope that these will lead to improved performance and renewed credit-worthiness. The conditions set have typically involved the provision of new loans and other assistance in return for implementation of structural adjustment programmes worked out by the international agencies.

Structural adjustment programmes have been intensely controversial. Their implementation has often involved cuts in social expenditure that have reduced the living standards of the poor;[58] they have led to governments selling off assets to Western investors in order to reduce debts and swap equity for debt;[59] and it is not clear that their economic goals have always been realised, through poor design of programmes and inadequate controls on privatisation and market development.[60] Their environmental impact can also be damaging: privatisation of state assets may simply mean that companies and land are sold off cheaply to TNCs, which then develop the assets with little or no regard for the environment.

Development aid and lower income countries

Compared to the huge sums owed by debtor countries in the Third World and ex-communist world, and to the capital flows in the international trading system, development aid is a relatively minor item. World development aid flows together make up only 1.4 per cent of the Third World's total GNP. As noted above, in the 1980s there was a net flow of resources from low income to high income countries: aid money was effectively sent straight back in the form of interest payments.

Nonetheless, the sums involved are large, and represent an important source of capital for the poorest nations. Bilateral aid from high income to low income countries in 1989 was some $41 billion; loans from the World Bank and its affiliates amounted to $28 billion.[61] In 1989, official development assistance (ODA) 'accounted for nearly two-thirds of new resource flows to low income countries and four-fifths of the flows to the poorest countries'.[62] ODA from a number of large high income donors – notably the US and the UK – fell as a proportion of their GNP in the 1980s, but the volume of aid from the OECD countries overall went up by around 3 per cent per year on average over the decade. With the reduction in lending by Western banks to debtor countries in the wake of the debt crises, the relative importance of ODA as a source of capital for the poorest countries has increased.

Much of the financial and technical assistance referred to as 'aid' comes in the form of soft loans from North to South, and thus actually amounts to a mild addition to recipient countries' debt. Moreover, aid is linked in other ways to the great structural inequalities between high and low income countries, and within low income countries. First, much Western aid money is provided with the intention not only of helping the recipient but also of assisting domestic producers and boosting economic performance at home. Aid projects supply machinery and services from 'donor' countries, and assist in developing jobs at home and export markets overseas.

Second, the aid business has been distorted throughout the post-war period by the Cold War and the linkage of development aid to what the superpowers and their allies regarded as their security interests. Vast sums have been spent on military aid to allies and clients. In many cases this resulted in enormous waste, as funds flowed to dictatorships that misused them in pursuit of disastrous economic policies, and through corruption: the Mobutu regime in Zaire provides a particularly grim example.[63]

Third, aid has often failed to help the poor in recipient countries and has played its part in promoting unsustainable development at the expense of the environment. This outcome stems from the combination of the two distortions noted above. Tied aid that benefits business in donor countries is unlikely to produce results that benefit, say, the rural poor in recipient countries. The kinds of projects that will result in the purchase of Western goods and services on a large scale tend to be big engineering ventures such as dam-building, or high technology agricultural projects involving imports of Western pesticides and fertiliser. Such projects have generally not involved either rigorous environmental impact assessment or consideration of their effect on the living standards of poor people.

Debt and aid: towards sustainable policy

The problems posed by debt and development aid are thus intertwined, and stem from a major failure of policy integration. The style and direction of lending and aid have often encouraged inappropriate use of resources. Industrial countries and multilateral agencies have not integrated environmental policy into their aid and debt policies. However, there are grounds for hope that new ideas emerging will lead to more environmentally sensitive strategies.

First, persistent criticism from NGOs and from lower income countries has had its effect on the multilateral agencies and on Western governments. The World Bank has taken steps to improve its expertise in environmental policy, strengthen environmental impact assessment for development projects funded by the Bank, provide support to countries devising National Environment Action Plans, and commit itself to the reduction of poverty in a way compatible with sustainable development.[64] Western governments now feel obliged to speak of sustainability as a key policy aim of their aid to low income countries.

Second, the end of the Cold War has transformed the aid scene just as it has changed the international security system. The former communist countries have largely withdrawn from bilateral commitments as domestic troubles have mounted; and Western states in turn have finally felt able to put pressure on dictatorial governments once tolerated in the name of strategic interests. Western governments and the multilateral agencies began in the early 1990s to link the provision of development finance to observance not only of market-friendly economic policies but also policies favourable to democratic politics. At the 1991 IMF/World Bank conference both agencies called for massive cuts in global arms spending as a key part of a redirection of aid, and of lower income countries' public expenditure towards education, primary health care, family planning, improved nutrition and environmental protection; and the World Bank's 1991 World Development Report stressed the association between democracy and economic progress.

Third, the multilateral agencies show signs, in the post-Cold-War world, of wishing to see equally dramatic changes in the policies of the rich countries as in the politics and economies of the low income ones. The 1991 IMF/World Bank conference saw attacks by the directors of both bodies on the military spending of the industrialised countries and on the failure of the West to agree on a strategy of debt relief for the poorest debtor nations. The head of the World Bank's Strategic Planning Division has raised the possibility that sustainable development may involve the imposition of forms of 'conditionality' on the industrialised world:

> The task now is to rethink the function and structure of international institutions to make them responsive to the new demands imposed by the emerging, fractured global order ... For example, in the same way that multilateral institutions impose economic policy conditions on developing countries in exchange for access to financial resources, is there any way a supranational institution could impose conditions on the developed countries on issues such as energy use, resource depletion and preservation of the environment? Can we devise alternative organisational and institutional arrangements capable of transcending the autonomy and sovereignty of industrialised nations and impose, if necessary, some of the changes that all of us agree are essential for human survival and a more equitable world order?[65]

These are straws in the wind, but important ones: these developments indicate that the climate is favourable for the progressive integration of policies for sustainable development into the mainstream policies of aid donors, whether governments or multilateral agencies, and for the application of conditions to lending and aid grants that go beyond the market-based structural adjustments insisted on by the IMF and World Bank.

Altering structural adjustment conditions on aid in order to promote environmental protection, cut military spending, reward democratic reform and improve the lot of the poor would provide a powerful impetus towards sustainable development. Such a reorientation of aid policy would need, however, to be part of a general recasting of Western approaches to the low income world. There needs to be structural adjustment on the part of the rich world too, especially in relation to the terms of international trade and to two further components of the emerging global economic order: technology transfer and the transnational corporations.

TECHNOLOGY TRANSFER

The process of industrialisation is all about the transfer (sale or donation) of technology. Technology in this sense does not just mean finished products and process equipment, but includes know-how, in the form of expert personnel, information services, training programmes, manuals, and so on. The key issues in technology transfer in the emerging global industrial system concern:

- the access of low income countries to technologies and to the international networks in the West;

- appropriateness of technologies; and
- integration of technology transfer with policies for environmental protection.

The access of low income nations to new technology is constrained by many aspects of the inequitable economic order described above. Although a number of newly industrialising countries have become important exporters of some technologies (for instance, South Korea in consumer electronics), they have done so by adopting more or less mature technologies already developed in the West; and the poorer low income countries remain constrained by their weak position in the international trading system. Their ability to import new technologies is limited by their economic weakness, as is their capacity to build up a home-grown technological base, which is a very costly way of lessening dependence on imports of technology. In this situation, a major role is played by direct foreign investment and technology licensing by transnational corporations. However, the debt crises of the 1980s, the instability of many low income countries, and the attractiveness of the increasingly integrated markets of Western Europe and North America have reduced direct foreign investment by transnationals in lower income countries. This investment is becoming more concentrated in industrialising countries with good growth prospects.[66]

Policy on improving low income countries' access to technology cannot therefore be based mainly on the decisions of corporations on investment and licensing, but must involve aid flows from the World Bank and other official agencies. This raises the question of the appropriateness of technology transfer through these various mechanisms.

Inappropriate and appropriate technology

The degree of appropriateness attached to any given technology depends on answers to the following key questions:

- how far a given technology serves a country's development needs in an environmentally sound fashion;
- how far it represents a productive use of resources;
- whether its use is likely to lead to sustainable wealth creation; and
- how far it can be maintained by local people rather than by overseas experts.

It is easy to see that much technology transfer from the high to low income countries in the form of aid and technical assistance has been wholly inappropriate in these terms. The 'mega-projects', such as massive dams and highways, favoured by donors, financial agencies and the elites of many low income countries have soaked up resources that could have been used on more productive and sustainable schemes. The most glaring example of inappropriate transfer is the diffusion of weaponry, on which low income countries spent some $38 billion a year in the late 1980s, mainly on imports from the industrial world.[67]

With the end of the Cold War and the growing pressure in the multilateral agencies to make development aid conditional on 'good government' as well as on structural adjustment in the economy, there is some cause to hope that the transfer of military technologies will be curbed. But inappropriate civil technology is also deadly for the environment and for the well-being of people. The modernisation of the Third World has seen a repetition of many of the features of industrial development in the West and the ex-communist countries that are now costing billions of dollars in environmental repair work: the gross pollution of air, soil and water by heavy industry, the profligate use of energy, the dumping of toxic wastes, and the obsession with the motor car. This is because the mature technologies that generate these problems have been the cheapest and easiest to import or develop on license from the West, and have been identified with 'progress'. Licensing agreements for new technologies are harder to conclude and command higher royalties, and the skills to exploit them are scarcer. Thus the low income countries are often in a poor position to 'leapfrog' stages of modernisation and go directly for state-of-the-art technologies that are cleaner, and less energy-intensive.

This issue is of course especially relevant to the global environmental threats recognised in recent years: the greenhouse effect and stratospheric ozone depletion. In the light of these threats, key mature technologies massively diffused in the industrial world and readily available to the low income countries are 'inappropriate' with a vengeance: the internal combustion engine, CFCs, coal-fired power stations, and so on. Appropriate technology capable of providing a partial solution to these problems is only now being developed and diffused in the West: for example, energy efficient lighting and heating systems and energy generation plant. Much of the new technology in these areas cannot be afforded by the low income countries, including the ex-communist industrial states.

The issue of inappropriate technological development also relates to the neglect of indigenous skills and local knowledge, which count as technologies in their own right. In the newly industrialising countries there is generally a view among governing elites that local skills and expertise are somehow primitive and thus need to be discarded in favour of Western products and processes. This 'top-down' view has of course been encouraged for years by Western commercial interests. The downgrading of local techniques in resource management and agriculture often means that potential sources of wealth are lost and are replaced with inappropriate imported technologies that are costly to develop and maintain. In agriculture, the introduction of 'off the shelf' Western technologies into Africa at the expense of local people's farming knowledge is now widely regarded as a prime example of inappropriate technology transfer.[68]

While there is evidently a role for advanced Western technology in improving agriculture in low income countries, it must be as a complement to long-established and sustainable local knowledge, not as a wholesale replacement for it. Appropriate energy technology for rural areas in low income countries will often best be developed as an 'intermediate' hybrid of Western or domestically-produced equipment and local fuel inputs, designed with the participation of local people. For example, the Harayana sustainable energy project in India, involves development of biogas generators, gasifiers and solar water heaters to make a village self-sufficient in renewable energy.[69]

Unfair technology transfer from South to North

The debate over technology transfer tends to be based on the assumption that the transfer is all in one direction – from the high income North to the low income South. In fact, massive transfers of technology have been going on for years from the Third World to the industrial countries in the form of genetic resources. Third World seeds for crop plants represent a technology of fundamental value to low and high income countries alike, for which the low income countries have had no means of charging. Seed varieties have been collected for decades by Western scientists and companies, and have been developed intensively in the industrial world, with no royalty payments going to the farmers who originally bred them in the low income countries. This inequitable relationship must change, since the industrial countries are now aware that their seed banks are inadequate to the task of conserving varieties and that genetic resources are being eroded at an accelerating rate in the Third World as forests and other crucial ecosystems are destroyed.[70] There is growing pressure on the high income countries to establish international funds for payment of Third World countries for conservation of genetic resources and ecological 'services' (for example, as performed by the rainforests), and for the patenting of traditional local knowledge, including plant varieties. Such developments would lead to large transfers of money and sustainable technology to the low income countries.[71]

Sustainable technology transfer

There is no single 'package' of appropriate technology that can be devised to suit the needs of all countries, but the key elements of a portfolio of appropriate technologies can be identified. These concern energy efficiency, minimal waste generation, maximum resource efficiency, and above all the 'soft' technologies for sustainable development such as technology assessment, environmental impact assessment, and training and research systems that involve local people in the analysis of problems and in devising solutions.

This last point is crucial: technology transfer should not be seen as a purely commercial and technical operation, but as a social transaction demanding attention to local circumstances and appropriate local management. The 'soft' technologies vital to effective technology transfer include new approaches to environmental management explored in Chapters 7–9, and in the case studies that follow. In essence this means that the transfer of technology must be *integrated* with policies in other areas designed to promote sustainable development. While this task demands the involvement of intergovernmental agencies, national governments and other public agencies, and the transfer of resources on a large scale through official mechanisms to the low income countries, it must also bring in the private sector. This leads us to consider the role of the transnational corporations (TNCs) in technology transfer and the development of sustainable industrial systems.

TRANSNATIONAL CORPORATIONS

TNCs are corporate networks with production facilities and subsidiary companies in more than one country. They almost all have headquarters in OECD countries and are a key force in the internationalisation of industrial production and of Western consumer tastes. The TNCs have been for many years the object of vehement criticism from the Third World and from Western NGOs as 'neo-colonialists', playing a key role in the despoilation of the environment and exploitation of working people in low income countries. The view of TNCs as leviathans trampling the earth is encouraged by contemplation of their weight in the global economy.

- The TNCs dominate international trade, and in particular they control almost all world trade in many primary commodities such as tea, coffee, copper, forest products and bauxite.
- They dominate direct foreign investment.
- Some have turnovers that exceed the GDP of small low income nations.
- They are a key source of technology transfer for industrialising countries.
- They are responsible for most of the world's technological innovation, including development of environmental protection technologies.

By any standard, then, the TNCs constitute a critically important element of the global economy, yet their global reach is not matched by international regulation. The environmental impacts of the TNCs are controlled by the regulations of the various countries playing host to them, and by whatever policies for self-regulation they devise on environmental protection. The microeconomic linkages forged by TNCs and their host country customers and suppliers amount in some cases to cartelisation of markets, but there is no international anti-trust law to regulate TNCs' competition. The international political and institutional capacity to deal with the consequences of globalisation at the level of the corporation is almost wholly lacking.[72]

The TNCs have an immense impact on the global environment, and in the absence of global regulations on their behaviour, it becomes crucial to know how they respond to international guidelines and national environmental law and how they develop internal standards for environmental protection. On this point, recent research reveals a patchy response by TNCs, but also considerable potential for postive development of corporate strategies. A survey in 1991 by the United Nations Centre on Transnational Corporations of over 200 TNCs with annual sales of over $200 billion indicated that their environmental policies were influenced most strongly by home country legislation and very little by international guidelines and global ecological problems. The majority had no integrated environmental policy.[73] The environmental challenges best understood were those on which Western countries had developed the most extensive legislation, such as air and water pollution. Those lowest on the agenda were the issues associated with the low income countries – loss of biodiversity, soil erosion and explosive population growth.

The main message from this research is that environmental policy in the largest TNCs is as yet unintegrated: the performance may go beyond legal requirements in any particular country, but there is a long way to go before TNCs develop proactive strategies that raise environmental standards on a company-wide basis, and take 'Third World' environmental problems as seriously as they have begun to take those of most concern in their domestic bases. Yet there are some grounds for optimism on this score.

- Respondents to the UN survey said they wanted more international standard-setting.

- The TNCs are conscious of public opinion in the West in relation to industrial accidents with severe ecological consequences and thus are keen to promote a 'greener' image.
- Perhaps most significantly, there is a trend towards centralised standard-setting within the TNC, whereby the parent company lays down environmental quality standards and targets for the entire operation. This development could offer opportunities to environmental lobby groups and international agencies to collaborate with TNCs in policy development and ensuring consistent implementation of corporate strategy in different countries.

The TNCs need to be regulated within an international regime that requires them to observe policies compatible with sustainable development and fair trade. This kind of international economic framework is a distant goal, and will take complex and lengthy negotiation. Meanwhile, it is crucial that TNCs be encouraged to live up to the rhetoric of high-profile international business groupings in favour of sustainable development, and adopt sustainable policies on a voluntary basis across countries.[74] For this to happen we need to go beyond confrontation between TNCs, Third World governments and environmental NGOs. While campaigning and tough criticism must go on, there must also be a recognition that the TNCs are a fundamental element in the global economy and will remain so. Their dominant position in international trade, research and development and technology transfer means that their co-operation in the creation of a sustainable global economy is critical. The scope for more proactive policies within TNCs and the tapping of TNCs' expertise and wealth in the development of sustainable policies is such that international agencies and environmental lobbies should look hard for ways of collaborating with TNCs as well as controlling them. The 'soft technology' for this may well exist in the form of the action-centred networks discussed later.

CONCLUSION

In this chapter we have considered the key features of the emerging global industrial economy. This consists of an intricate and interconnected system of networks that must be reformed on many levels if the process of sustainable development is to be realised. The global economy is characterised by dynamic but grossly uneven development, reflecting the outcome of colonial history and the scientific and technological ascendancy of the West; by Western domination of international trade and technology transfer; by the massive financial and technological power of the TNCs; by the dependence of many low income countries on TNCs and Western governments because of indebtedness, inappropriate aid, and the ruinous economic, social and military policies of many Third World elites; and by the export to the low income countries not only of welcome aspirations to democracy and improved living standards, but also of the profoundly mixed blessings of Western tastes in consumption, Western modes of industrial production, liberal market economic policies, and the pollution problems of affluence.

The key issue is how far the existing elements of the global industrial system can integrate environmental consciousness into their operations and thereby adapt to a sustainable development path. The overriding environmental failure of the economic order has been its lack of integration of ecological concerns with policy making. However, there are numerous signs of hope. The IMF and World Bank have begun to make important changes in policy to promote sustainable development. There is at least greater understanding of the ecological consequences of debt and aid. But more work is crucial on mechanisms for promoting the integration of environmental management into the core activities of the GATT, IMF, World Bank and the TNCs, as well as of national and regional governments throughout the world. In this context the analysis of organisational constraints and the proposals for organisational innovation and networking across sectoral and institutional frontiers developed in Chapter 7 and following chapters are of great relevance. Before turning to these, however, we examine further political constraints within which new approaches to sustainable development must be devised.

6   Top-down or bottom-up? The dilemma of development

Social mobilization at local levels needs to be backed by mobilization around policy issues that require national and even international resolution. A global capitalism requires a global approach to the environmental question.

John Friedmann, 1990[1]

People already have the knowledge; what they must have are the rights over their local environments. This is the big problem in the world today. The vast majority of people have become passive observers, and a few people are taking decisions for everyone else. That is the prime reason why the environment . . . is being destroyed.

Anil Agarwal, 1990[2]

It is a central contention of this book that good environmental management is not a technical exercise separate from everyday economic and political life, or something tacked on after the fact of development, but that it can only come about when environmental values are embedded within economic and political systems. For this to occur it is first necessary to understand something of those systems, and the basic tensions that affect them. In modern political systems, particularly democratic ones, an enduring tension exists between top-down forces and bottom-up aspirations.

This tension, essentially involving the forces of centralisation and decentralisation, is of concern in environmental management for two reasons. First, at a general level, it provides much of the political context for unfolding debates about the meaning of sustainable development in many countries. The range of tensions is growing as the world economy integrates but also as more and more ethnic or nationalist groups aspire to self-government. At the extreme, as in the civil war in Yugoslavia, society and environment are ruined, and nothing sustainable can hope to be created except in the very long term. But in many more, non-violent circumstances, the tension is also endemic, as with the gradual erosion of the basis for federalism in Canada, or the laborious forging of the European Community. In these cases the tension between centralisation and decentralisation is fundamental to the dynamic of the political system.

Second, and more specifically, is the meaning of *self*-management, where people define their own problems and take control of their own environments. This is fundamental to the network approach espoused here, but it begs the questions of scale and participation. Who decides how sustainable development is defined for what unit of territory: the neighbourhood, the town, the region, the province, the nation state or larger, and who participates in its implementation? In many cases sustainable development has no hope of realisation where the problem is defined at the wrong scale, either too grandly or in too limited a way, or where relevant stakeholders are excluded from participation. There are no ready answers, but a grounding in the arguments is needed if we are to try to tackle some of these basic questions.

CENTRALISATION AND DECENTRALISATION

It is in the interplay between two criteria for good government put forward by John Stuart Mill, democratic participation and efficiency, that fascinating issues arise concerning the relative advantages and disadvantages of top-down versus bottom-up action and control for sustainable development. In *Liberty* Mill argues for local self-government from a conception of the absolute priority of individual liberty, which he understands as the absence of restraint in relation to self-regarding actions of individuals, groups and local political authorities. Just as the individual has a right to liberty in personal matters, there is a similar '. . . liberty in any number of individuals to regulate by mutual agreement such things as regard them jointly, and regard no persons but themselves'.[3] Here local self-government provides an important institutional buffer against abuse of power by greater society.

The other great value of local control argued by Mill is efficiency in the management and delivery of local services by virtue of responsiveness to local need. He states '. . . it is but a small portion of the public business of a country which can be well done or safely attempted by the central authorities'.[4] Local officials could be held accountable and this ensured a measure of efficiency in meeting local needs.

Chapter 5 documented the integration of the world economy which increasingly impinges on all aspects of life, and which is experienced by individuals and communities largely as a 'top-down' transformation of social and physical environments. In this chapter we see how action by government to support economic development, and to buttress its own power, also tends to be centralising, but also how there are increasing demands for democratic participation and decentralisation of control.

Trends to centralisation within national boundaries are associated with:

- the rise of the modern state;
- increasing control by central governments of policy funding and redistribution of resources on a territorial basis;
- cultural homogenisation; and
- extension of administrative control through professions and bureaucracies.

Trends to decentralisation are often the result of:

- political responses to ideological regionalism or ethnic nationalism;
- measures for the promotion of regional economic development;
- measures to mobilise local resources and generate commitment;
- functional responses to government overload, bureaucratic unresponsiveness, or the continual failure of centralised policy initiatives.

At a deeper level, decentralising tendencies may also be a reaction against the socioeconomic forces in modern life producing homogeneity, concentration of power and centralisation of functions. They may reflect the deep-seated impulse in 'post-traditional' societies for political participation, emancipation, and the realisation of democratic values.[5] Both centralising and decentralising forces operate simultaneously in modern societies, and this creates a dilemma for environmental management.

The tension between centralisation and decentralisation is more complex than it may first appear. At a basic level it represents the difference, say, between top-down approaches such as that of the World Bank, IMF or national governments the world over, compared with very local, usually NGO-led, environmental initiatives. Examples of the latter range from the expanding network of Groundwork Trusts in Britain and Europe, described later, to the many thousands of village projects in lower income countries, such as the Kibwezi Women's Project in Kenya, which promotes small-scale, sustainable business initiatives such as brickmaking and honey production. Much of the debate is polarised around these two divergent approaches, centralised or community-based.

In reality the tension is more pervasive. It permeates our lives and our concerns for development, whether in higher or lower income countries. It is a basic problem of the modern state, in which demands for democratic participation and devolution of decision-making may clash with demands for economic efficiency and decisive policy-making at national or international levels. For example:

- In relation to the European Community, there is concern in some member states that the EC is over-centralising decision-making on environmental policy and impact assessment procedures, and rapidly encroaching on the sovereignty of the state. For others, however, the centralisation of many aspects of policy in Brussels has come not a moment too soon for the purposes of environmental protection, which they feel receives no more than lip service from national government.
- This type of issue will be replicated on a world scale over questions such as ozone depletion and global warming. Unless there is a great increase in willingness to enter into binding agreements, it may not be long before countries will need to be pressured into giving up large areas of environmental policy to supranational agencies.
- At the national level there is growing concern about how best to organise the state for the purposes of pollution control and sustainable development. For example, in Nigeria the recently established Federal Environmental Protection Agency (FEPA) is wrestling with the challenge of how to organise environmental policy, monitoring and scientific testing in the thirty Nigerian states, taking into account the very limited resources available for administration and the many political and cultural constraints. Their solution is to devolve as many functions as possible to the states while retaining a necessary degree of policy and control within the Federal Government. Many countries, Britain and Canada included, consider reorganisation of government functions as an important aspect of environmental control.
- At the local level, there are many examples where local NGO-managed projects are successful, in countries as diverse as Britain and Kenya, but also many other well-intentioned local projects that are undone by the effects of international economic integration. Urban renewal efforts may be undone by the effects of

decisions taken by multinational corporations headquartered in other countries. This lack of real control is a classic problem in local development.

There is, of course, no one right answer to the dilemma of how to balance top-down and bottom-up forces, either by reference to criteria of democratic participation or efficiency. Both forces must be harnessed to the needs of sustainable development, in a flexible and balanced approach sensitive to local circumstances.

There is also a broader issue at stake. This is the endemic tension between the powerful trend toward specialisation and integration, which characterises the modern industrial state, and aspirations for integration of social, economic and environmental forces on a regional or local basis for the purposes of sustainable development. In many cases, the very nature of environmental problems requires action on such a territorial basis, but within national and international contexts. Unfortunately the trend to centralisation is powerful, and it is difficult to turn to the real world for examples of genuine decentralisation in pursuit of sustainable development, at least at the scale of the region, often the appropriate level for carrying out environmental management tasks. In the next section we analyse an intelligent proposal by some 'new decentralists' for regional control for sustainable development, along with the powerful obstacles to its realisation. We examine below the main forces behind the demand for centralisation and international integration on the one hand, and that for decentralisation on the other.

Top-down: the trend to centralisation and international integration

First and foremost, government has to service the economic system as the ultimate source of the material resources upon which its political survival depends. Government must also monitor, control and organise its utilisation of these economic resources.[6] Clearly, central governments have an overriding interest in retaining responsibility for economic policy and demand management.

After World War I, and especially during the Great Depression, central governments in the West started to build up their monopoly of economic intervention and planning. This position was consolidated during World War II, and after the war most states assumed responsibility for economic stability through Keynesian management of the economy. This trend to greater government control coincided with the concentration of economic power in the hands of oligopolistic, multinational corporations. The state of any national economy thus became both a national and a supranational issue. Most national governments see it as in their interests to manage the economy on behalf of oligopolistic corporations, often by providing: the infrastructure upon which industrial production depends, access to natural resources, financial and tax incentives, and export credit guarantees, in addition to supportive monetary, fiscal and trade policies.

Market-friendly conservative governments have recently sought to decrease government expenditure as a proportion of GDP, and subject more aspects of society to market mechanisms, following the doctrines of economists such as Hayek and Milton Friedman. However, most central governments, whatever their professed stance on laissez-faire, are unlikely to diminish their hold over economic management without a struggle. Paradoxically, the rhetoric of the 'freedom of the market' is often used at the same time as policies on public spending drastically restrict the power of local government agencies. In Britain for example, more than a decade of attempts to impose a supposedly minimalist, laissez-faire state has only served to reinforce centralist trends. As Rhodes notes, Thatcherism '. . . provided the clearest assertion yet of the centre's belief in its right to govern'.[7] Jenkins puts it more dramatically:

> In order to liberate the individual from the State it has had to wield the power
> of the State . . . in order to devolve economic choice upon the sovereign
> consumer, his democratic possibilities have been narrowed.[8]

Following from this, Eversley makes the important point that so long as major decisions on economic management rest with central governments, these decisions will pre-determine all lesser decisions related to regional economic development and environmental management, and thus pre-empt much of the decision-making power in regions and localities.[9] In Canada, for example, central government decisions on the timing and location of oil and gas exploration and production, and the provision of generous grants and tax incentives to multinational energy corporations, seldom have anything to do with local needs and may run counter to them. This illustrates that local considerations often get short shrift when national issues are at stake.

Other centralising forces

The centralising tendencies in the modern state based on the imperatives of economic management are complemented by other factors. These include population growth, the drift from the country to the city as agriculture becomes more mechanised, and increased mobility of city dwellers responding to changing labour market conditions. In the West, and to an ever greater extent in the rest of the modernising world, these factors contribute to a decline in the individual's orientation around place and a rise in orientation around functional groups, such as professional colleagues. Centralisation is also reinforced by professionalisation and the growth of bureaucracies. Professional knowledge and the allegiances of bureaucrats to central government often transcend local allegiances and patterns of life and lead to their erosion.

A related factor is cultural homogenisation, brought about by improved transportation and development of communication networks, especially radio and television. Sharpe notes, for example, that where an emergent national media system carries advertising, centralisation and 'metropolitanism' is enhanced by the promotion of world-wide mass consumption.[10] The penetration of American consumer culture to every corner of the globe via Cable News Network is a case in point. Smith argues that such developments are '. . . a powerful socially homogenizing force that undermines parochial sentiment and interest in the uniqueness of regional cultures'.[11] Modern politics reflect the tension between such forces and attempts of cultural movements and organisations to preserve local culture and language, as in for example the struggle of native groups in Canada and New Zealand to preserve their cultural identities.

In every case, financial control is the acid test of the balance of power between the central and local. The potential for conflict is clear:

On the one hand, it is impossible to have meaningful local ... political autonomy without corresponding financial resources. On the other hand, many advocates of an energetic economic policy claim that central steering of sub-national expenditure policies is inevitable.[12]

It is probable that constitutional, or ad hoc, devolution of power is virtually meaningless without corresponding transfers of control over financial resources.

Finally, the advent of the modern state has raised expectations for territorial justice within the nation, and central governments are usually the only level of administration able to re-allocate resources between sub-national units, based on need. This process serves to concentrate power at the centre, and indeed constitutes one of the major ethical arguments in favour of central power. As Bogdanor notes: '. . . territorial justice is a fundamental aspiration in most modern democracies, and it can easily serve to reconcentrate powers at the centre'.[13] The same holds true for many aspects of environmental, transport and land use planning, for example in watershed systems, which cut across administrative boundaries and demand centralised arbitration and control.

Trends to decentralisation

Despite the powerful forces behind centralising trends noted above, the modern world is marked also by countervailing pressures on the centralised nation state and supranational bodies. There is general agreement that decentralisation should involve a genuine transfer of power, that is, the transfer of legislative, judicial or administrative authority. Decentralisation thus usually requires the creation of local political or administrative institutions. The notion of decentralisation covers a wide range of concepts. For example:

It can be defined as the transfer of responsibility for planning, management and the raising and allocation of resources from the central government and its agencies to field units of central government ministries or agencies, subordinate units or levels of government, semi-autonomous public authorities or corporations, area-wide regional or functional authorities, or non-governmental private or voluntary organizations.[14]

Within this conception of decentralisation, based on a number of country studies, Rondinelli and Nellis suggest four sub-categories:[15]

1　Devolution is the creation or strengthening, financially or legally, of sub-national units of government, whose activities are substantially outside the direct control of central government.

2　Deconcentration is the handing over of some administrative authority or responsibility to lower levels within central government ministries and agencies – a shifting of workload from centrally located officials to staff or offices located outside the centre.

3   Delegation involves the transfer of managerial responsibility for specially defined functions to organisations outside the regular bureaucratic structure.
4   Through privatisation or the creation of arms-length agencies, governments divest themselves of responsibility for functions either by transferring them to voluntary organisations or by allowing them to be performed by private enterprises.

Political or ethnic nationalism

There are many reasons for decentralisation. One is the increasing desire for political representation at the regional level. Outside the classic pre-1945 federations (Australia, Canada, Switzerland and the USA), political regionalism is a recent phenomenon, based on convictions that decentralisation is essential in true democracy, and that regional (or local) underdevelopment runs counter to notions of territorial justice. In many countries, political regionalism is a reaction against dictatorial regimes associated with a high degree of bureaucratic centralisation and lack of local autonomy.

The political form of decentralisation is generally shaped within a federation or a regionalised administrative system. The initial impetus may be political crisis, de-colonisation and/or liberation, and subsequent political bargaining. In any case, whenever sub-national units of government have been established, central government generally recognises that it cannot function solely on the basis of national minorities. Instead, two 'political logics' come into play — '... one, the classic democratic logic of one man - one vote, the other the logic of cooperation between entities differently constituted'.[16] The recognition of the two logics is institutionalised by either an organisation designed to facilitate central–regional (or local) bargaining, or through the representation of provincial units at the centre to secure the resolution of territorial conflict. However, the creation of a sub-national level of government sets up a new locus of power:

> Elected provincial assemblies will claim they are best able to represent public opinion in the areas of their jurisdiction, and their electorates may well support this claim. The assemblies will enjoy a degree of legitimacy arising from popular election, and those who have elected them are likely to resent intervention by the centre, whatever formal powers central government enjoys ... Even if constitutional theory dictates that ultimate legislative power remains with central government, the political facts may well indicate that power has been nearly irrevocably transferred.[17]

Another force towards political decentralisation is regional or ethnic nationalism, when groups with a common culture demand a greater degree of self-government and an enhanced share of national resources. To share a culture means to share a language or a religion or a history, and often the notion of cultural and especially language and/or religious heritage is seen as a fundamental democratic freedom which cannot be denied by the state. Such nationalism is often a reaction against over-centralisation in the modern state. In highly centralised and bureaucratic India for example, separatism in Kashmir, Punjab and Assam threatens the integrity of the state. Many commentators attribute this to the abuse of central power by New Delhi, particularly in the economic sphere.[18]

The experience of the ex-communist states in the aftermath of the 1989–91 period of revolution illustrates this reaction well. The weakening of central authority led to an explosion of demands for increased ethnic and regional autonomy within federal systems (the former USSR, Czechoslovakia, Yugoslavia) or for outright independence. Authoritarian over-centralisation in the communist years produced a dynamic trend towards ethnic nationalism once the dictatorships fell, often leading to a degree of political and economic disintegration that threatened to be ultimately destructive of local culture and economic prospects – as in the violent break-up of Yugoslavia and the wrangling between the ex-Soviet republics. During such radical and rapid disintegration, environmental considerations are likely to be laid to one side and it may be many years before any progress is possible.

In its most radical form then, outright separation is demanded by radical action, for example, by the Tamils in Sri Lanka, the Timorese in Indonesia, or the Sikhs in the Punjab. The problems of separatism in the Punjab (and Kashmir and Assam) have been laid at the door of over-centralisation:

> Yet a closer look at India's problems suggests that most of them have been aggravated precisely by the abuse of central power. The energies of a naturally entrepreneurial and hard-working people have been stultified. A monstrous bureaucracy has been created. Controls breed evasion and corruption, and corruption breeds violence.[19]

The list of more modest, non-violent forms could go on and on. The Polish journalist Ryszard Kapuscinski, considering fervent calls by near-starving refugees in an Ethiopian camp for independence for a region of Somalia rather than bread, muses:

> I thought about that powerful, dominating force: the need to feel at home, to be independent, to lock oneself within the four walls of one's own national, religious, racial or cultural home. It seems that in so far as the twentieth century was one of ideology, the next might become the century of nationalism.[20]

In some cases, interest in cultural heritage can diminish during a process of integration of regional economies and traditional cultures into the global economic system. A common result of that integration for cultural minorities and indigenous peoples is alienation from both tradition and from the modern lifestyle of consumerism. In Canada, for example, suicide, divorce and alcoholism rates among native people rose alarmingly following the 'opening up' and modernisation of Canada's north in the 1950s and 1960s. Such problems for native people continue in Canada and the United States to this day, but also out of this alienation arises renewed interest in the former traditional, usually sustainable, way of life. The act of asserting cultural independence can contribute to renewed self-respect within ethnic minorities, increased demands for self-government, and perhaps to some creative fusion of tradition and modernity.

The demands for more suitable forms of representation arising out of political or ethnic nationalism can take many forms, from neighbourhood committees to regional parliaments. Agarwal reports on the recent development of village-level control in Rajasthan, authorised under the state's Gramden Act of 1971.[21] This act, inspired by early Gandian leaders, allows a village assembly, the *gram sabha*, made up of all adults, to manage resources within the village boundary and to judge, prosecute and penalise those who violate a self-imposed environment and land use plan.[22] Given this degree of self-control, highly unusual within India's extensive bureaucratic structure, Rajasthani villages are devising effective means of sustainable management of their own environment. This is not, as Agarwal notes, for the purpose of increasing GNP in monetary terms, but to increase the 'gross natural product' upon which villagers' well-being depends.

At another level, regional parliaments have recently been created in Spain, in an effort to defuse Basque and Catalan separatism. The functions of such parliaments, for example, in taxation, spending or environmental control, then becomes an open question which increasingly needs to include discussion of the potential for sustainable development.

Finally, cultural nationalism is of interest to our purposes for at least two reasons. The first is that cultural diversity is as important to sustainable development as biodiversity, and for much the same reasons. The erosion of traditional knowledge and skills in the face of relentless modernisation is a grave loss to the repertoire of environmental management, whether in the case of the skills of Amerindians in Guyana, Inuits in the Canadian Arctic, or peasant farmers in Indonesia or India. These skills invariably represent knowledge evolved and refined over many generations, and once lost, are unlikely ever to be retrieved within the context of modern science and industrialism. Moreover, innovative thinking on management is moving in the direction of fine-grained, localised responses to the seemingly overwhelming range and complexity of the problems that face us. The erosion, and even extinction, of cultures and their knowledge reduces the range of possible responses we might make to the global *problematique*. Even in a strictly functional sense, this is a profound mistake.

Second, and again from an instrumental point of view, once a cultural group organises politically, the common symbolic system makes for efficient collective action because organisational costs are relatively low.[23] Political entrepreneurs often exploit this organisational advantage to make collective claims for resources and control. There is no particular reason why environmental activists could not do likewise. A common culture can circumvent the need for a lengthy process of searching for common meaning and definition of the nature of sustainable development. We are not of course claiming that this will necessarily happen, but only that cultural nationalism may provide an opportunity for defining and implementing local forms of sustainable development.

Functional decentralisation

Another spur to decentralisation is the remoteness of central government from its regions and its clients, which can result in poor communication, deficient design and implementation of programmes, and squandered resources from information overload, bureaucratic ineptitude, 'buckpassing' and political patronage. A whole literature on service decentralisation and implementation has arisen. Peeters, for example, argues that decentralisation may be the solution to overcoming government overload, which he argues is a common characteristic of the modern state.[24] Decentralists argue that assessment of needs and delivery of services can be made more efficient and effective by localising the administrative structure. Closely linked to this is the demand for more responsiveness and access through participation, for example, to counteract bureaucratic dominance and to ensure citizens' involvement in such areas as education or environmental planning as much as in the political act of voting.

CORE, PERIPHERY AND REGIONAL SELF-DEVELOPMENT

After ideology and ethnicity, impetus for decentralisation also comes from the need to mobilise resources for self-development. This can be a direct reaction against the integration of regional economies into the international economic system, a process which can debilitate sustainable local economies. This process by which peripheral, often agricultural, regions become the ultimate victims of apparent national economic progress is not new, but is part and parcel of the trend in industrial societies to *functional* integration of economies at the expense of *spatial* integration. For example, Weaver describes the process in nineteenth century England:

> Both the small scale territorial community and the biological family were alienated from the production process, and people in ever-increasing numbers were pushed off the land to become urban factory workers. This freed the countryside as well for organization along factory lines. The metropolis boomed, becoming itself an extended factory – surrounded by the squalour of working class housing. The countryside was first reduced to a position of political and economic subservience, and then, in much of the industrial West, it was all but obliterated as a social environment.[25]

There are many modern parallels, not only in lower income countries, such as in Africa, having to shift to chemically intensive monocultural farming of export crops, but also in the continuing dramatic changes in the rural economies of countries such as Britain and the United States, where communities have been profoundly changed by a shift to high technology factory farming. In the 1970s, some of the older industrial regions themselves, the 'rustbelts', became part of the economic periphery as a result of deindustrialisation and the rise of the service/office sector economy in new centres of economic growth.

This powerful conception of uneven spatial development as a basic element in capitalism is captured in the terminology of 'core–periphery' analysis, which holds that dominant regions are the locus of decision-making, and exploit and discriminate against less developed regions for their own gain. Residents of those disadvantaged regions thus become alienated from the national state. Although not without its limitations, this core–periphery metaphor is a helpful heuristic device for thinking about colonialism, the rise of the modern state and regional social movements in terms of power, managerial control and the dimensions of democratic action.[26] Some regions in the higher income countries are part of the periphery, and whole countries, such as many poor African states, are also part of the world's periphery.

Attempts to avoid or overcome peripheralisation at the level of the region have given rise to various attempts at regional development planning. Although the Scottish ecologist Patrick Geddes can be credited with an early conception of the viability of the region as a level of ecological understanding and action, regional planning *per se* is often traced to the early activities in the 1930s of the Tennessee Valley Authority in the United States, which harnessed hydroelectric power as a lever for improving the fortunes of one of America's poorest regions.

Although planning at the level of the region is probably critical to sustainable development, regional planning need not necessarily involve genuine decentralisation of power. All its institutional trappings, regional development departments or agencies, development grants, controls over industrial location and the like, can serve to centralise power in the national government. This is because regional development policy invariably institutes new financial and administrative instruments, ultimately controlled by central politicians and bureaucrats. It is for this reason that regional planning is sometimes disparagingly referred to as 'technocratic regionalism' by its more radical critics, such as the 'new decentralists' or eco-regionalists. It is instructive to look at their proposals for what they consider to be genuine regional decentralisation of power.

Proposals of the New Decentralists

This group of environmental planner-philosophers addresses these issues in relation to sustainable development. Hebbert suggests that the '. . . terms for this debate in the 1980s have been set by the emergence of a strong decentralist school whose leading exponent is John Friedmann'.[27] Friedmann sees development planning, including for the United States, as a field with technical, moral and utopian dimensions:

> The first dimension answers to the question of how we can best achieve the ends we seek. The second answers to the question of how we shall live with one another. It is fundamentally a question of social and environmental ethics. And the third addresses the long-term future and our vision of what life for all of us might be like. It is what inspires us beyond the mundane affairs of politics. Utopian visions enshrine our hopes.[28]

The new decentralism questions the very organisation and goals of the world development process as we know it, and the likelihood that it could ever possibly lead to sustainable development. Friedmann argues that function has superseded territory as the mode of economic organisation in the world. This has resulted in a global development crisis, in which ways of thinking and modes of action are based on false assumptions about the inevitability of the functional integration of the world economy.

Such integration is based on abstract, rational and large scale economic behaviour, as opposed to small-scale, local or regional patterns of integration. The latter take place in real, territorially delimited, places while the former takes place in increasingly abstract, functional space, bridged by high technology communication, and involving large-scale, impersonal human interactions. Functional integration in production, transport and technology is epitomised by vertically-integrated multinational corporations and international banking activities. In many cases the power of functionally organised institutions is supranational. The assumption made by proponents of functional integration as a development path is that smaller-scale communities (localities, regions or even nation states) can only develop through interaction with more 'highly developed' communities or countries, and then only by accepting the larger unit's definition of development. This is part and parcel of the paternalistic view of the 'under-developed' world by the 'developed', discussed in Chapter 2. Whether we accept this view or not, we must accept that, in current conditions, it is backed up by the sheer financial power and economic control of international capital.

The situation of Guyana in South America provides a stark example of the process of functional integration. Burdened by a debt of US$1.7 billion for a population of less than a million, Guyana has launched an IMF-sponsored Economic Recovery Programme which involves a massive sell-off of the natural resources of its near-pristine rainforest. First in line was an Anglo-Dutch company which purchased logging rights to 1.1 million acres of rainforest. This was followed by the purchase of 4 million acres by Korean and Malaysian companies, the latter said to be partly responsible for the dramatic deforestation of Sarawak.[29] Canadian, Australian and Brazilian mining companies are purchasing mineral rights, and Brazilian businessmen have paid for a US$30 million road which bisects Guyana south to north and will open up 140,000 square kilometres of rainforest to development.

Although the Guyanese have every right to determine their own path to development, it is an open question whether such events as these are compatible with long term, sustainable development benefiting the Guyanese people, including the Amerindians who already live a sustainable lifestyle. Chapter 11 reports one efforts by the environment agency for Guyana to establish a policy framework strong enough to deal with such issues.

The dramatic costs of functional integration in general are summarised by Friedmann as: apparent gains in production at the cost of the devastation of nature, ruthless destruction of traditional ways of life, exploitation of labour, inequality between rich and poor, and gross regional disparity.[30] Friedmann argues that even where the usual kinds of development planning are attempted, they invariably fail because they leave untouched the effective balance of power between core and periphery political communities.

The solution suggested is decentralised regional integration based on territorial units with the highest possible degree of economic sovereignty. Friedmann's proposal is underpinned by his earlier, influential, theory of societal planning, called 'transactive' to denote that knowledge is joined to action through personal transactions, and that theory itself is transformed by effective learning.[31] This 'learning society' is to be organised through decentralised control of the means of production and distribution, and the development of a cellular socioeconomic organisation that maximises personal interaction and dialogue and promotes the capacity for independent action by communities.

Friedmann has applied his concepts of societal learning to problems of regional development, particularly thinking about South America where he had worked. In *Territory and Function* he explores the dichotomy between functional and territorial integration of the regional economy as a prelude to arguing for an economically decentralised, territorial basis for sustainable development, which he calls agropolitan development.[32] The objective is 'an argument from political theory' and a 'fuller rationale for a decentered system of societal guidance' based on 'a dramatic devolution of power'. Here societal guidance is defined as a process of decision-making involving both state and private sector at the level of territorially organised social formations.

The fundamental, radical argument of the decentralists is that growth should be based on mobilisation of resources in an integrated way within a defined region, and not on criteria dictated by international market forces. This principle of territorial integration refers to 'those ties of history and sentiment that bind the members of a geographically-bounded community to one another'. Territorial communities are informed by 'deep attachment to their territorial base'. The ties between people in these communities are created by face-to-face relationships. The boundaries of territories are those of natural political communities which are defined as 'political parties, social movements, and other groups of citizens mobilised for a political purpose, to the extent that they are independent of the state'. Here, political community is explicitly defined as a territorial form of organisation that exists to the extent that it is free from state interference and manipulation by capital.

The basic objective of the decentralist approach is the development of a region's resources and human skills, for the benefit of the residents of that region. Policies are geared towards meeting basic needs, social development, labour-intensive activities and appropriate, intermediate technology. In this way development would be sustained by the territorial hinterland and its population, rather than by an uncontrolled 'trickle-down' of resources from national and international agencies. Considerable decentralised power would rest with regional government to carry out economic and social development policies and to counter the destabilising effects of functionally-integrated institutions. Such powers, Friedmann argues, would need to include strategic and selective protectionism, import substitution and a regional focus for transportation and communications.

Where functional integration is the dominant mode of development, Friedmann argues that planning is implemented 'from above' by the state, and meant to further the state's interests in maintaining its own legitimacy and serving the interests of capital. Where territorial integration is the dominant mode, planning is developed 'from below'. Friedmann feels that a move away from functional organisation will be precipitated by crisis and breakdown in the world economy and subsequent reconstruction along territorial lines. He finds evidence that this has begun in the ethnic nationalist movements: the Basques, the Corsicans, the Scottish nationalists, the Quebecois and others. These are taken as evidence of the emergence of a post-statist economy where the role of the nation state is on the wane in favour of territorially-based planning and governing organisations.

Radical decentralism: reasonable *and* utopian?

This new decentralist vision has many attractive features. Many proposals for sustainable development embody features of this conception, and they seem both reasonable and utopian. It is instructive to consider why apparently reasonable proposals can also be utopian, and examine the problems of implementation that confront them.

An obvious constraint is that the approach would be difficult to implement in regions or countries which have a high degree of dependence on exports for income and imports for development, for example, those with small internal markets or dependent on primary commodities such as copper, bauxite, coffee etc. Also, transport systems in most countries are physically oriented toward core areas or major cities and this reinforces the centre at the expense of the periphery.

Second, while the peripheries of many countries are irrelevant to the needs of international economic actors and are therefore grossly underdeveloped, there is no evidence that the situation can be redressed without action by the self-same central governments which connive in part (sometimes unwittingly) to exploit the peripheral regions. Indeed, curtailing the ability of central governments to exercise national economic and industrial policy may reduce the overall economic growth of the country, which may or may not be acceptable to the various regions. Also the protectionist measures that Friedmann proposes would run counter to any structural adjustment measures, such as described in the previous chapter, and could shore up unsustainable policies.

Third, any real increase in regional financial control diminishes the ability of central governments to shift resources or redistribute income. Indeed, central redistribution is usually necessary to pursue a measure of social justice, which, it can be argued, should be a fundamental goal for the modern state. Inefficiencies in the use of resources may result from the lack of central direction, and opportunities will be limited to redistribute income from rich to poor regions. In Canada, for example, the degree of devolution of control over natural resources puts the province of Alberta at an advantage over the poorer Maritime provinces in terms of royalties paid into the provincial treasuries, whenever the price of a barrel of oil is high. In the Canadian system, these royalties are not redistributed by central government, although other opportunities for redistribution exist.

In recent work Friedmann recognises that redistribution cannot be radically decentralised, but he questions which central state agency has the power to intervene effectively in the distribution of income:

> Is it the municipality? Its financial resources are extremely limited . . . Is it the state (as in the state of California)? Is it the federal government? . . . But when it comes to acting locally, the federal government is like a bulldozer . . . Perhaps my question is misguided and the search for an appropriate central state is less important than a search for a new politics of redistribution, implying political mobilization at all levels, from urban neighbourhood to the national (and even international) arena.[33]

Fourth, there is a problem with the territorial approach in so far as private corporate power may be more controllable by the nation state, and international agencies, than by localities. Certainly there is evidence that, despite the immense power of the multinational corporation, the international state system also has the potential to have a powerful effect on the character of domestic events. Friedmann also recognises this criticism of his proposals, as the quote at the beginning of the chapter shows. Friedmann's observation points to the need for what we will define later as 'nested networks' for environmental action, which link levels of policy and action from the local to the international.

Fifth, it does not necessarily follow that regional political independence will foster a locally-generated economic transformation. Even if it did, there is no further guarantee that the principal beneficiaries of decentralisation would not be established local elites. Although Friedmann argues that the state is always '. . . aligned with the dominant class in society and will use its powers to safeguard the basic interests of this class', he fails to explain how the same situation would not be replicated when power is devolved from the nation state to what must clearly be a territorial, state-like entity, whether it is called a province, a municipality or even a political community within particular boundaries. This ignores the likelihood that existing inequitable top-down power relations will be replicated in the regional bodies.

Finally, for better or worse, events have so far refuted the regionalist ideal, first of Geddes and Lewis Mumford, and now of John Friedmann. Their ideas are powerful, but the organised region has yet to prove a more potent force than the great functional mobilisation of the twentieth century around nation states and supranational entities. This is not, however, to denigrate their ideas, which many environmentalists are bound to find attractive, but only to suggest that reasonable debate about their possibility must reflect on the potent forces of centralisation weighed against the regionalist ideal. As with many utopian visions, there is a great gap between 'here' and 'there', and little in the way of guidance as to how even to begin the journey. This is not to say that, however difficult, it is not a journey worth attempting. In Chapter 11 we give examples of more modest regional frameworks for sustainable development, which draw on the network approach to environmental management.

CONCLUSION

Understanding the economic and political relations between centres and peripheries, territorially or functionally, is fundamental to understanding the wider contxt for environmental management. Management agencies stand in some relation to large-scale forces and most are in constant tension between the demands made on them for environmental policy and action and the institutional arrangements governing their ability to act.

While the relative degree of centralisation among levels of government is often dictated by judicial arrangements and/or legislation, there is often scope for altering these. On the one side, decentralisation can provide choice, differentiation, and local knowledge and responsiveness in meeting needs. Decentralisation of urban government to neighbourhood office has been a common theme in the last decade, for example, in Brussels, Rotterdam, Paris and Toronto. However, arguments for centralisation of some functions may be compelling as well because territorial justice, income redistribution or the need for large scale environmental management, for example to deal with acid rain, may depend on the existence of an agency with a national overview able to act as a national or international arbitrator. In other cases, functions like land use or transport planning are most effectively undertaken by regional and national authorities. In Toronto, the decentralisation of some functions of local government to the neighbourhood level is paralleled by the shifting of other functions, such as transport, to regional government. This recognises that the growing environmental problems associated with transport can be dealt with only at the level of the region, and in the context of national transport policy.

At the beginning of this chapter, we claimed that the answer to the decentralisation dilemma is that there is no one right answer. The appropriate degree of decentralisation in any situation is that point where major areas of both functional responsibility and political participation are maximised. This hypothetical equilibrium is described by the ungainly term 'subsidiarity', a principle of decentralisation first put forward by Kohr in 1957.[34] The subsidiarity principle states that tasks should be undertaken at the lowest level in society by which it can be effectively managed, and that higher levels should support lower ones to ensure they have sufficient means to undertake the required tasks. Ungainly or not in terminology, this is a reasonable approach.

From this it follows that functional responsibility for stabilisation and promotion or control of economic activity, and ultimate responsibility for sustainable development and national and international pollution control will reside with central governments. Central governments also have *enabling functions* including strategic monitoring, structuring power relationships, provision of incentives and influencing organisational culture. Conversely the provision and maintenance of many public goods and services, including the local environment itself, should be managed locally, especially where the costs and benefits are borne locally.

However, not all activities are neatly compartmentalised, and there are often cases where benefits are national or regional but environmental costs are borne locally. Hydroelectric projects are a classic example, but there are many others. Here there are bound to be disagreements over the appropriate level of government for adjudication and planning. As Mawhood notes, '... there is no such thing as a deductive theory of political decentralisation, working downwards from first principles to logical prescription'.[35] Rather, the only basis for resolving such a fundamental issue is a continuing process of negotiation and mediation among competing jurisdictions within the conventions of a democratic political framework.

This being the case, it is not surprising that the tension between top-down and bottom-up development is endemic in modern society. In many cases the quality of the relationships between central and sub-national levels of society are critical to the successful design and implementation of environmental policies. However, the decentralisation debate can also become confused where decentralisation itself is assumed to be the function of a central authority. In reality, of course, non-centralised and voluntary organisations and NGOs may be quite independent of the state and may well act for many local interests.

Problems of integrating levels of activity in environmental management are common to all but the simplest city states, and even the explicit constitutional arrangements in federated states have not saved them from addressing these issues. What remains under-appreciated is that all socioeconomic systems are products of compromises and adjustments between centralising and decentralising forces, and endemic tension is built into such arrangements because of the undecidable nature of these arguments. The essence of this contradiction therefore is that there are no perfect systems in which different tiers of government, and local and national organisations, relate as autonomous and independent entities.

Any notion that the contradiction is somehow resolvable in the longer term is entirely at odds with the fact that regionalism or federalism is an 'open-ended' contract, in which the balance of power shifts along with economic and social conditions. Continuing constructive debate over organisational arrangements is not therefore the exception but the rule in the modern state. As Bogdanor notes:

> There will, inevitably, be conflict and tension between different layers . . . the task of creative statesmanship must be not only to ensure that such conflict does not threaten the very basis of the state; but also to turn conflict into creative channels so that federal or regionalist states can achieve their aims of diffusing power and ensuring for the territorial groups in the state effective representation. How this is to be achieved is a task for the politician and not for the jurist.[36]

This point is echoed by Frenkel: 'Interdependence . . . is a result of the complexity of modern life. It cannot be spirited away by some clever constitutional formula'.[37] The case is reinforced by the fact that, except at the highest level of generality, there is no unitary public interest. Even the meaning and method of sustainable development will be vigorously and continually debated. Proposals that assume such unity of interests over the definition of sustainable development will never be implemented, attractive though they may be.

This is both the task and the context of environmental management: problem analysis and communicative action in what we will define in more detail as a turbulent environment, described in part by simultaneous and conflicting trends towards economic centralisation and political decentralisation. These forces are important factors shaping the context of environmental management and will invariably result in shifting organisational arrangements of the state.

An increasingly important aspect of these fluid organisational arrangements will be the action-centred networks recommended later in this book. These will form to accomplish particular tasks and evolve or disappear when those tasks are completed, or when the requirements themselves change. In terms of management style, the fluidity of the situation will be less threatening, and even exciting, to managers who understand that political, organisational and professional interactions in the management process often contribute more to social betterment than products or plans themselves.

It is also important to note that decentralisation within networks will have administrative and political aspects, and while these are sometimes overlapping, they are neither the same, nor substitutes for one another. They are, however, complementary. In Chapter 8 we look at the rationale for operational decentralisation. In Chapter 9, we will consider how this form of decentralisation relates to the more difficult political decentralisation discussed above, and how mediation can be applied within the context of environmental management.

PART IV

Innovative management for sustainable development

UNIVERSITY OF GREENWICH LIBRARY

Part IV Innovative management for sustainable development

The rapid evolution of environmental problems, and greater public awareness and concern, bring pressure on governments to unify policies and develop more credible environmental management systems. The main obstacles to this are political and organisational.

Some governments do little or nothing because of fear of internal conflict, or because political resources are fragmented or ideological divisions intense. Even in stable countries, governments regularly pursue contradictory policies, and politicians lack the will or a motivation strong enough to force them to undertake the difficult mediation among conflicting economic, social and environmental goals that diverge substantially from the status quo. Generating political momentum for new ideas is a major task, and one to which environmental managers contribute, within organisational and bureaucratic constraints. Campaigning NGOs make a particularly marked contribution to setting the agenda for political debate on the environment.

A main organisational constraint on management for sustainability is the idea of 'limits to governance'. For example, Peter Self notes:

> There is increased expectation of public administration, and indeed of political systems generally, in the post-1945 world. These expectations have led to a big increase in the formal tasks and responsibilities of government, but of course it does not follow that these tasks have been adequately implemented. Clearly they have not.[1]

Apart from the tension between centralising and decentralising forces, there are two other important factors in the limits of governance. One is the *dynamic nature* of the modern world system which gives rise to endemic uncertainty. Organisational analysts call this 'turbulence', and we examine this concept in Chapter 8. The other limiting factor is *fragmentation*, in policy and institutional terms, in our societies which remain largely compartmentalised. That fragmentation exists is no surprise: previous chapters have set out why it is a common condition and one likely to worsen before it gets better. These conditions mean that management systems depending on rigid, deterministic control are likely to fail. But it is the scarcity of political will and skills to overcome these conditions that is the critical issue:

> A widely recognised 'managerial gap' exists between the demand for and supply of indigenous management talent at nearly all levels, and this gap constitutes a major, if not the major, constraint in achieving economic (and) social development.[2]

One fruitful response to the problem of compartmentalisation is multi-agency networks, which we have called action-centred networks, that attempt to understand uncertainty and develop strategies to manage it. As the notion of self-sufficient organisations gives way to more complex networks, organisational and managerial skills in joint working become critical to environmental management and sustainable development, often as important as the substantive nature of any environmental issue. The development of localised management skills, entrepreneurial abilities and modes of partnership is therefore a critical but largely unaddressed aspect of environmental management. At present, Western (and westernised) societies are weak in such competence, even though their higher level of interdependence means that most traditional bureaucratic approaches to management are of limited value.

A key constraint in human resource terms, then, is insufficient skills in newer, 'integrating' styles of management. This is true for both higher and lower income countries, because where higher income countries gain in sophistication of training they often lose in terms of long-term, entrenched compartmentalisation in bureaucracies. Fortunately one does not need to go back to university to learn the new management skills: 'on-the-job' is often a good place to begin. At least three preliminary steps are necessary.

First, to think about and understand the main constraints on more integrated management approaches. These can be thought of as 'soft' organisational problems that are additional obstacles to the resolution of any 'hard' environmental problem. They are often a spanner in the works of good management, even where excellent science and adequate funding are available. Improvements in environmental management come about from an understanding of the true nature of constraints on integration, and from investment in human resources specifically to address those. The constraints then become part of the agenda for action for resolving any environmental problem. Chapter 7 begins this process of analysis, but it is not exhaustive; every environmental manager could add to the list from his or her own experience. In any event, a list of generic constraints is only useful insofar as it encourages us to analyse our own situation.

Second, having understood a range of constraints on integration, it is necessary to understand the potential of the modern management organisation to deal with turbulence. This means developing the required degree of innovation to manage successfully in a rapidly changing environment, and structuring organisational arrangements in a manner appropriate to the nature of the problems themselves. In particular, the action-centred network, engaged in consensus building and 'organisational learning', is an appropriate response. This makes the connection between our understanding of the constraints and what should be an evolving plan for action. Chapter 8 looks at the ecology of management organisations, drawing on recent thinking from organisational analysis.

Finally, it is necessary to take positive steps. Chapter 9 suggests basic principles and methods for action-centred networking for sustainable development. Following that, Part V goes on to illustrate, in a number of cases, how the basic principles of the network approach work in a variety of settings around the world.

7   Constraints on integrated management

Many failures in development are not failures of production or technology. Instead, they are institutional failures. An alternative view of development accepts the sustainability imperative and places the institutional dimension in the forefront.

David Gow and Elliott Morss, 1988[1]

There are any number of generic constraints on the development of successful, integrated environmental management. A main feature of the action-centred network approach set out in Chapter 9 is systematic identification of such constraints so that each becomes part of the focus of the environmental management task, and resources are devoted to understanding and overcoming them. This chapter looks at constraints on integration suggested by the recent literature of environmental management, development and public administration, and by field experience.

THE COMPLEXITY OF ENVIRONMENTAL PROBLEMS

Serious environmental problems are invariably part of socio-biophysical systems characterised by both complexity, that is many relevant factors in an unclear relationship, and a high level of interaction, which means the relationship is constantly changing. In such a system, organisations interact dynamically with the natural environment.

Complexity now extends to every level of analysis. For example, the Club of Rome argues that the world's economic, social, financial and cultural systems are highly interdependent, with the result that the earth is 'a stressed system'.[2] Interdependency is compounded by the uncertain nature of political and economic change at all levels from the international to the local. Complexity compounded by uncertainty is as a central challenge of the world *problematique*.

Complexity equally bedevils regional efforts at environmental control and planning. The water pollution problems in the Densu River basin in Ghana, mentioned briefly in Chapter 3, are a good example of this kind of complexity (Figure 7.1). These problems have been analysed by the Ghana IDEA team and are reported in more detail in Chapter 11. Although a small river by African standards, the Densu's function as a water supply for two million inhabitants of Accra and the packed river basin communities, as well as for drainage and irrigation, have caused it to be described as Ghana's most important river.[3] The main causes of pollution in this watershed arise from:

- rapid urbanisation, stemming from migration from rural areas, and resulting in direct, uncontrolled discharge of household and industrial wastes and sewage;
- intensification of agriculture stemming in part from structural adjustment, including deeper ploughing and the usual inputs of fertilisers and pesticides, resulting in reduction of natural vegetation, soil degradation, heavy run-off of silt, eutrophication and pollution;

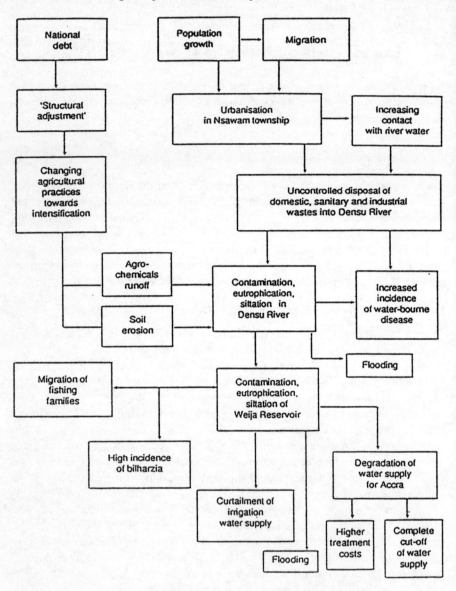

Figure 7.1 *Densu River and Weija Reservoir watershed management problem*

- legal and illegal logging activities in the upper reaches of the river basin, and fuelwood gathering and charcoal burning along the length of the river.

Problems are compounded because modernisation in Ghana is resulting in the erosion of traditional, sustainable methods of river management. In this example, many thousands of producers (businesses and larger industries, small 'backyard' industries, small farmers and so on) contribute unwittingly to either water pollution, or to siltation, which results in widespread flooding during the rainy season and drying out during the dry season. The environmental management system that might respond to these problems is nearly as complex as the problem itself: 11 agencies in central and local government have been identified by the project team as having substantial control over activities in the Densu basin, in addition to the complex mosaic of tribal controls. The river basin itself stretches over eight district administrations, each of which has an interest. But road connections between the lower and upper reaches of the river are poor or non-existent, and this hinders communication and recognition of the integrated nature of the watershed ecosystem.

This kind of complex environmental management problem is not unusual: equal environmental and organisational complexity might be found in virtually any river basin in the world with both urban and agricultural uses. This kind of complexity precludes straightforward cause-and-effect analysis of the problems, and also precludes simple solutions implemented by any agency acting alone. In dealing with this kind of 'turbulence', static, formal management approaches by one or two agencies are less useful than a network approach which gradually builds up a partnership of relevant stakeholders. Just as one agency is unlikely to resolve such a problem, so also is one government acting alone. Thus the team of stakeholders will often involve government in partnership with private and voluntary sectors.

The management approach will also need to stress continual feedback and adjustment in policy and action to suit the emerging needs of the many stakeholders. This 'adaptive' management often requires:

- the development of an emerging consensus among all vested interests as to the real dimensions and boundaries of the problem, and often a shift in professional orientation and organisational culture towards more holistic problem definition;
- a partnership approach to implementation among all the relevant agencies; and
- the development of new skills and responses as dictated by the changing nature of the problem, and the need to mediate among the differing objectives of various agencies.

Chapter 11 documents how an action networking approach by the Ghana IDEA team is overcoming the serious constraints of problem complexity in the Densu Basin, and gradually shifting an initial concern over water pollution to a commitment to a programme of sustainable development.

FAILURE OF THE COMMAND AND CONTROL MANAGEMENT STYLE

A primary requisite for public sector management and development is a competent bureaucratic system, and administrative reform is a near universal goal of contemporary societies. However, the record of achievement is poor. Jreisat, for example, remarks that '. . . the dilemma of administrative reform in these (lower income) countries lies in the mediocrity of results'.[4] This is not surprising as many countries acquiring independence in the post-war period will have had little or no experience in the operation of the Western-style bureaucracies bequeathed to them.

However, higher income status confers no special advantage, and administrative reform is equally difficult to implement in Western bureaucracies. Since the 1930s, unheeded administrative recommendations of various American presidential commissions have far exceeded the number adopted.[5] Numerous reviewers document the continual post-war failure to implement radical reform in the British civil service until the 1980s, despite '. . . endless royal commissions and other investigative bodies which have produced endless reports . . . and proposed numerous reforms'.[6]

The advent of more complex problems in the modern state has only served to compound the problem. A recent article entitled 'The Organisation of the '90s' in the business management journal *The McKinsey Quarterly* notes that, in the private sector, rigid, hierarchical 'command and control' (C&C) organisations are now 'competitively disadvantaged' due to slow response, lack of creativity and initiative, and excessive cost.[7] The same is true in the public sector. Such traditional C&C bureaucracies may be characteristically well suited to dealing with planned change, but not with the rapid 'unplanned' change which is becoming more typical of environmental problems, in which knowledge about the problem, and the problem itself, evolves rapidly, and for which any solution must involve overlapping public, private and voluntary sector initiatives. In this case:

> . . . successfully developing a high performing organisation requires that senior
> managers overcome commonly-held misconceptions and lead a change process
> that blends top-down with bottom-up initiatives.

With this in mind, many analysts are now proposing alternative, looser, task-oriented management structures. These have been called by many names, such as 'small scale administrative cadres',[8] 'multi-disciplinary project teams',[9] 'interorganisational approaches . . . to natural resource management'[10] and 'parallel structures to bureaucracies'.[11]

For example, Haas[12] argues that an important consideration in institutional design is the rapidity with which institutions recognise and respond to new environmental threats, which result in unplanned change. Knowles and Saxberg propose that unplanned change requires the development of informal organisations and temporary groups, to work in parallel with existing bureaucracies.[13] Zand suggests that managers of bureaucracies sponsor 'collateral organisations' – interdisciplinary task forces with members from several departments – to identify and solve problems not amenable to solution by formal systems.[14]

An important aspect of the action-centred network methodology proposed below is such an informal, task-oriented group, whose membership is free to grow or contract. This type of informal organisation:

> . . . must be differentiated from the formal structure and relationships in dealing
> with change. The networks of interactions in the informal organisation can
> reward, discipline and punish their members . . . They can and do absorb and
> accommodate changes which management cannot anticipate in the design of
> policies, systems, tasks and procedures. The informal organisation represents a
> dynamic aspect of the formal organisation. Though managers have regarded
> these networks with suspicion, many have recognized them as flexible adjuncts
> to all levels of the formal work organisation.[15]

As the case studies will show, the informal organisation, which is, or may be, part of a wider network, is also an excellent organisational vehicle for moving from specific environmental management tasks to broader tasks of sustainable development. This is for two reasons:

1   The informal organisation can expand or contract its membership to draw on the necessary political, bureaucratic or technical skills required to address the specific problem or task identified; and
2   The informal, task-oriented organisation is characterised by learning-by-doing, and can therefore 'grow into' more sophisticated tasks.

The potential to move beyond environmental control issues to long range development planning is also suggested by the development literature. For example, here is Sagasti's proposal for an 'unconventional' evolving institutional framework for national development planning:

> The institutional design required for a new approach to development planning is that of an evolving network that should be flexible, open and capable of restructuring itself over time. The planning units that compose the network would not conform to a hierarchical organisation and each would relate to the structure of political authority and power in a variety of ways that are also likely to change over time.[16]

Sagasti proposes some of the elements of such a network: a social intelligence unit, a planning unit, temporary issue-oriented task forces, co-ordination committees to link planning units with all types of non-governmental organisations, social science research centres and an international support network. The methodology put forward in Chapter 9 offers one option for developing such a planning framework.

UNWITTING FAILURES OF POLICY INTEGRATION

These failures often have their deep roots in the organisation of the natural and social sciences into compartmentalised disciplines, discussed in Chapter 3. One result tends to be inadequate definition of environmental problems based on single discipline perceptions and solutions: 'an agricultural problem', 'an economics problem', 'a transport problem', and so on. It is not that discipline-based science is not essential to the process of understanding, but that another, higher order of analysis is also necessary. This is to enable critical recognition of the inevitable limitations of our perceptions, and to integrate scientific knowledge with the many sources of social, economic, cultural and intuitive knowledge relevant to complex issues.

This failure of perception is compounded by the compartmentalisation of government and international support agencies into poorly communicating departments or sectors pursuing divergent and often competing objectives. It is common that government departments do not interrelate policy or action; indeed there is seldom reward for doing so. The result is an unwitting failure of 'horizontal' integration (Figure 7.2). For example, a consequence of the introduction of high-energy agriculture in India has been increased food production, but this has also increased income disparity because of a failure to implement land reform.[17]

The lack of links between environment, energy and transport policies in the UK provides another example. Britain's road vehicles produce about 100 million tons of

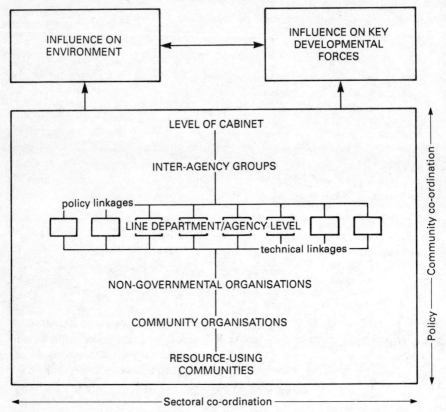

Figure 7.2 *Inter-organisational linkages which contribute to policy integration*

carbon dioxide annually, one-fifth of the UK total, as well as the usual toxic cocktail of carbon monoxide, nitrous oxide, hydrocarbons and lead. On current trends, a 15 to 24 per cent increase in miles driven is likely by 2000, mainly due to increasing car ownership and a dramatic dispersal of urban land uses of housing, retailing, employment and leisure across previously rural countryside. Many people think that the problem of traffic congestion and and erosion of rural land has reached crisis proportions.

The UK Government's response to this crisis is a classic example of the unwitting failure to integrate policy. The Transport Department, which has no energy or environmental policy, continues to promote a road building programme out of tax revenues, including a £2.8 billion expenditure on widening the London orbital motorway. This is in spite of the fact that it is now common knowledge that new roads generate new traffic flows, and none more so than the London orbital highway. At the same time, Britain's rail fares are the highest in Europe and its rate of subsidy the lowest, further encouraging passengers on to the roads. British Rail, which must run like a private business to fulfil the Government's hopes of selling it off, closed 65 freight terminals in 1991, resulting in 70,000 new lorry loads per annum on the already choked roads.

Meanwhile, the Environment Minister continues to sanction the building of new, green-field housing and office developments, theme parks, retail warehouse parks and out-of-town shopping malls, some of the latter with parking for 9000 cars. The Energy Efficiency Office is forbidden to study petrol consumption and ways of reducing it, as this is the remit of the Transport Department, which has no interest. For ideological reasons, the government is pressing ahead with plans to privatise all the rest of Britain's bus lines. This is in spite of evidence from a House of Commons subcommittee that previous bus privatisation has resulted in fewer passengers and an older, less well maintained and more polluting national bus fleet. It is also in spite of the evidence that the car driver produces about six times as much carbon dioxide per passenger mile as does the bus passenger.

THE ADMINISTRATIVE TRAP

A failure of integration often results in what has been aptly called the 'administrative trap' by Randall Baker[18] (Figure 7.3). This describes the common mismatch between the nature of environmental problems and the sectoral problem-solving structures in government, which disaggregate ecological problems, recognise and treat symptoms as the problem itself, and generally remain inadequate to the task. Baker describes how the current administrative trap in lower income countries was inherited lock, stock and barrel from their colonial predecessors:

> The administrative structures of the LDCs were generally inherited intact from former colonial powers, and are typically organised vertically into sectoral, or functional, ministries and departments (Agriculture, Education, Health, etc). This works reasonably well until the system encounters a problem of a very broad and highly integrated nature – such as desertification. Then it tackles on the parts which are identifiable to each ministry and then each ministry tackles the symptom as a problem in, and of, itself.

Government departments caught in the trap single-mindedly tackle complex ecological problems by way of their vertically integrated, single sector systems (farmer; Extension Service; Ministry of Agriculture; UN Food and Agriculture Organization). This results in consistent, expensive failure to resolve problems which, by their very nature, require multi-sectoral responses.

For lower income countries, a persistent case is the failure of 'donor co-ordination'. This is reported to have been the Achilles heel of assistance in the 1980s:

> Countries with a weak institutional base, exposed to multiple donors' institutional development efforts – sometimes contradictory – and presenting conflicting guidance, face a potential nightmare.[19]

Co-ordination among donors is unlikely due to differences in long term goals, and even to short term, local objectives, sometimes due to a sense of competition. Whittington and Calhoun argue that donors who regularly and rhetorically call for co-ordination simply do not mean it, and that it is one more exercise in what has been called the ritual of planned development.[20] They argue that at the heart of the problem is a patronising attitude of donors based on a mistaken belief in their own bureaucratic efficiency and in the inefficiency of the host country's bureaucracy.

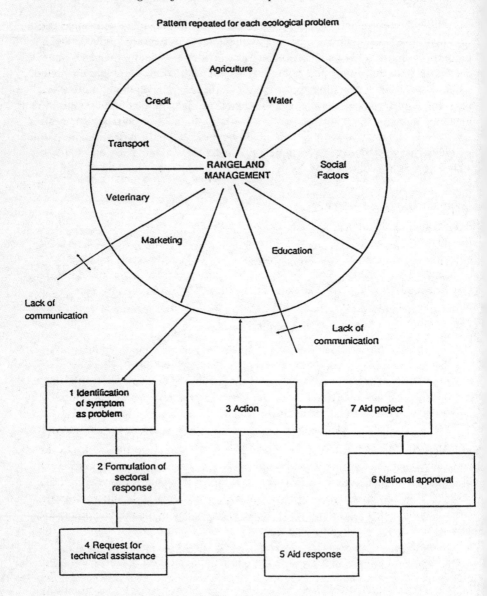

Figure 7.3 *The administrative trap: a sectoral approach to ecological problems*
Source: Baker[18]

Failures of horizontal integration bedevil every environmental management and sustainable development task. Virtually the first step therefore in any action programme must be to invite representatives of a range of relevant government departments and agencies to join some kind of an advisory group to address the specific, visible environmental problem identified. This provides an organisational base from which to begin a process of horizontal integration. The issue is taken up further in Chapter 9.

FAILURE OF VERTICAL INTEGRATION

Poor vertical integration is the result of the common failure of understanding and information flows between the policy levels of government and small scale production units or individual resource users, who may generate substantial, cumulative environmental impacts. A real challenge of sustainable development is to maintain the economic contribution of small producers, while also keeping to acceptable environmental standards. But the sheer number of producers and their independence of government control systems challenges traditional approaches to management. Often the motivations and constraints under which such small producers operate are little understood at the policy making levels of government. For example, Montgomery notes that:

> Millions of small-scale household-level actors produce most of the environmental degradation in the [lower income] countries. But environmental policy planners are almost entirely unaware of details about whether and how current practices that are encouraged by government destroy or conserve natural resources.[21]

This ignorance results in policies which appear reasonable but often prove difficult or impossible to implement. Failures of vertical integration can be compounded by the large economic and cultural gap between the policy making level and the reality of life at farm or village level, a reality which is often characterised by the drive for basic survival. The fine distinctions of policy and law are not applicable and government control structures are weak or non-existent. A gulf between the public and private sectors, indicated by different organisational cultures and different objectives, can also heighten this constraint.

An important aspect of the network approach is that environmental action teams attempt to overcome compartmentalisation by initiating action only on specific, highly visible environmental tasks, and by attempting to develop new levels of both horizontal and vertical integration around those tasks. Such tasks are usually environmental problems about which there is considerable agreement that 'something must be done', such as obvious and damaging water pollution. The specificity of the task gives a measure of credibility to the effort of integration, while confining the initial effort to the stated task can disarm potential critics who may be threatened by the idea of a parallel organisation to the traditional bureaucracy. Network-based advisory groups can become a kind of a low-key, non-threatening task force with a specific environmental objective.

LACK OF REWARD IN BUREAUCRACIES

A related constraint, which reinforces others, is the lack of a reward in bureaucracies for goal-oriented, inter-sectoral approaches. At the most basic level, in lower income countries, there is often simply not enough money available to pay an adequate wage to civil servants. For example, one Nigerian NGO is blunt about the difficulties of environmental enforcement: 'Most of the enforcers are pretty poor and are more interested in making extra money in order to make ends meet, rather than do what they are paid to do'.[22]

But the reward problem is hardly confined to lower income countries. In many countries, an enthusiasm for an inter-sectoral approach can jeopardise a career, and within most governments, there is little impetus to liaise with departments competing for influence and limited resources. Brandl, considering public administration in the United States, comments:

> ... the sorry condition of the public policy domain ... lies in the fact that the great bulk of the government's policies are implemented through bureaucracies – that is, through organisations in which workers are managed by being subject to directives, but rarely rewarded, penalised or inspired.[23]

Although hardly a panacea, the network approach, which includes a system of regular, inter-disciplinary peer reviews, can provide a measure of systematic support or non-pecuniary reward, and is therefore a useful adjunct to the bureaucratic structure.

OVER-RELIANCE ON INSTITUTIONAL REFORM

Although institutional reform is often part of a high quality management approach, there is a common tendency to assume that if only the 'right' institutional arrangements can be brought into being, that adequate environmental management will result. This is not only fallacious, but risks diverting attention away from the need to meet environmental challenges by attention to the broad range of national needs in terms of legislation, human resources, and finance as well as institutional structure.

Of particular concern in many countries is the question of whether an environmental agency or a ministry will deliver the best results. There is, of course, no correct answer. Baker[24] thinks that this is a red herring, which can perpetuate the administrative trap for a host of reasons:

- A environmental ministry is like every other ministry, and probably less powerful than the main financial and industrial ministries, unless it has some powerful statutory authority which gives it power over others. Creating a new ministry does not change the weakness of existing horizontal linkages.
- Much of the environmental legislation will already belong to other ministries such as Health, Agriculture, Industry, Mining and Resources and others, and there is no clear reason why any new ministry should have any control over this legislation.
- The creation of a new ministry or agency can divert attention away from real needs, such as for inter-sectoral planning.

- The potentially conflicting roles of an environment ministry – as policy maker, policeman, co-ordinator or project inspector – may not be resolved productively.

Probably most important, the usual absence of any clearly stated national policy regarding the relationship between environment and economic development invariably marginalises environmental concerns. This leaves the ministry unable to affect major structural decisions, while fighting a rearguard action against damaging developments with inadequate weapons.

FAILURE TO LEARN FROM EXPERIENCE

Within the traditional bureaucracy there is often little motivation to learn from past experience and even less to admit, analyse and learn from past mistakes. Raking over past failures is generally considered poor form, and seldom brings any career benefit. But accepting the need for such learning is essential for the type of adaptive environmental management argued here, for it provides the rationale for active monitoring to generate feedback for making the necessary incremental adjustments to policy and implementation.

What we will describe in detail in the next chapter as action learning leading to innovation can assist this process. The rationale is set out by Hulme:

> If . . . project evaluation is to contribute effectively to the process of 'learning from experience' then a new focus is required. It will be necessary to move on from the cosy ground of formal structures, techniques and procedures to the more ambiguous and less clearly defined task of analysing learning processes within and between agencies involved in development initiatives. *It will recognise that the lessons of experience are not neutral data, but a strategic resource* [our emphasis].[25]

FAILURE TO CONFRONT THE MANAGEMENT PROCESS

There is a variation of the previous constraint, which is that most politicians and bureaucrats involved in public decision making and management have little interest in improving the processes of decision making, and indeed, little interest in considering the process at all. For example, Baker[26] summarises the concerns of delegates at big international environment conferences:

> The delegates, representing administrations, made fairly sure that their national position papers presented their actions in the best possible light, rarely looking at the public management system per se . . . There was rarely, if ever, any explicit discussion of policy and management issues for the public sector, and certainly no criticism of existing policy.

There are obvious reasons for this. There are few votes in reviews of management and administration, progress takes time and politicians seldom look past the next election. Bureaucrats have little motivation to upset the status quo. There is a larger issue also, which is that there is seldom any public pressure for reform, unless the 'organisational culture' of the society itself values forward thinking, strategic planning.

CONTEXTUAL CONSTRAINTS

These constraints arise from the specific nature of national political systems, and from religious, tribal and other cultural factors. Such factors are part of a grey area of environmental management. For example, the influence of corruption must be addressed, if only obliquely and diplomatically. Once again the Nigerian IDEA team is forthcoming on problems of environmental enforcement in the face of what it calls 'bigmanism': 'The enforcers are very much affected by this concept; they would rather not enforce anything against somebody occupying a position of power or influence'.[27]

However this type of constraint is hardly unique to lower income countries. The main lesson must be that it is important to make a particular effort to understand contextual constrains in formulating objectives and actions. Frank, face-to-face, and off-the-record discussions are a helpful means of considering issues which may not normally be discussed or committed to paper. This is another area in which a network is a valuable means of support for difficult areas in management.

TECHNOLOGY AND LOCAL MANAGEMENT

In Chapter 3 we noted the process by which apparently benign technologies, like the automobile, can become, by their very attractiveness, structural imperatives in societies, and thus virtually impervious to social control. A related point is that, in many countries, imported Western industrial processes and technologies are tending to eclipse historical, indigenous environmental management skills, and social, cultural and legal control structures, which will have developed over many generations.

This is not surprising, for technologies are not culture-free. For example, Ghana has a long history of small scale, agroforestry. Historically, trees were felled only after careful communal deliberation with the tribal chief and priest and a lengthy ceremony to mark the significance of the act. In the past few decades, with the importation of industrialised forestry, both the environmental knowledge and spiritual concern represented by this process is disappearing. Similarly, past agricultural practices in Ghana based on shifting cultivation and sustainable agroforestry have been replaced by intensive, industrialised farming of monocrops which rely heavily on inputs of chemical fertilisers and pesticides. Soil erosion, eutrophication and chemical pollution are the by-products of such processes; these are rapidly and seriously degrading water supplies in the country.

In future, the successful integration of indigenous skills and knowledge with new technology will become even more important as other powerful technologies, such as biotechnology, hold out the promise of increasing the volume of food production, as well as improving food quality. Brenner, considering the question of technological innovation in agriculture, notes:

Technological change is inherently difficult to measure or evaluate, all the more so when technologies have pervasive or synergistic effects . . . Technologies can be 'embodied' in physical products or in skills and people. They can also be, in the case of agricultural production, land-saving, labour-saving, cost-reducing, input-reducing or quality-enhancing. Institutions, decision-making processes and diffusion mechanisms also have an important bearing on technological change.[28]

In all countries, there is a pressing need to diffuse technologies to serve the needs of development. The question is: how can societies ensure that technological change serves as a means to sustainable development, and how can management systems be devised which allow us the benefits of technology without our becoming its unwitting victims in the longer term?

8 Organisational ecology and innovative management

To explain global environmental change it is necessary to examine the direct human actions which influence it, as well as the indirect human actions that set in motion complex chains of events which also affect the environment.

Roberta Balstad Miller, 1989[1]

The future is not written anywhere – it is still to be built. It is an uncertain, multiple and indeterminate future. In fact, without this uncertainty, human activity would lose its elements of freedom and its meaning – the hope of a desired future.

Michel Godet, 1989[2]

In our Preface we suggested expanding the definition of environment to include the interaction of human society with natural ecosystems, the combination of which can be called human ecology. In this chapter, we examine organisational ecology, and the challenge of planning for the future given endemic uncertainty and organisational constraints. To do so, we draw on some concepts from organisational analysis. These insights help explain the limits to governance, that is, the inability of our current management and planning systems to cope with the dynamics of rapid change and interaction between numerous organisations and entrepreneurs and the environment.

Organisation theorists use the term 'turbulent environment' to describe the conditions which give rise to the limits to governance. Here the term 'environment' includes interactions between the natural and the social worlds, and the interactions between organisations. In a 'full world' economy, these interactions increasingly impinge on, or even determine, the quality of the natural environment.

THE TURBULENT ENVIRONMENT

Previous chapters discussed the challenge of complex environmental problems. In the literature of organisation theory these are known as metaproblems. We have seen how metaproblems are really many-sided clusters of problems, with interrelated symptoms, that are beyond the capabilities of existing organisational arrangements to grasp and tackle. They have also been described as 'wicked problems' because they are hard to define, and because, in pluralist societies, we lack objective definitions of equity from which to fashion consensual solutions to them.[3]

Metaproblems are not amenable either to simple cause-and-effect analysis or to one dimensional responses. Such problems are not only bigger than any one organisation acting alone, they are seldom the responsibility of any one body. It is common for governments to excuse inactivity on a metaproblem by arguing that not enough is known about it, or because it spans functional departments and political jurisdictions. The 'wickedness' of these metaproblems has been heightened by the increased pace of change since the 1973 OPEC oil price rise, which ended a period of relative stability and ushered in a period of increasing turbulence. Metaproblems both exist in, and are the result of, turbulent environments which compound uncertainty, the root of the world *problematique*.

The notion of the turbulent environment was first discussed in organisation theory by Emery and Trist.[4] In a condition of turbulence, systems of interrelated problems are exacerbated by the independent actions of many unrelated organisations or entrepreneurs, and change can be rapid and complex, and even bewildering or apparently chaotic. Organisations will often act in unco-ordinated and dissonant ways in attempting to meet their individual objectives, typically externalising as many of the costs, and internalising as many of the benefits, of their actions as they can.[5] Trist has defined turbulence as 'a kind of contextual commotion that makes it seem as if the "the ground" were moving as well as the organizational actors'.[6]

A turbulent environment is characterised by:

- uncertainty;
- inconsistent and ill-defined needs, preferences and values;
- unclear understanding of the means, consequences or cumulative impacts of collective actions; and
- fluid participation in which multiple, partisan participants vary in the amount of resources they invest in resolving problems.

For our purposes, the turbulent environment is a socio-ecological system, which is defined as any system composed by a societal (or human) and ecological (or biophysical) subsystem.[7] The levels of aggregation may range from a local community and the surrounding environment with which it directly interacts, up to the system constituted by the whole of mankind and the ecosphere. The ability of managing organisations to plan in the face of turbulence is constrained, partly because turbulence grows as a result of the activities of individuals and organisations attempting to respond to it.[8]

As we have seen, at the same time as complexity in urban and regional systems is growing, the number and complexity of international and inter-regional linkages and dependencies associated with the world economy have never been greater, nor has the rate of technological change. These lead to more turbulence, further uncertainty and a loss of local control. This condition has been aptly called the loss of the stable state.[9] It is a characteristic of modern societies in conditions of global industrialisation and makes it difficult for organisations, especially in the public sector, to deal with their environment. The only realistic response has been described as 'permanent innovation'.[10]

ORGANISATION AND ENVIRONMENT: LEGACY OF GENERAL SYSTEMS THEORY

The relationship between any organisation and its wider environment, natural and social, has been described as one of the most powerful and pervasive metaphors in the language of organisation theory. This can help us understand the complex interrelationships between environment and development.[11] The distinction first arose in the early 1960s as theorists began to examine economic and societal forces external to organisations, rather than focusing solely on their internal dynamics. Soon after, the theories of Gregory Bateson on learning in complex animal, family and wider social systems formed the basis for consideration of the role of learning in organisational systems.[12] At the same time influential concepts in general systems theory were subsequently applied to a range of social science disciplines, including the study of organisations. This step marked an important paradigmatic shift in many fields of enquiry.

Systems thinking contributed some basic concepts to organisation theory:

* a more holistic viewpoint, which encompassed the organisation–environment relationship;
* the importance of the boundaries between the two;
* the idea of constructive feedback; and
* the concept of 'requisite variety', which suggested that environmental complexity needed to be matched by an equal sophistication in organisational response.

These concepts are helpful to understanding, and deriving appropriate responses to, environmental metaproblems.

Systems theory views an organisation as an 'open' system, differentiated from its environment by some sort of boundary.[13] An open system tends towards a state of dynamic equilibrium with its environment through a continuous exchange of material, data and energy. Both system and environment can affect the exchange, giving rise to important interactions.

The boundaries of environmental problems

A basic tenet of the systems approach is that organisations are *processes* striving towards survival, which can be understood in terms of inputs, throughputs, outputs and feedback. Units within an organisation are subsystems with their own systemic characteristics. Boundary transactions, by which inputs are altered into outputs, are critical organisational activities, both internally between subsystems, and externally via the environment. Boundaries can be expanded to draw in more resources or participants, or tightened to strengthen existing participation.

This idea of 'bounding' environmental problems is a fundamental one, for if a problem is defined too narrowly, relevant factors and connections will be excluded; too widely, and the problem will seem too diffuse and incomprehensible. The appropriate boundary definition will change over time, depending on the problem itself and the changing competences of the organisations concerned. Continually bounding and re-bounding (or redefining) any environmental problem is therefore a primary task of environmental management.

The process of continually re-bounding problems runs counter to the normal working of bureaucracies, which tend to define any problem as either within their own area of competence, and therefore 'their' problem, or outside their area of competence and therefore not their responsibility. Once a problem is defined in a particular way, a superstructure of programmes, political and funding commitments and careers is usually built around that definition. But every environmental problem or problem of sustainable development has these characteristics:

- The problem will inevitably evolve according to changing circumstance, and as a result of every interaction which has any effect, positive or negative. What a problem cannot do is remain the same, and neither therefore can its definition.
- If a problem will not remain static, then neither can the adequate response to that problem or the team needed to develop and implement that response. In other words, responses must be as dynamic as problems.

Bounding the problem in the right way, for a particular point in time, is therefore a key factor in determining who are the right stakeholders to participate in a problem resolution network. Again, a list of too few stakeholders will exclude important participants; too many will dilute the process to the point of uselessness.

In systems terms, this redefinition process depends on feedback, which describes the process whereby information concerning the system is fed back as input, leading to alteration of the behaviour of the organisation and thus the system. Feedback is a critical concept for organisational learning. This is a point to which we will return.

For the purposes of considering the role of organisations in environmental management, five concepts from organisational analysis are useful:

1   The sources of endemic uncertainty in environmental management.
2   The idea of the 'resource dependence' of organisations.
3   The potential role of action-centred networks in environmental management, and how they differ from other kinds of networks.
4   The role of conflict and consensus in management.
5   The importance of organisational learning, which gives rise to innovation in management, and the contribution of action research to this innovation.

These are considered below.

THE SOURCES OF UNCERTAINTY

A concern of organisational analysis centres around the extent to which organisations are able to 'manage' in what is clearly an uncertain world. In this situation, the traditional rational planning model (study the problem, develop alternatives, choose one, implement, move on to something else) is of little use, since the environment is an interactive, dynamic phenomenon which cannot be manipulated by unilateral action:

> Complexity cannot be managed, intellectually or practically, through increased control. We have to learn to understand and manage complex systems while respecting the autonomy of the processes and the elements within these systems.[14]

Robins argues that this uncertainty is a classic problem of social order and integration in modern societies and that this has been close to the 'heart of social and economic theory since the Enlightenment'.[15] The intractable problem of uncertainty has led analysts to speak of the 'poverty of prediction' in public policy making.[16]

The poverty of prediction

Each organisation will have a definite impact on the environment, but it will be impossible to predict that impact precisely because all other organisations will be acting at the same time. Therefore, although organisations may influence what is called their environmental 'niche', the larger context of their actions will always include a full range of phenomena which are important but which cannot be controlled. This gives a dramatic twist to the notion of uncertainty:

> Environmental uncertainty has roots that lie deeper than the problems of collecting and evaluating information, directing organisational activity, or any of the other features discussed in the analysis of strategic planning and control. An uncertain environment exists precisely because the consequences of organizational activity are not realized until after the activity has taken place.[17]

Uncertainty therefore is not simply a lack of adequate information relevant to a problem or management task; there is no body of knowledge which, if acquired, would unlock solutions or dissolve uncertainty. Nor is dealing with uncertainty simply a matter of organisational restructuring or revised management direction. Uncertainty exists because the impact of human, organisational activity cannot be predicted in a way which allows those activities to be altered to control environmental effects. The human ecological environment is therefore by nature uncertain. While this uncertainty can be managed it can never be overcome. Rather, management and planning organisations must be prepared to take maximum advantage of the resources available to them and to adapt continually as new information (feedback) from the environment becomes available. This is *adaptive management* which is concerned with the process of learning, and continuous decision making, rather than with plans and projects alone.

RESOURCE DEPENDENCE IN ORGANISATIONS

All organisations must interact with others which control the resources required for their survival. Four propositions describe this dependence:

1 Any organisation is dependent upon other organisations for resources.
2 In order to achieve their goals, organisations have to exchange resources.
3 Although decision-making within the organisation is therefore constrained by other organisations, the dominant coalition in any organisation retains discretion. The culture of the dominant coalition will influence which relationships are seen to present an opportunity to secure resources, and which resources will be sought.
4 The dominant coalition employs strategies within known rules to regulate the process of exchange.[18]

Organisation theory argues that organisations experience power and dependence, success or failure in policy areas or positive results in conflict and strategic bargaining depending on their access to the following major types of resource: finance, political access and support, information and expertise, legal authority and organisational relationships. Of these, information (feedback) and expertise (human resources) are potent resources which can strengthen the power of management organisations even where they are subordinated in jurisdiction or administrative relationships. Conversely, a shortage of information and expertise can undermine formally delegated powers. In an increasingly interdependent world, a pool of new resources is offered by inter-organisational relationships.[19]

Increasingly therefore, innovative management organisations are prepared to devote resources to productive, if temporary, linkages with other agencies, and other sectors: public with private sector, private with voluntary sector, and so on. These initiatives may be called partnerships, joint ventures or networking initiatives. In the next section we look at some different kinds of networks, before discussing the action-centred network in some detail.

INTER-ORGANISATIONAL NETWORKS

DiMaggio argues that the more centralised the resources upon which organisations depend, the greater the degree of interaction in that field, and the greater the degree of uncertainty likely to arise.[20] The expansion of responsibilities in the modern state has clearly caused a centralisation of resource dependencies in many areas of life. A consideration of resource dependence in a highly interactive field leads directly to the concept of inter-organisational networks for the exchange of the resources needed for problem solving. In technical terms, networks are non-hierarchical social systems which constitute the basic social form that permits an inter-organisational coalition to develop.[21]

The development of networks in any field involves four steps: first, an increase in the level of interaction among organisations in a field; second, an increase in the load of information on organisations; third, the emergence of structures of domination or patterns of coalition; and fourth, the development at the cultural level of a dominant ideology of the field, usually accompanied by competing, minority ideologies.

Rhodes suggests some key features of networks:[22]

1 Constellation of interests – the interests of participants in a network vary by service/economic function, territory, client-group and common expertise.
2 Membership – membership differs in terms of the balance between public and private sector; and between political-administrative elites, professions, and clients.
3 Vertical interdependence – intra-network relationships vary in their degree of interdependence, especially the dependence of central government on sub-national actors for the implementation of policies.
4 Horizontal interdependence – relationships between the networks vary in their degree of horizontal articulation: that is, in the extent to which a network is insulated from, or in conflict with, other networks.
5 Distribution of resources – actors control different types and amounts of resources and such variations affect the patterns of vertical and horizontal interdependence.

In the face of complex issues and a pressing need for action, networking has become commonplace. For example, in the environmental field, an intense structuring process has been binding organisations into a complex web of information flows, computer links (such as the environmental information network GREEN NET), interests and resource exchanges, all encouraged by the integrating force of world conferences such as the 1992 UN Conference on Environment and Development in Brazil.

It is important to distinguish between a range of networks serving different functions. The following four types can be identified:

Policy networks are based on the major functional interests in and of government (energy, transport, education, housing and so on). They are characterised by stable relationships, continuity of restricted memberships, shared responsibilities for service delivery and insulation from other networks.[23]

Issue networks are considerably less integrated, with a large number of participants and a limited degree of interdependence. Some are based on the need to share technical information, such as the agricultural development network AGRONET; others are based on shared concern over issues, such as conservation of the rainforest.

Professional networks cut across policy and issue networks. National professional associations, such as the United Kingdom's Royal Town Planning Institute, may periodically formalise professional opinion, disseminate professional practice and regulate entry into a field. Professional influence is exercised in lobbying and in institutionalised policy networks.

Where a particular group of professionals has operational control in government or quasi-governmental agencies, their views may coalesce around some political or professional ideology. This is especially the case in authoritarian or totalitarian regimes where freedom to publish and lobby is severely curtailed or non-existent. In the former Soviet Union, for instance, the ideological professionalism of technological elites contributed greatly to the near–total failure to integrate ecological concerns into agricultural and engineering developments, even in the face of major public health problems (described in Chapter 1). In democratic systems too, the ideological assimilation of professionals may be harmful. For example, Dunlevy argues that the concentration of nuclear engineers in regulatory bodies like the UK Atomic Energy Authority, which works closely with nuclear power plant manufacturers, has distorted the operational conception of the public interest in the nuclear power industry.[24] But professionalism can also work in the public interest. For example, it has been reported that Britain's Nuclear Installations Inspectorate agitated behind the scenes for tighter safety at the Sellafield Nuclear Reprocessing Facility when government ministers tried to block inspections for purely political reasons.[25]

Producer networks are concerned with economic functions, and the relationship between private and public sector. Here private industry, through links with government and trade associations such as the UK Chamber of Industry and Commerce, may exert an influence on policy. For example, private industry, through the Chemical Industries Association, has had a major influence on pesticide analysis and control policy in the UK. In both producer and professional networks there have been particularly strong links between public and private sector.

If we accept the proposition advanced earlier that inter-organisational activity itself generates unpredictable policy impacts, then the emergence of a complex web of networks with the growth of modern states helps account for the notion of increasing turbulence. It also suggests why it is insufficient for environmentalists to be 'issue-oriented'. For example, it may not be enough to understand and argue the relative merits of nuclear power, hydroelectric dams, and coal-fired power stations. Rather, what Vickers[26] has called a 'policy appreciation' may require an integrated perspective on an issue and the promotion of cross-cutting networks to provide a dynamic analysis of policy issues.

There is also a strong core-periphery dimension to the growth of such networks:

> The emergence of policy networks with the growth of the modern state could be interpreted as the triumph of functional over territorial politics. Thus, channels of communication between centre and locality are not based on territorial representation but on professional–bureaucratic contacts: dispensed territorial justice rivals the politics of place; uniform standards challenge local variety.[27]

The functional orientation is also reinforced by the professional one, creating tension between the drive for centralisation and the need for local service delivery. In any event, what it does suggest is that only inter-organisational activity itself, which requires resources such as mandate, staff time and funding, can unravel policy problems which are interwoven and demand attention across departments and specialisms.

Action-centred networks

As we have seen, management organisations are forced increasingly by turbulence and complexity into a range of temporary alliances, formal or informal, with other organisations. The capacity to do this productively is described as 'connective' capacity, which results in collaborative problem-solving. These alliances are the 'administrative cadres', 'multi-disciplinary project teams' and 'flexible adjuncts to all manner of work organizations' described earlier as unconventional institutional frameworks for environmental management and development planning.

There is growing evidence that such inter-organisational collaboration is emerging as a clear feature of successful management. This trend also fits theories of responses to turbulence in the early organisational analysis of Emery and Trist. Following that early work, Trist suggests that management will increasingly be undertaken by such task-oriented networks.[28] The possible functions of action- or task-oriented networks are:

- regulation – of present relationships and activities, establishing ground rules and maintaining values;
- appreciation – of emergent trends and issues, developing a shared image of a desirable future;
- mutual problem solving – by tapping into the extended range of knowledge, expertise and experience available from members of the network;
- infrastructural support – resources, research, information sharing, and support of innovation;
- mobilisation – of resources including finance, political access and support,

information and expertise, legal authority and administrative relationships; and
- development – of a network of external relations for interactive planning and mutual support.

A key issue in any such network is the degree to which the partner or stakeholding organisations are loosely or tightly 'coupled'. Coupling can be defined in terms of the strength of vertical or horizontal ties between organisations, and whether relations are voluntary or mandated. The degree of coupling also depends in part on the degree of hierarchical control, if any, exercised by a central authority. Following a review of networks within social service delivery systems, Aldrich[29] summarises the position:

> Advocates assert that a loosely coupled structure is most appropriate under conditions of environmental change where decisions must be taken rapidly and where a high degree of responsiveness is desired. Advocates of centralisation attack these arguments on the grounds that a decentralised system caters to local interests at the expense of societal interests and is more costly to administer because of duplication of administrative overheads across many semi–autonomous organisations.

Linking-pin organisations

There is something else which distinguishes the action-centred network from other, less task-oriented networks. This is some central focus to the network, which is not management *per se*, but a centre of communication, co-ordination and 'drive'. In organisational analysis, this factor is called a linking-pin structure. It may be an existing organisation which gives birth to, and nurtures, the network, or it can be established by network members who recognise the need for a central focus. It will play a key role in integrating the loosely coupled system, even if it has no formal status.

Five functions of a linking-pin organisation can be identified:

1   it serves as a communication channel between nodes or stakeholders within the network and to the wider world;
2   it provides general services that link third parties to one another by transferring resources, information or clients;
3   if it is a high status organisation it may secure resources for the network and it may also use the dependence of other organisations on it to actively direct network activities;
4   with the agreement of network members, it serves as catalyst to drive the network forward towards its task or objectives; and
5   it may encourage different nodes within the network to develop specialised areas of expertise for the benefit of the network as a whole.

A linking-pin organisation may also use its stature or authority to link more than one network, and it can help prevent the isolation of smaller organisations within any network. Linking-pin organisations play an increasingly important role in difficult environmental management tasks. For example, the World Wide Fund for Nature (WWF) plays such a linking-pin role in a number of different national and international networks. Internationally, WWF pioneered 'debt-for-nature' swaps that linked interest groups in tropical countries and wealthy industrialised countries. In Britain, WWF is drawing together and providing a focus for a variety of organisations concerned with loss of rural farmland to suburban development. In the case study in Chapter 10, the parent Groundwork Foundation provides a linking-pin function to the semi-autonomous offspring Trusts that it helps to establish. And in Chapter 11, we will see how the Commonwealth Consultative Group on Technology Management (CCGTM) has carved out for itself an important linking-pin role for a number of action-oriented networks, one of which is the IDEA network.

A linking-pin function can also be pursued at the societal level. Trist, for example, calls for advances in institution-building at the level of inter-organisational domains, which occupy a position in social space between society as a whole and the single organisation. Such domains manifest themselves in concrete organisations to reduce and regulate turbulence. For example, in Canada the regular interprovincial meetings among premiers and senior ministers constitute the framework of an inter-organisational domain, which attempts to regulate endemic turbulence in a political system so fractured that the future of the country is at risk. In Britain, the non-profit NGO, The Environment Council, works to establish linkages between campaigning environmental groups, business and government. In many lower income countries, where linking-pin institutions are non-existent, an early step by government is to establish some kind of arms–length environment council to set the environmental agenda and to draw in the competences of other organisations, such as business or university, to the environmental management task. This is the approach of the Government of Ghana, which saw the establishment of a national environment council as an early step towards developing support for a national environmental policy.

In the remainder of this chapter we consider how organisations, faced with difficult management tasks, can improve their corporate abilities, and their members' abilities, for fostering innovation in management. Within the term 'organisation' we now explicitly include the action-centred network, whether formal or informal. In the arguments over the meaning and method of sustainable development, we see the opportunity for organisations and their members to improve their abilities to manage conflict to mutual advantage through a generic process of organisational learning. The rest of the chapter sets out a rationale for organisational learning; the next chapter covers a set of practical steps for initiating such a process within an environmental action network.

CONFLICT AS AN OPPORTUNITY FOR INNOVATION

In defining and implementing sustainable development, 'conflict between organisations is an inevitable result of functional interdependence and scarcity of resources'.[30] In all action-centred networks therefore, bargaining to resolve conflicts is likely to be a central mode of political action. Organisational dynamics will involve a relationship between positional power and authority derived from possession of resources and their use in bargaining.[31] Bargaining in turn can be made more effective by processes of organisational learning, facilitation and by types of mediation.

Conflict among organisations over resources, power and influence is inevitable. If we take, for example, organisations concerned with regional development and environmental conservation in Canada's Northwest Territories, the following areas of inter-agency conflict can be found:

- between Federal Government departments with different mandates, for example, the Department of Indian Affairs and Northern Development and the Department of Environment;
- between Federal, Territorial and Municipal Governments;
- between Native organisations and all levels of government;
- between environmental pressure groups and government agencies; and
- between private industry and environmental groups.

In fact the list could be longer, for there is a strong measure of centre-periphery tension between Ottawa, the federal capital, which is 2000 miles from the region, and Yellowknife, Inuvik and other regional administrative centres.

But it would be mistaken to take such situations as one of constant and evenly spread conflict among competing agencies. There is also a constant shift of organisational alliances among groups. For example, native organisations find it in their interest to align themselves with central government against the aspirations for provincehood of the Government of the Northwest Territories. A federal department with a mandate over environmental conservation, the Department of the Environment, falls naturally into an alliance with the similar Territorial Department of Renewable Resources against federal and territorial agencies aligned with private industry to promote industrial development.

These 'situational' alliances are constantly altering as agencies make progress towards, or review, objectives. All this takes place against a background of:

- shifting world prices and preferences for the region's commodities (oil, gas, gold, furs, etc) which, in this case, means a 'boom and bust' economy;
- the long term constitutional struggle over the region's future and the future of Canada itself; and
- the democratic aspirations of the majority of native people for an independent political entity within or even outside of the Canadian federation.

In late 1991 the federal government announced that such a political entity, within the federation, would be carved out of the Northwest Territories. It is to be called 'Nunavut', and in this region 18,000 Inuit will have unrestricted right to hunt, fish and trap, and presumably to fashion their own version of a sustainable, natural resource-based society.

Canadian political scientists have reviewed this complex melange in all its fascinating detail.[32] For the purposes of environmental management, there are two key observations. First if, as we have argued, conflict is inevitable in attempting to realise goals of sustainable development, the nature of conflict itself is worthy of study if organisations are to manage better. Second, many empirical studies of management find in conflict a beneficial opportunity to improve the effectiveness of inter-organisational relations, providing managers accept that conflict cannot be eliminated. Rather organisations may find in conflict the opportunity to redefine norms and identity, and to reassess ineffective structures. This view is echoed by Godet who finds in system crisis both a threat and an opportunity for beneficial change.[33] Gemmill and Smith argue that it is at the point when there is a major thrust towards disorder within a system that genuine learning and transition can occur.[34]

Types of conflict

It would be a mistake to assume that all conflict over environmental policy is based on disagreement over substantive issues. Five types of conflict have been identified by CDR Associates during assisted environmental mediation processes in the United States and elsewhere (Figure 8.1), distinguishing between unnecessary and genuine, or unavoidable, conflict.[35]

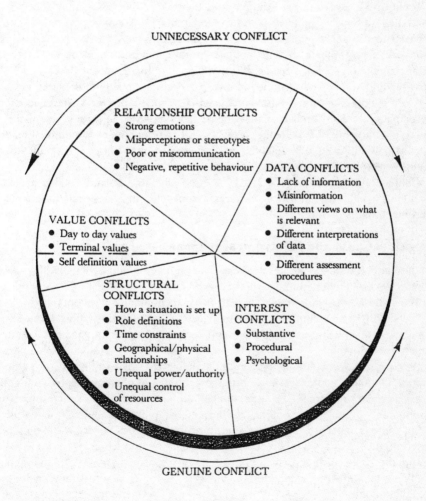

Figure 8.1 *Types of conflict*
Source: CDR Associates, Boulder, Colorado[35]

There are three types of conflicts which are, on the whole, unnecessary. **Relationship conflicts** are reported to occur because of misperceptions or stereotypes, miscommunication or habitual negative behaviours. These are unnecessary in that they may occur even when genuine conditions for conflict, such as limited resources or mutually exclusive goals, are not present. **Data conflicts** occur when people lack information, are misinformed, disagree over the relevance of data, intrepret information differently or have competing assessment procedures. Most can be resolved by better communication. **Value conflicts** represent incompatible belief systems, but again these need not lead to genuine conflict unless people attempt to force one set of values on others, or assert that divergent beliefs are not allowed. Conversely, people with quite different values systems can live together in harmony, unless their self-definition is threatened by conflict.

Structural conflicts are genuine and therefore difficult to avoid. They are caused by oppressive patterns of human relationships, usually shaped by forces external to the participants in a dispute. Participants may be disadvantaged by economic arrangements, lack of political control, organisational or professional arrangements or spatial peripheralisation. Finally, **interest conflicts** are also genuine, and occur over substantive issues (the decision), procedural issues (how to arrive at the decision) and psychological issues (perceptions of trust, fairness, need for participation, etc.). Conflict occurs when parties believe the satisfaction of their interests is incompatible with the satisfaction of their opponents' interest: 'For an interest-based dispute to be resolved, all parties must have a significant number of their interests addressed or met . . .'[36]

Chapter 9 describes two related methods, facilitation and mediation, for identifying conflict and moving toward resolution of disputes via the establishment of action-centred networks.

Organisational and behavioural responses to conflict

In summary, conflict presents opportunities for positive action, particularly if types of conflict can be identified and addressed in a manner intended to diffuse tension, isolate genuine from unnecessary conflict, and meet as many interests of participants as possible. This is important for managers who constantly find themselves confronted with what seems to be one 'sub-system crisis' after another, sometimes called 'firefighting'.

Appropriate organisational responses to conflict may be institutional or behavioural. The former attempts to improve organisational effectiveness by changing organisational roles, mandates, legal obligations, communications systems, reward systems and other characteristics. It is equally important to engage in parallel behavioural change: of stakeholders' culture, attitudes, values, norms, and so on. This involves participants in a cycle of discovery–invention–production and evaluation of knowledge. The purpose is to increase human resource capability for managing conflict in a number of areas relevant to difficult tasks. These capabilities include:

- analytic – to formulate a view of the key problems facing the organisation;
- target-setting – to have clear objectives in the sense of preferred future states of the operating environment;

- innovation – to devise appropriate strategies in non-traditional forms for the achievements of these futures;
- corporate – to be able to take an overall view of the resources and requirements for action in a given situation;
- functional – to develop and implement specific programmes within a corporate framework;
- monitoring – to evaluate changing conditions in the operating environment and the effects of interventions with a view to assessing their impact and further reviewing policies; and
- connective – to devise productive relationships with other bodies whose operations are relevant to the achievement or frustration of environmental goals.[37]

This list provides an agenda, focused on the *innovation* function, for improving skills within any organisation, but it does not provide the method. At its simplest, the method is based on self-development through organisational or 'action-learning', by which we mean participants or stakeholders engaging in a self-directed, mutually supportive and iterative process of understanding organisational constraints and experimenting with options for overcoming them.

ORGANISATIONS AS LEARNING SYSTEMS: THE PATH TO INNOVATION

As noted above, organisations addressing environmental metaproblems cannot help but be influenced by the activities of other organisations influencing the environment and each other. For this reason, organisations need to be aware of the changes which occur in their environment and to learn or adapt their behaviour to accommodate this flow of information. Such organisational learning is not mechanistic, as the cybernetic analogy might suggest, but must involve what can be called 'cultural change', that is accepting the possibility of altering what may be deeply held beliefs or entrenched patterns of organisational culture.[38] This gives rise to innovation:

> Innovation involves new behaviour, new habits, new interlocking expectations which we call roles in social theory, and it even involves new interlocking patterns of roles, which we call institutions or practices ... Innovation is collective action.[39]

Organisations that do not engage in cultural change which gives rise to innovation remain immured in what have been called 'culturally programmed strategies'. These emphasise continuity, consistency, and stability in order to maintain the status quo. However, when such an organisation experiences turbulence it faces an array of internal and external disorders and is unable to deal effectively according to its accustomed patterns of operation. Bureaucracies, for example, have not been structured for learning, adaptation and change, but rather to carry out a predetermined range of tasks.

Innovation: learning to learn

The essential definition of innovation involves the notion of learning to learn, what

Gregory Bateson called higher-order learning.[40] The concept of organisations as learning systems is a valuable contribution of organisation theory to innovation in management. For example, Argyris and Schon propose a 'theory of action' which describes a process of human learning in which knowledge is continually tested and reconstructed.[41] Morgan argues that the application of these insights has resulted in a major reorientation in organisations: goal-oriented rationality is superseded by an ethic which stresses the need to facilitate the creative interplay and development of contextual relationships, or action learning.[42]

Here the primary task of managers is to create capacity for learning, which becomes a pre-eminent organisational function. Action learning strategies address three objectives:

1 informed and effective decision making through the changing of organisational culture;
2 the unification of theory (or systematic reflection) and practice through action-research, which leads to replicable learning across a range of similar problem areas;
3 professional development.

Action learning is the means by which organisations can deal with rapid and complex change which causes process outcomes and organisational objectives to be mismatched. Turbulent change can be seen as systems of problems, or errors which need to be dealt with through learning and alteration of individual, professional and organisational beliefs. This is seldom easy, but the rewards are tangible in terms of enhanced management capacity and flexibility in the face of uncertainty, and in terms of personal and professional development:

> Action learning strategies enable us to deal with systems of problems without having to solve them, and to do so in a continuous, adaptive and non-synoptic manner which meets the rapidity, complexity and uncertainty of turbulence.[43]

Figure 8.2 summarises the differences between traditional approaches and action

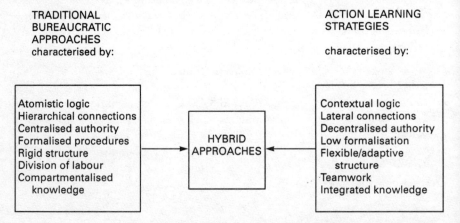

TRADITIONAL BUREAUCRATIC APPROACHES characterised by:		ACTION LEARNING STRATEGIES characterised by:
Atomistic logic Hierarchical connections Centralised authority Formalised procedures Rigid structure Division of labour Compartmentalised knowledge	HYBRID APPROACHES	Contextual logic Lateral connections Decentralised authority Low formalisation Flexible/adaptive structure Teamwork Integrated knowledge

Figure 8.2 *Bureacratic and action learning approaches*

learning strategies. This is, of course, a simplification: many agencies have other, often statutory, functions which do not demand innovation, and operate somewhere in the middle ground.

The innovation process

Organisations generally do not adopt a specific blueprint for an innovative activity, but rather adopt a general concept, the operational meaning of which gradually unfolds in the management process. The stages in this process of unfolding have been identified by Rogers and Kim.[44] Five steps are grouped into two main sub-processes, initiation and implementation. Initiation consists of all the information gathering, conceptualising and planning. Implementation is action, from which the initiation process can re-start:

Initiation sub-process
1 Agenda setting: a general organisational problem creates a perceived need for innovation as defined by members of the organisation.
2 Matching: specific aspects of the problem are matched to alternative solutions (forms of innovation), and their fit is tested by members of the organisation.

Implementation sub-process
3 Redefining: reinvention or modification of the innovation based on feedback about the fit.
4 Structuring: organisational structures may need to be altered to implement the innovation. For example, a new organisational unit may be created.
5 Interconnecting: relationships within and between organisations are clarified. As this happens the innovation may lose its separate identity and become institutionalised.

The process is not linear, of course, but circular, involving as many interior loops as necessary to ensure the fit of the innovation to the problem.

Innovation in government

Each partner in an action-centred network makes a contribution of relevant expertise and enthusiasm to this innovation process, including representatives of government departments and agencies. But government also has an important overall societal role, which we can only begin to touch on in this book. This is a strategic role, which Godet calls *la prospective*.[45] It is not mathematical forecasting, nor is it reactive in the sense of attempting to respond to technological and economic imperatives thrown up by the market-place. Rather, it is the *proactive* attempt to throw light on present action by looking at possible positive futures. It begins with some sense of the possibilities of the future, call it vision, and uses this vision to initiate the sub-processes of innovation: the agenda of the future – what kind of society we might want to have; and commitment to implementation based on desire to realise this future and not some other, less satisfactory one.

First and foremost, *la prospective* is a way of thinking; it is reflected in the strategic vision a government communicates to society. Figure 8.3 shows how strategic culture

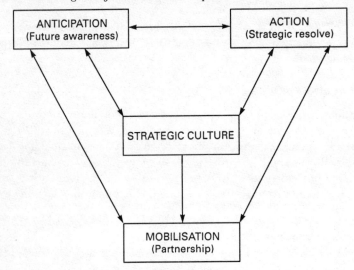

Figure 8.3 *Anticipation – action – mobilisation*
Source: after Godet[2]

is the pivot which links the 'Anticipation–Action–Mobilisation' functions of a modernised society. Godet suggests why it is imperative:

1   the acceleration of technical, economic and social change necessitates long-term vision, because 'the faster you drive, the further ahead your headlights must shine'; and
2   factors of inertia inherent in structures and behaviour mean that we must sow today in order to be able to harvest tomorrow.

Prospective thinking involves two commitments by government, to be reinforced by organisational culture:

1   commitment to strategic management, which involves monitoring major issues in society, including issues just appearing on the horizon, and making use of that information in planning for the future; and
2   commitment to partnership, recognising that no agency of society can manage on its own, and that partnership, or networking, processes require and deserve support from public as well as private resources.

With all these terms – management, planning, partnership – it is the participation in the processes they represent which generates both policy innovation, and the capacity to innovate. By promoting such innovation, government begins to define a new, sophisticated role for itself, beyond the failures of bureaucratic over-control and beyond the naivety of laissez-faire. The experience of action-networking is that the benefits of the process, in terms of new productive linkages in society, and individual growth in ability to take a wider perspective, continue after any particular aspect of the process is complete.

The Growth Management Consensus Project in California, described in Chapter 12, is a good example of this constructive role for government. This process of formal mediation, initiated (but not controlled) by the State of California, has been able to propose recommendations for policy and legislation based on consensus among many of the major stakeholding agencies in the state, ranging from environmentalists to property developers. This is reported to have brought the legislative programme, and the level of statewide debate over these issues, forward by many years.

We now return to the concept of learning, and show how a specific methodology of 'action research', arising out of the action learning perspective, can link anticipation and action in a single effective framework. This is also a methodology for policy making and implementation which works well in the action-networking approach.

ACTION RESEARCH

Action learning is specifically concerned with integration: theory with practice, and research with action. Its underlying assumption is that there is an emergent quality to this process. It is not therefore either theoretical or anti-theoretical, but theory grounded in practical experience, and experience directed by theoretical reflection. Action learning:

> . . . addresses head-on social inquiry's fundamental problems – the relation between theory and practice, between the general and the particular, between common-sense and academic expertise, between mundane action and critical reflection, and hence – ultimately – between ideology and understanding.[46]

Action learning in organisations produces direct results in terms of innovation. It can also produce knowledge, or transferable learning, when linked to the parallel tool of action research. This new approach to research needs to be contrasted with traditional social science which requires:

1   that the primary objective of research remains unaltered during the research process;
2   that there is precise and measurable control over dependent variables;
3   that intervening variables be controlled or excluded from the research framework;
4   that the researcher remains neutral and dispassionate throughout the process.

The problem is that (2) above is impossible in any dynamic policy situation characterised by turbulence, and that (1), (3) and (4) greatly reduce the value of social science research to real time management problems because they negate the value of feedback, and prohibit the researcher from contributing the benefits of experience and intuition to the process. All four criteria ensure that qualitative aspects of environmental problems will be ignored or undervalued. For these reasons, traditional approaches to research in the management field are often unrealistic, cumbersome, unresponsive and unable to bridge institutional barriers to understanding.

The action research approach, on the other hand:

1   makes use of the social context of a specific environmental problem or development challenge to increase its own effects;
2   redefines the research process towards a rapid, interactive cycle of problem-discovery-reflection-response-problem redefinition;

3 replaces the neutral social scientist/observer with a multi-disciplinary team of practitioners and researchers, all working together in a process of mutual education;

4 proposes that pluralistic evaluation replace static models of social processes. This is characterised by concern for: institutional functioning, continual monitoring of project implementation, the subjective views of major constituent groups, and methodological 'triangulation' by which a variety of data sources are brought to bear for evaluation; and

5 generates replicable learning from the above elements, which is constantly tested against both past experience and the results of current action.

Action research therefore differs substantially from research or action alone. From research, in its avoidance of the static, controlled and contrived model and its emphasis on a fluid, on-going approach which generates conclusions at the most appropriate time in the process rather than waiting until the bitter end. It differs from action alone in the constant feeding back of evaluation resulting in crucial shifts in the direction of action. It is fundamentally about collaboration and dialogue:

> Action-research is a collaborative endeavour in which groups of practitioners work together to understand better their own practice, to increase their awareness of the effects of their practice, and of their control over the situation in which they work.[47]

There are personal and professional, as well as organisational, benefits. Participants in action research strategies and/or in action-centred networks tend to become sensitised to the diversity of motivations for human action, and constructive and sustainable means for altering them. The result is what Schon calls the 'reflective practitioner'.[48]

CONCLUSION

This chapter has argued that the context of environmental metaproblems is turbulence, which is characterised by uncertainty about the nature of complex problems and the consequences of collective action, by inconsistent and ill-defined preferences and values, and complex networks of participants with a varying interest in problem resolution. A mistaken belief in a stable state, in which planning can act as a buffer against change and uncertainty, gives rise to institutional dysfunctions caused by organisations attempting to fulfil individual objectives, while maximising their own benefits and externalising costs.

The main conclusion to be drawn is that complexity and fluidity are inevitable in the modern state, often reinforced by instability in the world's economy. Any organisation faces not only system complexity but is dependent on other organisations in that environment, each of which are probably pursuing unrelated objectives. Such interdependence of organisations and environment is compounded by political, economic, cultural and psychological changes. This has caused the range of governments' problems to increase dramatically, made it more difficult to respond appropriately, and is thus responsible for the limits to governance. This, in turn, is manifested in concern over poor management, deficiencies in service co-ordination, poor quality of service and an inability to establish a conception of the public good which commands confidence. Kirby argues that the problem is exacerbated by a rise in pluralism and a changing value system which reduces willingness to co-operate with government.[49]

Here we arrive at the argument that the management of complexity is a continual process of innovation, rather than a product. It is a journey which can be done poorly or well, but where each arrival is a point of departure. Managers must work towards a synthesis of knowledge and promote a common problem conception and an evolving consensus on a series of pressing issues. They must relish the rough and tumble of inter-organisational negotiation and accept the indeterminate nature of their calling. Collaboration and a drive towards consensus, rather than subordination, is the preferred approach. The situation was excellently summarised by Whalen, writing more than thirty years ago:

> The law of life is the law of change, social activities breed and transform social and political arrangements . . . The achieving of an acceptable balance between change and order involves a continuing tension between institutional effectiveness – interpreted as operational efficiency in relation to a matrix of communal skills, resources, demands and skills – and group images of institutional legitimacy. Given the complex, changing, independent and potentially unstable conditions common to most democratic states, and given the public measures required to secure social stability in such an environment, the condition of government may be described as a crisis of effectiveness.[50]

The challenge is much the same whatever the field to be managed: natural environment, transport, land use, energy, resources or any other. This supports Webber's contention that good management is about a 'cognitive style, not a substantive field'.[51] The next chapter suggests one distinctive organisational framework for nurturing that style in the service of sustainable development.

9 Developing action-centred networks for environmental management

It is widely assumed that environmental issues can be dealt with in the same way as other government activities. But the complex inter-relationships demand holistic thinking and a new multi-level, multi-organisational approach – presenting a challenge to traditional government organisational and management structures.

J D Stewart, 1991[1]

The substitution of open communication for bureaucratic authority in informal groups and temporary or parallel organizations, encourages creative thinking. This may equip the organization to move from chaos to order as it needs to begin a new phase in its existence.

H P Knowles and B O Saxberg, 1988[2]

The inability of command and control bureaucracies, working on their own or vertically with international bureaucracies, to deal with complex environment and development problems should be a major concern worldwide. This calls for examination of the processes of decision-making, including the organisational culture of governments, as well as the products of policy making. Unfortunately, as was noted in Chapter 7, process issues are of little interest to politicians and bureaucrats who already have power, and therefore a vested interest in maintaining the status quo. Also, process issues are more difficult to conceptualise than substantive environmental issues. Finally, to be honest, process issues do not rank very high on many people's list of exciting things to talk about. None of this negates the need for radical improvement of the processes of decision making. Fortunately, there is growing concern among people addressing environmental and development challenges that good work is continually undone by lack of attention to process. There is much interest in the possibilities for inter-organisational innovation, in what we call 'action-centred networks', linking the public, private and voluntary sectors.

Alternatives or improvements to the existing situation have been suggested under many names, but they all boil down to innovation in what has been described as an evolving network that should be flexible, open and capable of restructuring itself over time.[3] Unlike the loose linkages in the more usual information-sharing networks, the action-centred network is focused on the goals of its management and research tasks, and engages in regular, critical review of its progress towards those goals. The networks function at a number of levels:

- as growing constituencies for sustainable development, fostering an ongoing political process of mediation and the building of consensus even where conflict is bound to be pervasive;
- as a vehicle for new partnerships between government, business and non-governmental and community groups;

- as groups of public administrators and natural and social scientists with a commitment to mutual learning to develop a new range of skills in environmental management; and
- in multi-layered, 'nested' networks, as a means of integrating efforts at sustainable development from the local to the international level.

Increasingly, forward thinking government officials are sanctioning the involvement of such task-oriented, less formal groups in environmental management. These groups define environmental problems in a more holistic and practical fashion, and work to develop consensus on the way forward. These kinds of innovation are not, however, a replacement for the traditional bureaucracy, as they do not carry out any routine functions of government. Rather, government will find it helpful to participate in such networks, as a partner with business and community groups in tackling problems in environmental management.

The characteristics of these parallel, action-centred networks are:

- flat, flexible organisational structures involving teamwork or partnerships;
- equality of relationships among all relevant stakeholders;
- vision and value-driven leadership;
- emphasis on participation and organisational learning;
- undertaking continuous performance review and improvement; and
- a method of network development in which events progress at a pace which is politically and culturally sustainable given local conditions.

Within the IDEA network (Chapter 11) the application of these principles to real time management problems in member countries is called the 'quality management' approach, drawing on concepts from business studies.[4]

The action-centred network approach is concerned with both sustainable development and the sustainability of the innovations identified as necessary to improve environmental management. As such it addresses substantive and process issues simultaneously. This chapter describes some of the fundamental principles and mechanisms involved. These are divided into underlying assumptions, operational tactics and methods of working, as listed in Figure 9.1. The case studies to follow each suggest a similar methodology for developing action-centred networks at widely varying levels of decision making.

UNDERLYING ASSUMPTIONS OF ACTION-CENTRED NETWORKS

Redefinition of environment

A basic premise is that common definitions of environment are often too narrow in their focus on biophysical factors, at the expense of the social environment and of environmental, economic and social objectives for human development. Such definitions also narrow the management task unacceptably and lead to failure because of the large number of uncontrolled intervening variables outside the working definition.

The action-centred approach redefines environment, and thus the tasks of environmental management, in the context of national development, as *a mediation*

MAJOR UNDERLYING ASSUMPTIONS

- Redefinition of Environment
- Stakeholder Equality
- Action Learning
- Grounding in Real Problems

OPERATIONAL TACTICS

- Enrollment of Stakeholders
- Problem Reiteration
- Interdisciplinary Analysis
- Institutional and Organisational Development
- Role of Key Individuals
- Linkage between Public and Private Sectors
- Linkage with Non-Governmental Organisations

METHODS OF WORKING

- Management as Planning
- Role of Consensus
- Facilitation and Mediation Procedures
- Concept of Nested Networks
- Generation of Replicable Learning
- Paying for Networking

Figure 9.1 *Basic elements of action-centred networking*

process between economic/industrial needs and the maintenance of the biosphere, with the objective of an increased level of integration. In this way projects attempt to operationalise the concept of sustainable development in a practical manner as a dynamic process of good decision making and management, not a static product of policy or a distant vision of future policy.

Stakeholder equality

Underpinning the structure of these networks is the assumption that stakeholders are equal in terms of the validity of their values and perceptions and in terms of their right to participation in, and power over, the process of decision-making and implementation. This is a simple principle to articulate but one that is difficult to implement. As noted in Chapter 2, it implies that old hierarchical arrangements and patterns of paternalism or domination must be swept away in the new structure: for example, North over South, 'developed' over 'less developed', professionals over non-professionals, business over NGOs, men over women, rich over poor, urban over rural, government over community, and so on. There are many ethical reasons for doing this, but even purely pragmatically, there is little chance of progress unless stakeholders are strongly committed to 'ownership' of problems and solutions based on a feeling of genuine participation.

Implementing stakeholder equality is hard. In a very unequal world, it is easiest to start with a limited task and to rely on progress on that task to promote change in other areas of life by 'good example'. It is important to note that equality is not to be equated with a lack of strong leadership. Network participants understand that challenging outdated perceptions and accomplishing difficult tasks requires leadership, in terms of the resources offered by a linking-pin organisation. Finally, government or other public sector officials tend to find it difficult to relinquish status and control; business and community groups may be less concerned about hierarchical distinctions and the status they confer, but are still likely to find it difficult to achieve a sense of equality.

Action learning

At the most basic level, the action-centred approach works in two ways: realistic environmental problem definition and redefinition as circumstances change; and individualised, adaptive responses designed to improve management capability relevant to specific tasks. In short, the network teams intervene in the process of management, learn about it and improve it, hands-on:

> . . . combining past experience, organisational intelligence and future goals in a mode of action-oriented management which is intended to produce valid information, informed choice and, most importantly, a commitment to action based on consensual knowledge.[5]

Grounding in real problems

The action-centred approach grounds transferable learning about environmental management strategies in practical development challenges. This accords with Hirschman's advice that 'uniform solutions to development problems invariably lead us astray'.[6] In the IDEA programme for example (discussed in Chapter 11), the environmental problems first identified, such as river pollution, have been redefined into a series of positive 'management and action' projects in watershed, waste and natural resources management, supported by a second-level network providing information services, environmental advisory services, and training and action research methodology.

This underlines the point that, although countries face many enormous environmental problems, most of these will only be resolved by the development of local skills and solutions. Problems may be analysed at a global or national scale, but the resolution of big problems will be the result of aggregating smaller projects. The process of local problem redefinition generates the necessary local commitment and an understanding of the skills needed to implement solutions. Even the partial implementation of more productive management approaches builds confidence in local abilities in environmental management.

OPERATIONAL TACTICS

Enrolment of stakeholders

An important aspect of the network approach is to address the range of identified constraints on good management more or less simultaneously. Some constraints will require institutional development, others the development of a new consensus as a basis for action. These are discussed below. Two fundamental constraints usually found in any environmental management task are lack of political commitment and a failure of integration.

One way of addressing political constraints is campaigning, such as that undertaken by NGOs like Friends of the Earth. The action-centred network takes a different, but complementary, approach, by gradually drawing in relevant stake-holders – affected interest groups including politicians and government officials – thus building up a momentum and commitment to change in an emerging constituency for sustainable development. Some people will join the process because they recognise its potential in addressing a serious environmental problem; others would rather not join but will be afraid of being left out of something. Still others may need to be induced into coming along once because an important or expert speaker is addressing a topic of national or international significance. Some people will come because the Minister is making a brief appearance, and for no other reason. Most people will have no idea what an action-centred network is like, but once exposed to the stimulating discussion in a non-hierarchical setting, become attracted to the process.

How stakeholders are attracted is a tactical decision: the important point is that the right stakeholders are invited or even lured into the process. The IDEA projects tackle urgent problems of national significance, and then use widespread media coverage, senior Ministerial speeches, addresses by international experts, and invitations to a broad range of possible participants to convince people of the relevance of the approach and the urgent needs it is addressing.

Drawing in the right stakeholders tackles problems of integration at the same time, assuming that participants are empowered to represent their organisations and report back to them. In the more formal mediation approach, described below, it is a requirement of the process that participants can commit their organisations to the solutions that emerge from discussion. This was the case in the Growth Management Consensus Project in California.

The major areas of integration which usually need to be addressed by drawing stakeholders into the team are between

- different government departments;
- central and local government;
- public and private sectors;
- government and the academic/scientific community; and
- government policy level and community level, particularly smaller scale businesses, agriculture and community-based NGOs.

Problem reiteration

Policies seldom address comprehensively the problems they are intended to solve.

This is because the initial problem assessment is faulty – often biased to fit into preconceptions or an existing party political programme, or because the nature of problems changes while administrative responses do not, when too much is committed in the initial response. Problems change because circumstances change: the economy goes up or down, other organisations intervene for better or worse, or some progress is made on some aspects of the problem.

A simple but important tactic therefore is regularly to re–examine and redefine the nature of the problem, with the critical but constructive assistance of network members and other experts. There is no other way to ensure that the response is appropriate to the task. This is easier said than done – once we think we know what the problem is, we are not inclined to have this certainty disturbed. We will definitely be loath to admit that a change of direction is required or that our responses have been inappropriate to the problem. We will be inclined to defend what we have done because we have done it – where is the reward for admitting failure? The solution lies in changing organisational culture within the network to make the admission of failure a positive, constructive act, as it surely is, and to make problem redefinition an exciting challenge. Incentives may be required. The network, because it carries little baggage of organisational history, can refashion its culture in light of what works.

The main criterion in these decisions is to make progress in the task at hand rather than stick rigidly to a particular boundary definition. In particular, the informal, parallel organisation has the flexibility to redefine its mandate in this way during an unfolding process of problem redefinition.

Interdisciplinary analysis

The scale and interactive causes and effects of most environmental problems require holistic analysis which can appreciate the complex inter-relationships which define those problems. It is from these that damage and further risks arise; it is holistic thinking that can tease out the linkages which environmental policies need to recognise. Drawing in the right stakeholders, complemented by expert advisors to the network, ensures that an interdisciplinary team is assembled.

For example, the need to shift from an initial focus on pollution to the development of commitment to watershed or ecosystem management, and the institutional framework to accomplish this, means that tasks which originate from knowledge and expertise in the natural sciences, say of water quality, soon require complementary knowledge and expertise from the social sciences, such as regional land use, urban planning and economic analysis.

Institutional and organisational development

Institutional development, broadly defined, addresses legal and organisational constraints and limitations in human resources. As with other constraints, improvements may need to be pursued more or less simultaneously by networks for maximum effectiveness.

Legal institutions underlie the fabric of development and environmental control. For example, the property system and land use planning controls are a vital factor in any rural or agricultural development or conservation initiative, yet very often programmes are initiated without any analysis of these fundamental systems.[7] Legal systems include the necessary laws, regulations and environmental standards, and the framework of government to implement them. These are necessary but not sufficient conditions for successful management. The legal system also embodies formal arrangements for centralisation or decentralisation of planning and implementation, often a critical issue in development, and the institutional arrangements of government.

The term 'inter-organisational development' covers the shaping of the new formal and informal linkages within government, and beyond government to business, and the voluntary and community sectors. Investment in individual and team skills is the key to organisational innovation. This is crucial to improving the management process, both in terms of personal and professional development, and in terms of the development of all other organisational, institutional and legal structures of support.

We noted above the built-in bias of administrative systems towards maintaining the status quo. Those who favour innovation must therefore develop a reinforcement system which does three things:

- rewards people who try innovations, whether they succeed or fail;
- insures against losses, such as blame, if the innovation fails; and
- insures against losses even if the innovation succeeds.[8]

Incentives must therefore be given much more consideration as a means of generating commitment. At higher levels, the process of networking and achieving consensus must be made to be so stimulating and essential to good decision processes that senior officials feel that they would not like to be left out. They in turn can stimulate changes in organisational culture which can ripple throughout their organisations.

The role of key individuals

When initiating a network, there is a need to identify individuals who have the potential to mobilise people in a situation often characterised by tension, conflict and stalemate. A premise of the network approach, validated by case studies, is that senior people with the right outlook and human relations abilities, whether scientists or administrators, can, with the support of the network, move beyond their normal professional boundaries and become important agents of change in the improvement of the quality of management. This understanding, and particularly the means to achieve it, is a major output of the network approach.

Linkage between public and private sectors

The waning of socialist ideology, and obvious advantages of linkage between public and private sectors in economic development, have made this a challenging area for improved management. For example:

New forms of public-private relationship are sought to replace the traditions of techno-bureaucracy which grew up with the post-war welfare state. The state itself is struggling to restructure itself, ideologically and institutionally in response to these demands. This in turn destabilises the established practices of interest mediation through which claims in respect of land and environmental issues are recognised.[9]

The result, as suggested in a review of the future of public administration and development in Tanzania, is:

> For most economic activity, it will be an enabling administration, promoting private sector solutions or partnerships with the private sector, and only intervening where the market or the private sector will not carry the risks involved.[10]

These changes are in keeping with the notion of sustainable development as a process of mediation between production needs and environmental goals. Such new linkages between government and the business sector, encompassing small scale and medium enterprises as well as big business, will therefore be at the forefront of organisational challenges.

Linkages may prove somewhat easier to foster with multinational corporations eager to prove their environmental credentials, and their branch plants which are part of an international organisational culture; they may be more difficult to foster with heads of small businesses, who may be suspicious of government. The task of working with, and developing, organisations of small scale businesses is similar in many ways to tasks of community organisation and requires similar skills of diplomacy and empathy. Equally, any government which hopes to pursue sustainable development objectives in any field will need to learn to work with the private sector.

Linkage with non-governmental organisations

In Chapter 7, the common failure to extend vertical integration downwards and upwards between policy making levels of government and small scale natural resource users, such as farmers or small businesses, was identified as a cause of failure in policy making. The failure stems from governments' lack of knowledge of motivations and constraints which need to be influenced, lack of appreciation of the cumulative impacts of even small resource-using actions, and a failure to enlist these resource users in implementation. They are obvious candidates for network membership.

While organisation of small scale stakeholders can be difficult, it is important, and it will probably occur through either local government or non-governmental organisations. As with any other organisation with a hand in development, the ability of NGOs to participate productively in development tasks depends on their organisational capacity. Strong NGOs can be active partners in development and environmental management to redress failures of vertical integration. In a discussion paper, the World Bank suggests:

> People's propensity for organising is an immense development resource and NGOs are an adequate vehicle for tapping it . . . NGOs should not be regarded just as a conduit for funds or as a means of implementing programs, but as a

resource in themselves, a type of development capital. Thus building them up is development.[11]

It is helpful to distinguish between environmentalist NGOs and community-based NGOs. Environmentalist NGOs now engage in research, lobbying, public education, co-ordination of funding and protest actions at the international and sub-national level. They can target specific issues, generate widespread public interest, lobby key politicians and pressure public agencies. Community-based NGOs are usually much more local in orientation, but can have a wider brief than environmentalist NGOs in that their concerns will be more geared to the overall development of their locality.[12] In this sense they are 'people-oriented' and this is a major strength:

> They organize people to make better use of their own local productive resources, to create new resources and services, to promote equity and alleviate poverty, to influence government actions towards these same objectives and to establish new institutional frameworks that will sustain people-centered ... development.[13]

For the purposes of the action-centred network, it is important that every effort be made to extend the partnership to encompass relevant community-based NGOs. In Britain and the USA, for example, the late 1980s saw a flowering of involvement of community-based groups in successful urban renewal efforts, of which Groundwork (Chapter 10) is only one example. These are all predicated on the realisation that it is no good doing things 'to' or 'for' people, particularly in single sector approaches, like housing renewal, which had failed so dismally in the past. The alternative is to build up networks that encompass community groups, government and business.

The new partnership approaches, as they came to be called, recognised that local people, with appropriate assistance from a range of partners in government and business, could analyse their own problems and fashion their own solutions. These approaches, while difficult to build up, are potentially more relevant, more integrated and more sustainable than any which have gone before. They also generate multiplier effects, both for local people who have new confidence and new skills, and for neighbourhoods and cities at large, which become better places in which to live and do business, and which are better equipped to attract inward investment. Urban partnership approaches in the UK, which are clearly action-centred networks, are a tremendous source of innovation but still face a struggle in recruiting private sector participants and in overcoming suspicions in local government and the voluntary sector over working alongside business.[14]

The question of which NGOs to involve is a matter for local decision in any network. National or regional level NGOs, such as Friends of the Earth, could be expected to contribute to initiatives at that level, while community-based NGOs could initiate development at their own level. What is important is the understanding that local (or national) solutions are appropriate to local (or national) problems, and it is inconceivable that appropriate solutions would surface without partnership with the community through their NGOs.

METHODS OF WORKING IN NETWORKS

Management as planning

For reasons set out in Chapter 6, sustainable development is unlikely to be realised through initiatives based solely on the functional integration of the space economy. It is for this reason that network approaches are always grounded in some real, spatial or territorial concern, be it an urban neighbourhood or a watershed region, or some larger unit such as a state. With environmental issues too, the fundamental need for planning on a regional ecosystem basis is inescapable. Rowe argues that:

> In practice sustainability has to be a regional concept. We used to call it land use planning . . . Fortunately we can substitute for its two–dimensional flatness a better, more inclusive concept, perceiving a world surfaced with three-dimensional ecosystems in which we are immersed. These creative spaces are the focus of regional planning, whose ecological aim is a sustainable earth.[15]

In a similar vein, Fairclough argues:

> Most . . . countries have . . . economic plans, forest plans, plans for tourism, industry, services, ranching etc – not to mention plans for rural agricultural development. All these plans and development efforts impact on one another; and can conflict with one another. My simple thesis is that, in any attempt to harmonise economic development with sectoral objectives, a land use planning overview is essential . . . a planning framework within which public bodies, the private sector and individuals can all operate.[16]

Fairclough argues that only such a framework can provide the vehicle for mediation among competing objectives, such as economic development and environmental protection. The alternative, he says, is a recipe for 'continuing conflict'.

The role of consensus in the network

A key expected outcome of the network approach is an emerging consensus over the real nature and extent of the problem at hand, and a consensus about, and commitment to, the means of resolution. This drive towards consensus is quite different from the standard adversarial approach of parliamentary politics and law, based on simple majority rule, and which invariably leaves a large minority, or even a majority, dissatisfied with the outcome of the process and potentially alienated from the decision-making process. It is also quite different from the top-down administrative style of the traditional bureaucracy. Both can contribute to lack of confidence in decision-making procedures and active or passive resistance at the stage of implementation.

However, the context of sustainable development is one of pervasive conflict of interest, and therefore any shift towards consensus-building raises many challenges. The situation arises for two reasons:

1 the issues raised in considering sustainable development question ways of living that have been established at the expense of the environment and will not be discarded easily; and

2   some environmental issues raise questions of values that may have to be treated as absolutes and cannot therefore be traded off.[17]

In spite of these constraints, there is ample evidence that a consensus-based approach is workable and practical, and, more important, that it delivers environmental policy decisions appropriate to sustainable development.

First and foremost, consensus-building approaches are based on face-to-face interaction, and informed and guided discussion. The purpose is to arrive at a resolution which meets the needs of all the participants, and during which stakeholders become committed to, and accept greater responsibility for, the solution. Such consensus-building is a learned skill, either mutually learned by network members working with a facilitator, who will be a member of the network, or more formally, in a process of mediation under professional guidance. In no case is a third party decision maker involved, as is common in the adversarial approach.

At the operational level, there are four broad requirements for achieving consensus:

- the effective mobilisation of organisational self-interest as a basis for bargaining and exchange;
- the legitimation of wider interests in the goals of sustainable development;
- the creation of a broad, rather than narrow, base for inter-organisational relations; and
- recognition of the role and dynamics of trust.

Webb argues that the mobilisation of real, rather than apparent, self-interest is difficult and requires awareness, ability and skill, especially when those interests can best be maximised through bargaining and negotiation. Both self-interest and the interests of others have to be perceived and understood, and mutually satisfactory opportunities have to be sought:

Many in the public sector are not used to thinking in these terms and lack the necessary motivation and skills. The upshot is all too easily a failure to recognize the possibility of mutual gain or a failure to achieve it because relationships become one-sided, deteriorate and end in avoidance and conflict.[18]

The legitimation of wider interests is also challenging, particularly as politicians and administrators have a tendency to pay lip service to these without any real motivation to engage in processes that would lead to long-term societal change. Webb argues that the consistent involvement and leadership of senior administrators and politicians in shaping a more appropriate organisational culture must be supplemented by direct mobilisation of a wider public interest. Without this attendant pressure:

. . . inter-organisational and inter-professional collaboration may appear to be underpinned by a broad commitment to the wider good only to be shattered at the level of detail by divergent interpretations and priorities.[19]

The facilitation and mediation procedures described in the next section, and in Chapters 11 and 12, are one way of beginning a process of generating commitment from politicians to longer-term strategic initiatives and policy changes.

Similarly, collaboration and inter-organisational working at operational levels are likely to be undermined unless senior officials in departments, agencies and NGOs are committed to the process. Once again, consensus-building approaches set out at the onset to involve senior staff and politicians, to 'co-opt' them to the cause of sustainable development, while recognising that their time may be severely constrained. Here it is the case that top-down efforts are often required to generate a broad, sustainable framework for subsequent, more balanced efforts.

Finally, Webb argues that trust is the *sine qua non* of collaboration, and in its absence, conflict or avoidance are the likely outcome:

> ... small successes in joint endeavours may be needed to generate a virtuous spiral of expanding trust. Regard therefore has to be given to group dynamics, to the symbolic importance of including ... particular interests and individuals, and to showing proper respect for the joint activity and all the partners involved in it (eg by avoiding an 'inner core' of the 'senior' parties).[20]

The development of consensus, and subsequently joint implementation, is a challenging task. It cannot be treated as a peripheral activity. Fortunately, new skills and knowledge about the means of building consensus are becoming available every day, especially from trial and error field efforts, driven by the growing need for consensus on environmental issues. The next section outlines a 'facilitation' approach to networking and a more formal 'mediation' procedure. Both are gaining recognition as practical means of achieving consensus, notably over problems of environmental management.

Facilitation and mediation

The recent history of formal approaches to consensus building is described by Chapman:

> In the United States, Australia, Canada, and a host of other nations, mediation approaches have permitted and encouraged traditional foes to work together to develop creative and more satisfying solutions to challenging environmental problems. Even where scientific data are uncertain and policy objectives are conflicting, mediation techniques help clarify the scope and sources of parties' disagreements leading to more effective results. Disputes over the location of power plants, dam construction, water conservation and land use have all been mediated successfully.[21]

Consensus building by facilitation or mediation involves a dynamic process based on realisation of the broader nature of organisational self-interest and the potential for changing minds. The idea of changing perceptions is a key to the process: it assumes that most intelligent people are prepared to listen to reasonable arguments and to engage in an iterative cycle of learning which narrows the scope of disagreement and clarifies the difference between parties. The approach also assumes that a process of decision making will need to be newly fashioned to fit the issue at hand, and that it is unlikely that the existing institutional framework will be appropriate. Consensus building requires skill and perseverance, and is concerned with how things are done (process, thoughts and feelings) as well as what is done.

The following are guidelines for the types of issues which are amenable to facilitation/mediation techniques:

- A significant, visible environmental issue in which a response is needed and for which progress and resolution is possible.
- An issue which is of managable proportions related to the skills available for resolution.
- An issue which can generate commitment from participants with full decision making powers in their organisations.
- Potential commitment of stakeholders to long term participation and to the outcomes of the process.
- An issue with funding available to initiate the mediation or facilitation process.

There are basic differences between facilitation and mediation. Mediation is formal and carefully structured, focuses on clearly defined and contentious issues, and makes use of one or more trained mediators (as in the example of growth management in California discussed in Chapter 12). The facilitation approach is more useful when issues are ill-defined, when apparently smaller problems will need to be re-appraised and linked to larger issues of development, or when stakeholders or politicians are likely to be suspicious of the implications of the consensus-building process. The approach is more subtle and less direct than mediation and takes longer in order to allow key features of local politics and culture to be accommodated fully within the process. It is usually built into a process of 'unfolding' the issue, and of mutual self-discovery within a network, relying on one or more trusted, unbiased facilitators (as in the Chapter 11 case study).

One of the main tasks of the facilitator is to ensure equal participation among stakeholders. From this process, which may take some time, network members derive, through extended discussion, collaborative problem resolution which meets their individual and joint needs. The role of the facilitator is to:

> ... act as a catalyst to stimulate awareness of common interests, to introduce communication techniques that facilitate analysis and to provide information on organisational strategies employed in similar circumstances elsewhere.[22]

Mediation, on the other hand, is a form of assisted dispute resolution. While the facilitator generally assists parties in maintaining open and constructive dialogue, the mediator may challenge entrenched views, suggest alternatives and help parties bargain more effectively. Participants in a mediation process:

> ... learn to listen to each other's views and to communicate and identify their interests, sources of conflict and areas of agreement. The parties engage in joint fact-finding where appropriate, invent options for mutual gain, and reach voluntary, binding agreement based on trading or 'packaging' the options created.[23]

Three examples of the growing interest in mediation initiatives to contribute to environmental policy making are given by Chapman.[24] One, in Louisiana, involved senior officials from local and federal government, business, industry, civic organisations and environmental groups who negotiated a 'consensus risk-based ranking' of the 33 main environmental issues confronting the state, based on scientific studies and public concern. The result is a ten year action plan which commits the state to balance environmental protection and commercial development. In a second example, the Australian Resource Assessment Commission, charged with resolving resource use and environmental conflicts, has decided to use mediation to 'develop policies which meet the demands of sustainable development'.[25] In the third example, the United States Environmental Protection Agency (EPA) has decided to make a major shift of resources from defending its regulations against industry or environmental groups' attacks in the courts to involving these groups in the formulation of policy. Recently the EPA used this new initiative in formulating provisions relating to the Clean Air Act, with the result that the parties in the mediation have agreed not to bring any lawsuits to upset the settlements they reach.

Whether by facilitation or mediation, the achievement of consensus is satisfying for participants, and produces more sustainable decisions. The main outputs to be expected include:

Substantive outputs
- Incorporation of the maximum range of information into decisions.
- Politically realistic, practical and workable policies.
- A framework for further policy, legislation or judicial action.

Process outputs
- Legitimation by participants and their organisations, and strong commitment to implementation of policies and decisions.
- Increased co-operation, trust and collaboration among participants.
- Productive working relationships among participants in an action-centred network.

Nested networks

When the benefits of action-centred networking become apparent, layers of networks may begin to interlink or spawn new levels, in what we term 'nested' networks. By tapping the potential for vertical and horizontal integration, these can: contribute to sustainable development strategy and implementation, assist governments wrestling with questions about how best to allocate functions among jurisdictions, and help with the organisation of administration, monitoring and pollution control for effective action at various levels. For example, Holdgate argues that any sustainable development strategy requires components on at least three levels:

1 international (trade, economic, aid);
2 national (economic policy, education and training policy, arrangement for supply of commodities and marketing of goods; general infrastructure); and
3 local (resource survey and evaluation, resource development and management, training and support systems).[26]

This need for a linkage of levels of knowledge and action in the face of burgeoning complexity is, as yet, a largely unmet challenge of sustainable development. King and Schneider argue that the challenge posed by the emerging global environmental crisis requires that problems be simultaneously and comprehensively addressed at many different levels, by engaging in many possible solutions and by monitoring their impacts on other initiatives for the purposes of feedback and learning.[27] This challenges us to devise far more sophisticated organisational and information systems.

1   paring down complex bodies of information to their essential, interactive effects so as to avoid contributing to the already overwhelming problem of information overload; and

2   'translating' technical and scientific language so that the message is accessible to other disciplines, to politicians and to the public at large.

While this revolution in organisation and information constitutes a major world project for the early twenty-first century, and is part of the organisation–environment paradigm change we have identified, we believe the network approach can make a valuable contribution. The question is how to link initiatives at various levels, and how to carry out objectives in the most effective and efficient manner while avoiding traditional bureaucratic pitfalls and constraints and wasteful duplication of effort. In political terms, this parallels the question of subsidiarity among different levels of government, extending it beyond the allocation of political functions to the linkages between science (or systematic knowledge) and action (governance, [de]centralisation and empowerment).

The need for nested networks arises not only from the nature of the problems we face in attempting to realise sustainable development, but also in the possibility of increased effectiveness of management where networks reinforce one another at different levels. The five-level model from the Dutch National Environmental Policy Plan gives us an idea of the range of ecological tasks in a systematic framework towards sustainable development (Figure 9.2). The tasks cannot be isolated from one another, as there are two many linkages and interactive effects. But nor can all the tasks, at all the levels, be undertaken by one organisation or one network - the law of requisite variety, as relevant to organisations as to biosystems, would be violated and the complexity and challenges to control would result in management failure, even if political commitment did exist.

The notion of a series of nested, action-oriented networks provides an organisational framework for consensus building, co-ordination and reinforcing organisational learning at many levels. The concept of nodes of excellence with the nested networks would further contribute to the required learning process. Among the world's advanced scientific organisations, such network formation is already occurring around the issue of global climate change. What has not been done, however, is to devise an effective means of linking scientific knowledge to integrated action at various levels.

The concept of the nested network has already been tested in the field in a modest way in a few of the case studies. The IDEA programme (Chapter 11) linked seven 'country tasks' in Africa, Asia and South America with three international support networks of natural and social scientists and legal advisers in about thirty-five

THE 5-LEVEL MODEL

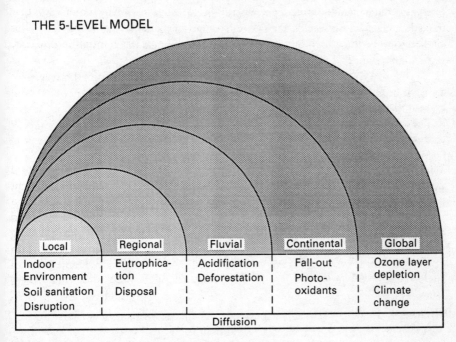

Figure 9.2 *Linkage of levels in sustainable development tasks*
Source: National Environmental Policy Plan of the Netherlands[29]

countries, within the broad framework of the Commonwealth Consultative Group on Technology Management. The following benefits were observed:

- communication, without organisation in a hierarchical structure, enhances the creativity of members and sharpens discussions to the task at hand;
- an interdisciplinary diversity of expertise and advice, often from senior people with a wealth of experience, can usually be provided at low or no cost, to back up local efforts and link them into a wider knowledge base;
- regular and supportive reviews of country task progress, by members of the network, results in constructive criticism and interactive peer review. This provides both motivation (which can wane when local teams feel isolated) and reinforcement, and generates confidence in local actions;
- continuing systematic analysis (via action research) supports and critically reviews the projects and consolidates aspects of transferable learning which are disseminated to, and beyond, the wider parent networks; and
- the international network, especially when members are on field visits, provides much credibility to the local team and enhances their status, thus contributing to the visibility of the environment problem or development task addressed and drawing new members into the local network.

Within the IDEA programme, the notion of nested networks also explains why local network members, say in Guyana, also see themselves as members of the wider IDEA network, and the still wider CCGTM networks, with members in about thirty-five countries. Each member and each network can call on the entire network for support, free advice and peer review. This support is not external to the management process, as the more traditional consultant might be, but expands the team addressing any particular task to include expertise from other countries.

The team in Guyana, for example, in developing the country's first national system for environmental management, was thus able to draw on field-tested information on environmental standards, impact assessment and training expertise from the Malaysian government, national environmental reporting skills from the Zambian government, private sector scientific expertise on chemical analysis from India, and legal expertise from London, all at little or no cost to the Guyanese. The international network also provides a means of diffusion of additional knowledge generated in areas such as environmental legislation, pollution control technology and environmental monitoring, throughout the network.

Generation of replicable learning

A recent seminar in Washington on 'Improving Management in Developing Countries', hosted by the American Consortium for International Public Administration, noted:

> There is a rapidly growing experience . . . of institutional development . . . However, there is a great need to document such experience as a basis for in-depth analysis of both successes and those less successful. At present there is just not enough known to provide the kind of firm knowledge base necessary to approach new institutional development undertaking with confidence. There is no adequate kit of management tools for people-oriented projects.[28]

As stated above, a corollary of action learning is action research, in which any case study generates not only direct action, but provides a field experiment for studying environmental management. The benefits to action researchers from attachment to active networks are obvious, and their key task is to generate transferable knowledge about the programme. This is done by recording the process as it develops, analysing the recording, making connections with other developments in the area, referring to the wider academic literature of institutional development and environmental management, and returning that information to the project teams and the wider network. The research team also provides the opportunity for members of the network to publish the results of their work in learned journals and to consider innovative means of dissemination. In all cases, unless we are to continue to reinvent the wheel, and thereby waste scarce resources, we must review what has been accomplished and assess the degree of success or failure.

Paying for networking

The case studies below demonstrate the potential for cost-effective network support for national or regional action on environmental management tasks. However, it would be misleading to imply that successful, task-oriented networks do not require considerable nurturing and maintenance to survive and prosper, and therefore a source of outside funding. Any network made up of senior people from government, business and the community, and researchers, consultants and facilitators, requires administrative support, financial control and, most important, some central focus.

The networks reported in the case studies below are mainly supported by enlightened governments and agencies, including business in the case of the Groundwork Trusts. We cannot point to any examples of wholly self-funding management networks in the environment field. Part of the problem is that it is difficult to attract interest in process innovation, compared to more sympathetic causes. The charitable organisations know this well and gear their fund-raising campaigns accordingly.

In addition to government and multi-lateral funding, there is potential to raise funds from business and from charitable foundations, or to put together consortia of funders. Multiple funding is increasingly common in research, but the experience is that a lot of resources can go on administering to the needs of the numerous funders themselves. Businesses may be sympathetic, but many have a strong interest in long term strategic planning in their locale. They will need to have visible outputs, and it is possible to envision 'sponsored mediation' of serious environmental disputes. The California growth management project, for example, (Chapter 12) received major financial and in-kind support from a consortium of funders including: the state assembly, a major bank, a large property developer, a charitable foundation, the California Housing Council and two universities. Additional support came from local government and public agencies, as well as from NGOs concerned about environment, conservation and housing issues.

The whole question of financial support for sustainable network (and other process) initiatives requires much more consideration. One rule of thumb is to start with smaller, highly visible problems, and to earn credibility. Otherwise potential funders will be dubious about permitting the required degree of financial control.

CONCLUSION

The action-centred network can be seen as an emerging 'soft technology' for environmental management in many different fields. The approach is an appropriate organisational tool for managing sustainable development because it fits the nature of the challenges posed by shifting to sustainable development paths. In the face of turbulent, shifting problems on many scales that cross administrative, political and disciplinary boundaries, it allows the construction of flexible teams, which also cross those boundaries. Such teams can generate new information and pool resources that would otherwise not be brought together. The case studies in the next four chapters illustrate different forms of action-centred networking, at scales of activity from the local community to the nation-state.

PART V

Case studies in innovative management

Part V Case studies in innovative management

This section describes four case studies of innovative management for sustainable development. All demonstrate major aspects of the action-centred network approach, particularly partnership between government, business and community groups, and consensus-building as a pre-condition for action on issues relevant to sustainable development.

The projects these case studies describe put the action-centred network model into practice at different geographic levels and in very different ways. At the local or neighbourhood level, the Groundwork Foundation has established 23 Groundwork Trusts in Britain and four more in Europe to rehabilitate the environment in derelict industrial areas, to attract new businesses, and to encourage local people to become involved in environmental action. Groundwork also mobilises the private sector, locally and nationally, in new and innovative ways.

At a city-wide or regional level, the IDEA (Innovations in Development for Environmental Action) Programme is involved in building organisational and human resource capacity in watershed management in Ghana, Zambia and Zimbabwe; in waste management in Nigeria and Malaysia; and in resource management in Mauritius and Guyana. These projects are experiments in improving local management skills by the development of action-centred networks, and are integrated internationally through the Commonwealth Consultative Group on Technology Management. IDEA projects begin with specific environmental problems, such as water pollution, and then steadily build up interest and teamwork to the point of tackling real challenges in sustainable development, such as watershed management.

At the provincial or state level, in California, the Growth Management Consensus Project is working to break a classic political deadlock between proponents of economic growth and environmentalists. The environmental risks are enormous – already pollution, water shortages, congestion and urban sprawl are engulfing large areas of this beautiful and prosperous state. By a highly structured and innovative process of mediation, the Legislature of the State of California is attempting to fashion a new consensus on the nature of sustainable development, and the policies needed to prepare for it over the coming decade.

At the national level, a striking example of consensus-building and integrated environmental planning is provided by the National Environment Policy Plan (NEPP) in the Netherlands. The process of developing the ambitious Plan involves discussions between different environmental constituencies and different departments and tiers of government. The Plan generated from this process is as yet unmatched in the industrial world in its environmental goals, the degree of integration between areas of policy, and the level of consensus achieved, and aspired to, among interest groups and parties.

10 Groundwork Trusts: environmental rehabilitation through business – community partnerships

It is at the community level that most is being done to protect the environment. We can all too easily get caught up in global negotiations whilst forgetting that people need to be free to pursue sustainable development for themselves. The reconciliation of environmental protection with economic advance essentially comes down to a mass of local problems.

HRH The Prince of Wales, March 1991[1]

The Groundwork Trusts are widely regarded as a highly effective networking initiative in the field of environmental management. The network develops projects for environmental improvement in run down industrial areas and derelict urban land. It brings together companies, public agencies and community groups in partnership ventures. Groundwork originated in the United Kingdom, where it now has 28 operating trusts across the country. The Groundwork approach is currently being introduced into continental Europe and it is set to be the model for similar developments in other European Community countries. Groundwork is important because it is a successful and growing operation based on the principle of action-centred networking, partnership and improved mutual understanding between community groups, public agencies and business, and takes an integrated approach to environmental management and community development. Groundwork projects aim to improve local quality of life, foster links between companies and communities, and involve all parties, notably businesses, in environmental management.

ORGANISATION AND AIMS OF THE GROUNDWORK TRUST

Development of the network

The Groundwork movement developed in the early 1980s from initiatives in environmental regeneration launched by the Countryside Commission, a public agency concerned with rural development in England and Wales. The Commission devised Operation Groundwork, an experimental initiative in the renewal of rundown and derelict areas on the fringes of two towns in North West England, St Helens and Knowsley. The aim of this venture was to demonstrate how abandoned and neglected land could be regenerated for leisure, encouragement of wildlife and flora, agriculture and general benefit to local communities. The Commission's concern was to find ways of 'greening' the towns by rehabilitating wasteland.

The problems that the initiative set out to tackle are well-known and extensive in all industrialised countries, and will be increasingly familiar in the newly industrialising countries: the degradation of urban environments as old manufacturing industry declines; the impoverished natural features of industrial areas; the low quality of life of communities in areas deprived of both green space and employers. The relentless post-war decline of British heavy industry accelerated in the 1970s with the oil price shocks, fierce competition from overseas, and widespread failure to modernise plants dating from earlier phases of industrial development. The deep recession of 1980–81 in the UK saw factory closures and the abandonment of much industrial land; this added to long standing problems of derelict land in the old manufacturing areas of the country.

The original Operation Groundwork was managed by a 'Groundwork Trust', and the success of the project led to the establishment by 1983 of six Trusts, all in the North West of England, a region that had suffered many factory closures and had large areas of derelict industrial land. By 1992 the network had grown to include 28 Groundwork Trusts in England and Wales. As the Trusts developed their role in 'greening' cities, towns and suburbs, sponsorship by the Countryside Commission became inappropriate, and a new framework for funding was set up. Since 1985 the network has been co-ordinated nationally by the Groundwork Foundation, based in Birmingham and supported by funding from the Department of the Environment and other sources. The network is especially extensive in the North of England, but Groundwork Trusts have been established in southern cities such as Bristol, in the old mining valleys of South Wales and around London. The large areas of derelict land in Britain's cities and urban fringes provide considerable scope for continuing growth in the network.

The Groundwork Foundation plans to expand the network to reach 50 Trusts by the mid-1990s. The Groundwork movement will also develop in other member states of the European Community. By 1991 feasibility studies on the export of the Groundwork model to the rest of Europe had been carried out and European Commission funding had been obtained to support project work in Lille, France and in Nijmegen, Netherlands. Experts from two Groundwork Trusts in northern England are involved in the development of these projects and in providing training for local staff. Exploratory work has also been undertaken with potential partners in Japan.

The partnership approach

The guiding principle of the Groundwork network is the development of projects in partnership with business, public authorities and voluntary agencies and community groups. Groundwork's corporate logo stresses the theme: the slogan *Partnership for Action* is as prominent as the name Groundwork. The network's projects are all designed to foster partnership projects that contribute to environmental improvement leading to enhanced quality of life and local prosperity. Environmental renewal and economic development are seen as complementary rather than as irreconcilable. The Foundation's Chief Executive has said that the aim of Groundwork activity in a community should be '... to encourage residents to take a pride in their surroundings once more, encourage industry to stay or move in, and gradually to renew environmental and economic prosperity'.[2]

Groundwork recognises that, working alone, it cannot achieve the enormous changes needed to transform degraded environments. Nonetheless, Groundwork projects have a crucial role to play in demonstrating the potential for environmental improvement within relatively short timescales given co-operation from business, public agencies and local communities. The practical demonstration of environmental regeneration can give confidence to communities that have suffered economic decline and ecological damage. It also is a key part of the long term process of winning local commitment to sustainable environmental management.

Funding and organisation

The funding of the network reflects the emphasis on partnership: at the centre, the Foundation receives an annual sum for the support of the Trusts (over £4.2 million in 1991/92) from the British government through the Department of the Environment. This sum is trebled by contributions to projects involving local Trusts by business and local government bodies. A key aspect of Groundwork funding is the use of public sector funds to lever in resources from the private sector in the form of project funding and sponsorship deals. Groundwork Trusts also receive funds from the European Commission. Large private and public sector employers provide management expertise, through staff secondments. Funds are also generated through Trusts' professional commercial work in landscape design and project management.

The Groundwork network comprises the national Foundation and the local Trusts. The individual Trusts, which develop and manage local projects, are all separate registered charities and limited companies with no share capital, and operate with considerable autonomy. The Groundwork Foundation manages the development of the overall network, acts as a support system for the Trusts, liaises at national level with government, industry and other partners, and negotiates the creation of new Trusts. A key role for the Foundation is to develop national initiatives that can be implemented locally by the Trusts. The Trusts are represented on the board of the Foundation, and the Foundation is a founding member of all the Trusts.

The Groundwork Trusts are established by the Foundation in response to local demand, which can originate from local government agencies, businesses or other organisations. The process of setting up a Trust may be lengthy, as the Foundation is concerned to ensure that a new Groundwork initiative receives commitment to partnership from local government, key local businesses, public agencies, environmental groups and other voluntary bodies. Considerable negotation may be required to overcome any initial suspicion, for instance from established environmental groups and their funders that a new competitor for local resources is appearing. If such difficulties cannot be resolved, a Trust will not be established. Trusts are designed to have a long term role, and so a special investment of time and effort is made at the outset to establish the partnership ethos among local stakeholders, and to win support.

The Trusts operate autonomously within the broad framework for development set out by the Foundation. Each has a board of directors composed of representatives from different sectors, typically from the relevant local government body or bodies, businesses and voluntary groups. In addition, the Groundwork Foundation is always a founding board member and sponsor. A key aim is to ensure that the board reflects the range of interests in the area. The Trusts have Executive Directors with a small team of professionals expert in fields such as landscape design and project management, and financial and administrative staff. Groundwork Trusts may be centred on a city or town, or on a wider area cutting across administrative boundaries.

GROUNDWORK IN ACTION

The range of Groundwork activity

The partnership approach means that a Trust is concerned to act as a catalyst, facilitating the work of its partners as well as carrying out project work itself. Trust directors have a key role in raising sponsorship for projects and liaising with partners, and in contracting work in landscape regeneration to other voluntary bodies. There is particular stress on obtaining volunteer support from local residents and employees of sponsor companies. Trusts are essentially in the business of orchestration of environmental projects: securing a mix of national and local sponsorship from private and public sources, and deploying the physical and human resources of the private sector, voluntary groups and individual volunteers to blend with the expertise of local Groundwork staff.

The range of project work carried out by the Groundwork Trusts and their local partners is wide, covering the following areas:

- environmental improvement of derelict industrial sites and other rundown urban areas such as housing estates;
- landscape improvement for industrial sites;
- development of urban fringe sites to encourage wildlife;
- consultancy to business on environmental policy;
- creation of leisure trails and parks on former industrial land;
- tree and flower planting schemes;
- consultancy on landscape design;
- development of urban farms;
- training courses in conservation skills and environmental management;
- assistance for voluntary bodies in developing local projects;
- environmental education projects in local schools.

Groundwork uses the network to transfer information about different projects and examples of good practice between the Trusts, resulting in a continuous process of learning. All projects are implemented at the Trust level, but the Foundation also develops programmes that can be piloted locally and then implemented across the network. These are designed to attract private sector sponsorship: after an idea has been tried out successfully within the network the Foundation will seek financial support from major corporations. While funding from public sources is also sought, special emphasis is placed on bringing the private sector into initiatives in a significant way, backing schemes locally with money, expertise and publicity. National programmes include the 'Greenlink' initiative.

The Greenlink initiative

Groundwork is involved in many schemes designed to improve education and training in environmental management, and a key element of the network's strategy is to raise business and community awareness of environmental issues. Building up environmental awareness in schools is an increasingly important part of Groundwork's programme. The Greenlink initiative is a notably innovative example of this aspect of the network's activities. Greenlink is a Groundwork venture developed in partnership with Esso UK and with the help of Television South Education. The scheme was launched in 1991 with Government encouragement. The aim is to develop long term partnerships between schools and local industry built around a shared concern for the environment. The scheme allows great flexibility in the choice of projects by schools and companies, but there is a common framework of activity. The partner school and company choose achievable aims connected with the company's environmental policies. These involve the development of a teaching plan by the school, including site visits and classroom work, and the integration of environmental issues affecting the plant in the agenda of both school and company. The aim is increased mutual understanding between schools and businesses, and the development of environmental education across the whole school curriculum.

The scheme was piloted in four Groundwork Trust areas around England, under the guidance of a steering committee of experts from education and industry. Partners in the pilot projects included small junior schools, large comprehensive schools (high schools), small firms, major corporations and local government bodies. The pilot projects have been concerned with the integration of environmental issues across the curriculum, and the investigation of environmental questions from a variety of points of view. Promotional literature for the Greenlink initiative emphasises the benefits that can accrue to both partners. For schools, there is the opportunity to experiment with new methods of project work and new techniques for delivering the curriculum, and to give teachers more experience of industry. For the participating companies and other employers, there is the chance to improve their 'environmental friendliness', public relations and staff morale. They can meet children face to face to explain what industry does and why.

Because Greenlink is a new venture with the aim of fostering long term partnerships, its full value cannot be assessed yet. However, the pilot projects are considered a success. Stereotypical views on both sides can be challenged and awareness of the scope for environmental improvement raised in companies and schools. There is no limit to the range of projects that could be developed by partner schools and companies. Moreover, the link with the Groundwork Trust network should allow for effective dissemination of lessons about good and bad practice around the country, facilitating a process of learning from experience as new partnerships are created.

Case study: the Groundwork Trust in Britain's 'Black Country'

How does a Groundwork Trust put the concept of partnership into action? Below, we examine the experience of one of the Trusts, based in the so-called 'Black Country' in the English Midlands, the original heartland of the Industrial Revolution. The region is full of: run down inner city districts in need of greening and improved community leisure facilities; abandoned industrial land in need of rehabilitation and landscaping; degraded land in urban fringe areas capable of being converted into parkland or wildlife refuges; and functioning factory sites with derelict or ill-used land.

The origins of the Black Country Groundwork Trust (BCGT) lie in the decline of the region's industrial base. The recession of the early 1980s led to a dramatic rate of closure of manufacturing plants and to widespread dereliction, with ensuing vandalism and pollution, and the reinforcement of an already poor environmental image for the region. The four boroughs that fall within the area have a combined population of over 9 million people, and cover some 34,000 hectares. The region falls within the 'West Midlands Assisted Area', a zone designated by central government for public expenditure to stimulate local economic redevelopment and urban renewal.

The four boroughs have set up joint ventures to promote the area's potential to investors and to improve its public image through initiatives for new jobs and environmental regeneration. The Groundwork Trust was established after much local discussion and negotiation, once senior officials in the boroughs became convinced that Groundwork could play a major role in facilitating partnerships for environmental renewal in the area, especially by securing private sector sponsorship for projects, helping to secure additional funds from central government and other public agencies, and bringing in new ideas from the experience of the nationwide Groundwork movement. A further consideration was that the BCGT could carry out projects that crossed local political boundaries in a way that would have been very difficult for the individual borough authorities to tackle in an integrated way. One example is the regeneration of environments in the valley of the river Stour, which runs across borough boundaries.

The BCGT was set up with the backing of the local boroughs, private companies and voluntary agencies, and declared its aim to be the development of projects that would support the overall environmental strategy already devised by the boroughs. A board was set up including representatives of the four boroughs, local business and local environmental groups. Board meetings are held alternately in each of the boroughs and board members are also involved in visits to project sites, though not in detailed project management. At the district level there are meetings involving local government officials to discuss the progress of individual projects and improve co-ordination and exchange of information.

The BCGT measures its achievement of objectives against a set of performance indicators covering five key areas of activity: improvement of the environment; partnership with other organisations; active involvement of local residents; work and job creation; and public awareness, education and training. The performance indicators used by the Trust place great emphasis on impact on people as well as on the physical environment.

The BCGT committed itself at the outset to developing the established range of Groundwork activities and also to providing support and guidance to local community groups carrying out environmental projects. In addition it planned to raise revenue from 'design and build' landscaping services for the private sector in order to supplement grants from the local sponsoring organisations. A crucial element in the approach developed by the BCGT is the determination not to duplicate or compete with the work of other environmental bodies in the area. This involves sub-contracting work to other voluntary agencies, passing ideas on to community groups, and taking up suggestions and ideas from them in turn.

The BCGT has established an initiative called 'GreenCare', which is a mechanism for picking up ideas for environmental improvement from local residents, schools, employers and community groups and helping to realise them with the backing of the BCGT's skills in technical support with landscape design, project management, publicity, provision of tools and equipment, and fund-raising. GreenCare deliberately downplays the 'Groundwork' name in order to minimise feelings among local environmental groups that the BCGT is 'taking over'; and it is designed to give a sense of ownership and achievement to groups in the community which might otherwise feel marginalised and unheard by local government and business. Groups of local residents, schools or employers can thus form their own 'GreenCare Groups' that can draw on the skills of the BCGT in order to develop their own ideas for improving the community environment.

KEY LESSONS FROM THE GROUNDWORK EXPERIENCE

The main elements of the Groundwork approach comprise a model of objectives and values for networked multi-sector projects in environmental management.

National level:
- develop policy to facilitate network growth;
- develop national and network-wide initiatives;
- provide support service to local Trusts;
- facilitate transfer of information;
- secure public and private sector finance;
- form links with private sector, voluntary sector, and public agencies;
- attract and develop personnel.

Local level:
- win trust and commitment from public, private and voluntary sector bodies;
- attract private sector funding to add to public funds;
- act as a catalyst for environmental projects linking business, public bodies and community groups;
- implement local schemes based on national initiatives.

Key values:
- emphasis on multi-sector partnership;
- non-threatening to other voluntary sector interests;
- non-confrontational approach to business;
- long-term commitment to raising awareness in business, schools and the wider community of the need for sustainable environmental management.

What lessons can be gained from the progress of the Groundwork Trusts? It is clear that the Trust model has become a recognised pattern of good practice among policy makers in central government and is increasingly winning support in local government and business. As mentioned above, the model is now ready for 'export' to the rest of the European Community. Several elements of the Groundwork approach stand out as good practice for other initiatives in environmental management.

The Groundwork Trusts' working method exemplifies what we have termed 'action-centred networking' – the cultivation of partnerships between organisations and sectors and the exchange of information with a view always to developing practical projects. The approach also emphasises and facilitates learning between Trusts and between them and their partners.

Groundwork is itself an action-centred network. The Trusts have great autonomy of action within a general strategic framework developed by the Foundation. National programmes are devised by the Foundation in partnership with Trusts and others, and local piloting allows experiments and discoveries about good practice that can flow around the network. In funding and policy development Groundwork has created a fruitful blend of 'top-down' and 'bottom-up' approaches to environmental management.

Groundwork also practises an integrated approach to networking: its activities bring together urban regeneration, environmental education and community development in cohesive projects and programmes. Projects are never just about physical development or repair work: they also are designed to assist in achieving greater awareness in companies and communities of the importance of care for the environment.

The emphasis on bringing in private sector funding means that Groundwork tends not to be seen as 'confrontational' by the private sector. The approach to private sponsors is always based on a commitment to businesslike partnership aimed at producing mutual benefits. This approach may draw criticism from environmental campaign groups on the basis that Groundwork does not challenge industry's values enough. However, there is clearly a need to encourage firms to take action on their impact on the local environment in such a way as to increase the chances of making the experience popular with employees and local people. In this way, the 'cosmetic' projects of landscape improvement carried out by Groundwork Trusts may create a bridgehead in companies for more radical ideas on production methods and product lines.[3] Groundwork can help companies go further: the network has an 'environmental review' service, sponsored by British Petroleum and the Department of the Environment, intended to help small and medium-sized firms understand their impact on the environment. Linked to this is the emphasis on long term development of understanding of environmental issues in local communities: Groundwork is, through its involvement in environmental education and volunteering schemes, engaged in the business of 'winning hearts and minds' to the cause of taking the environment seriously.

An important aspect of the Groundwork approach to setting up Trusts is the focus on careful preparation of the ground for networking in order to avoid, or at least minimise, suspicions and jealousies on the part of other voluntary sector bodies and from local public agencies. This is a fundamental problem in partnership building in areas of policy where many voluntary and community groups exist and newcomers may be suspected of 'parachuting in' and trying to impose their patent solutions for the community's problems.

Finally, the Groundwork experience reminds us that the city and the town are environments too – something often in danger of being forgotten as we debate the fate of the rainforests and other wildernesses. Initiatives to improve the urban environment are critical to sustainable development: we need to keep people in the cities in order to preserve countryside and the dynamism of city centres, and this will only happen if the urban environment is enhanced.[4] Groundwork projects cannot 'green' whole cities, and their regeneration strategies may focus on very long range improvement, but what they achieve with specific projects is visible, valuable and accessible to large numbers of people: it brings tangible improvement to people's lives as well as to wildlife, flora and buildings, and it encourages widespread participation in environmental management. Again, in this respect Groundwork activity provides a basis for long term environmental education among individuals and companies.

NETWORKS BEYOND THE GROUNDWORK MODEL IN THE UK

The success of the Groundwork Trusts has been paralleled by the development of other forms of networking and partnership for local environmental improvement in the UK and beyond. In the UK, many places have Wildlife Trusts, focusing on wildlife conservation and habitat protection: some have set up consultancy arms, as has Groundwork, in order to generate revenue and assist in the spread of information and development of partnerships.[5] The various Wildlife Trusts frequently work in close collaboration with their local Groundwork counterparts.

In the late 1980s a new variation on the theme of partnership with business emerged in the shape of the Industry and Nature Conservation Association (INCA). INCAs, promoted by the public nature conservation agency English Nature, are intended to be 'bridge building' organisations formed in the same spirit as Groundwork Trusts. INCAs will encourage companies to do more to protect natural sites and wildlife affected by their operations. An INCA is a forum in which industry and conservation groups can come to a better mutual understanding, and can develop projects for improved wildlife and habitat protection on industrial land. In 1989 the UK's first INCA was established in the county of Cleveland, a heavy industrial region in the North East of England. The area contains massive chemical plants run by the giant corporation ICI, and also estuarine sites for waterfowl and flora of international importance. The INCA partners include ICI itself, local government bodies, the local Wildlife Trust, and several other companies, mainly from the chemicals sector. The Cleveland INCA is likely to be the first of a number of similar partnership ventures around the country.

Groundwork is thus accompanied by a variety of initiatives designed to foster partnerships between environmental agencies and the private and public sectors.[6] These ventures are a valuable complement to regulatory systems and campaigning criticism of industry. Groundwork and other partnerships provide bridges between companies, communities and environmental protection groups. They allow for learning and gradual stimulation of interest in and commitment to environmental protection. The local work of the Groundwork movement and of initiatives such as INCA is of modest scope, and is unspectacular and unglamorous. But the local projects add up to a major nationwide development in the regeneration of environments in decline. This is essential to achieving a long term change of heart in business in favour of the integration of commercial concerns with respect for the environment, both natural and urban. The Groundwork partnership approach is no substitute for campaigning action against polluting industries, or for public regulation of industrial environmental impacts. However, it serves as a valuable complementary force in the slow process of fostering commitment to environmental management and social responsibility among businesses, their employees, and local communities. Wider diffusion of the Groundwork model and of network schemes such as INCAs would be a valuable step in helping to make new industrial development and modernisation sustainable.

11   The IDEA Programme: Innovations in Development for Environmental Action

This chapter describes an experimental programme to enhance local management capability for addressing serious environmental problems in seven lower income Commonwealth countries. The programme is called IDEA – Innovations in Development for Environmental Action. IDEA has developed action–centred networks led by senior scientists or public administrators in Malaysia, Mauritius, Zimbabwe, Zambia, Ghana, Nigeria and Guyana. There is also a small, worldwide interdisciplinary support team which, together with the seven local teams, constitutes an international IDEA network.

The seven projects represent a cross-section of challenges to environmental management. They can be grouped under three headings as follows.

Watershed management: the development of mechanisms to reduce pollution and promote co-ordinated watershed management in the Densu River Basin and Weija Reservoir in Ghana; improved institutional co-ordination to reduce pollution in the Harare watershed, Zimbabwe; and improved management of the Copperbelt and lower reaches of the Kafue River in Zambia.

Waste management: the establishment of an innovative co-operative arrangement for common wastewater treatment facilities among small metal finishing industries in the Klang Valley of Malaysia, and the development of policy guidelines and institutional arrangements to reduce unregulated waste disposal in Lagos State, Nigeria.

Resource management: promotion of the use of replacement construction materials as an alternative to coral sand depletion in Mauritius, and the development of a legal and policy framework for management of mineral exploitation in Guyana.

For each of these projects, management issues have been addressed at the policy, strategy and project levels by both direct and indirect action (Figure 11.1). Direct action includes, for example:

- the development of better policy and legislation to control the environmental effects of gold mining in Guyana;
- new institutional arrangements, such as the new co-operative of small scale industrialists for pollution control in Malaysia; and
- direct links to community leaders and NGOs, as in the towns and villages of the Densu Basin in Ghana.

Indirect action includes, for example:

- building awareness in field visits and meetings of industrialists, local government officials and the IDEA teams;
- using various media such as newspaper articles, posters and slide presentations; and

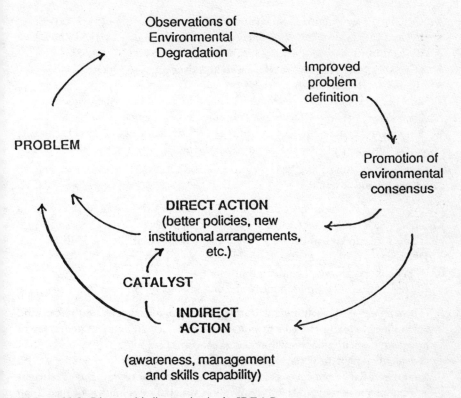

Figure 11.1 *Direct and indirect action in the IDEA Programme*
Source: Carley and Smith

- developing management and technical skills, for example, with the Science
  Council of Zimbabwe or the National Council for Oceanographic and Marine
  Research in Nigeria.

Within a project, action is taken only after careful analysis of the problem and of
potential constraints that could inhibit successful management. In keeping with the
network approach, each IDEA project promotes new formal and informal linkages
within government, and beyond government to the business, voluntary and
community sectors. This structure is fostered by informal communication channels
and working methods not always available to line departments and other
government agencies.

IDEA is of interest because it validates a number of the concepts described above
for improving performance in the management of environment and development
planning. In particular, it provides an illustration of the non-hierarchical, action-
centred network as a complement to traditional bureaucratic structures. Because of
its grounding in topical environmental issues, IDEA contributes to an understanding
of a practical methodology for generating these networks.

IDEA also validates the usefulness of the action research methodology for learning
about good management. The benefits of this learning are relevant to:

- the pilot project countries, which now have local nodes of professional experience in innovative problem assessment and management of environment for development;
- other countries, which could share this knowledge and experience;
- the entire IDEA Network, which provides the opportunity for diffusing this knowledge within and outside the Commonwealth, and which channels new knowledge back to the local nodes of professional experience; and
- funding and bilateral aid bodies, who can use the knowledge as part of criteria to assess the degree of good management in the use of their funds for development.

THE IDEA PROGRAMME

IDEA is part of, and administered by, the Commonwealth Consultative Group on Technology Management (CCGTM), recently established by the Commonwealth Heads of Government within the Commonwealth Secretariat. The pilot programme of IDEA has been funded by the Natural Resource and Environment Department of the UK Overseas Development Administration.

The objectives of the programme at the outset were:

1 To examine both institutional frameworks, and management strategies and techniques, which constrain or enhance the implementation of development programmes with major environmental concerns.
2 To identify pilot projects in African, Asian and Caribbean Commonwealth countries. Each project was to be an example of a clear cut, current environmental problem which requires institutional mechanisms for mediation at the policy, strategy and project levels. Each case study was to represent an environmental issue sufficiently important that failure to promote such mediation mechanisms could seriously hinder development.
3 To identify lessons at both country and overall generic levels for management and assessment of development programmes which will assist in a review of current management practice.

The IDEA Programme has taken a broad view of the components of institutional frameworks as encompassing organisational, legal and human resources development. The areas of critical concern in institutional development as identified by many international agencies are relevant to IDEA:

- the host country policy environment;
- the potential of various forms of organisation;
- the importance of institutional learning capacity;
- the problem of transferring knowledge, co-ordination and linkage among agencies;
- the improvement of management systems; and
- the role of local initiative and participation.[1]

To this list, the IDEA team added the importance of parallel local and international networks to support initiatives in sustainable environmental management. Within IDEA, paramount importance is attached to local initiative and participation. IDEA addresses the organisational and human resource constraints which operate on government policy and implementation systems, in the specific context of the tasks identified.

The IDEA programme has developed so far in two phases. Phase I, a period of six months in 1988–89, was initiated at a meeting at the Commonwealth Science Council in London, which identified themes for individual country tasks, and a research team leader in each country. The agreement of the relevant authorities (for example, the Office of the Prime Minister or the main Financial Ministry) in each country was also secured during this period. This gave political credibility to each project at its initial stage, and encouraged (but did not ensure) a process of horizontal integration among relevant government departments.

It was also agreed by the first members of the network that no project would be selected which could be construed as destabilising to the government of the host country. In one case, a project which had religious and ethnic overtones was rejected by the Office of the Prime Minister. This was accepted by the local team, and thus by the network, because the main aim of IDEA is to generate new management skills, rather than to solve any particular problem.

Phase II, lasting a further two and a half years, consisted of implementation of each of the management and action projects identified, and a series of joint meetings of all the IDEA country team leaders and representatives to review the progress of the research teams and to offer guidance on possible future steps. In addition to the tangible outputs of each country task, reported below, both phases of IDEA have been subject to monitoring and analysis. This provides both a vehicle for additional learning for IDEA teams, and a means of generating transferable learning from the overall process.

One strength of IDEA is that it grounds transferable learning about environmental management strategies in practical development activity, thus fulfilling a basic criterion of the action research methodology. Rather than attempting to adopt uniform solutions, the environmental problems identified as critical in the seven countries have been redefined into a series of positive 'management and action' projects, supported by IDEA's network and information services, environmental advisory services, and training and research methodology (Figure 11.2).

Key concepts

1   An individual, called the **team leader**, serves as a catalyst to the entire process. The team leader is invited to participate by the larger network, and selected for his or her ability to take a broad, process-oriented perspective on local environmental problems. The team leader is usually a senior scientist, administrator or professor from a potential linking-pin organisation.

2   The **selection of a serious environmental problem** is crucial. The choice is made by the local team, of a problem of national importance which it is also possible to reduce or resolve. The problem provides a case study for learning about the environmental management process and for developing new skills.

3   A local '**project advisory group**', is formed, which provides relevant stakeholding agencies and individuals with the opportunity for participation in

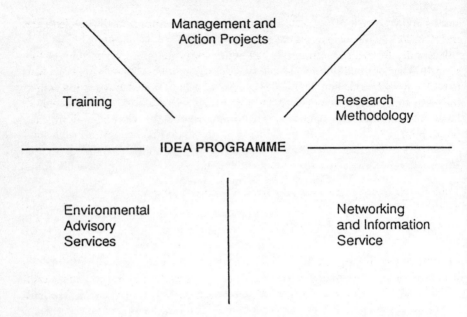

Figure 11.2 *Components of the IDEA Programme*

the definition of the problem and in its resolution. Each group is typically 8–14 people.

4   An **IDEA researcher** is hired locally to develop the project under the guidance of the team leader and advisory group. These three, together, make up the local IDEA team.

5   The local team has a **facilitating and/or mediating** role among the various stakeholders as necessary. Iterative problem definition broadens the perspective of team members and gradually builds up consensus and commitment to the resolution of the problem.

6   As the local network develops, it receives financial and administrative support, advice and peer review from the **international IDEA/CCGTM network**.

7   Because any new organisation may appear threatening to existing institutional arrangements and individuals in positions of power, IDEA local networks are developed only at **a pace which is politically and culturally sustainable**, by a process much akin to traditional community development, but at a regional scale.

THE IDEA PROJECTS

The IDEA projects have been extensively documented and the intention here is only to summarise the main points to arise from the case studies.[2] It is also important to note that, although this is a report on a research project of limited duration, by the very nature of the networks, a dynamic process has been initiated which will continue, although not necessarily in its present form. This is true of all the case studies in this book, and a general feature of the network approach. The projects are therefore mostly reported as ongoing.

Naturally the degree of progress for each country task varies according to the severity of the original problem and the individual national characteristics relevant to problem resolution. The extent of progress is reported below. However, it is within the methodological expectations of IDEA that this variety provides a cross-section of likely institutional constraints and thus contributes to learning within the programme.

Watershed management

Watershed management in the Densu Basin of Ghana*

The original concern, arising out of the project leader's scientific studies, was with the long term effects of pollution and siltation in the Weija Reservoir on the Densu River, which supplies about half the drinking water of Accra, as well as irrigation further downstream. The project objectives are:

- to rehabilitate the Densu River basin ecosystem and thereby improve the flow of the river, minimise flood risk, and improve the quality of the water in river and Weija Reservoir;
- to document the methodology and findings of this study and to disseminate them to target audiences and communities via discussions, seminars, audiovisual presentations and field demonstrations; and
- to publish the results in appropriate form and media for wider dissemination and possible application.

The main causes of pollution in the watershed arise from rapid urbanisation as a result of rural to urban migration at Nsawam Township, and intensification of agriculture and logging activities along the banks of the Densu River. Eleven agencies in central and local government have been identified by the project as having substantial control over activities in the Densu Basin, and their management structures and legal and institutional frameworks have been analysed. The project team also extended the initial boundaries of the study area to include the whole of the Densu Basin from its estuary to its source, a distance of 116km. This brought two more agencies, responsible for forestry and mining activities in the upper reaches, into the framework.

As water quality continued to deteriorate, the project team initiated a programme of awareness creation to alert people to the severity of the problem and to the implications of their actions on water quality. This included visits to agencies, and the use of newspaper articles to raise the level of problem acceptance. In 1990, the project team organised a seminar on Densu River Basin Development. This was attended by 40 people, representing 26 agencies and organisations with an interest in the Densu Basin. This seminar was described by the IDEA team leader as the first ever meeting of agencies involved in diverse developmental projects within a common ecological zone in Ghana. Out of this seminar arose a series of recommendations, the foremost

* See also pages 151–153.

of which are the establishment of a river basin authority, a public awareness programme, agency actions to reduce environmental degradation, and the institutionalisation of environmental impact assessment (EIA) procedures.

The project team is based in the Institute of Aquatic Biology, but works in collaboration with other technical institutions and agencies including the Water Resources Research Institute, the Institute of Renewable Natural Resources, the Forestry Department, the Ghana Water and Sewage Corporation, the Industrial Research Institute and the Environmental Protection Council. The team has set itself a series of tasks stemming from the above recommendations and others more detailed. District administrations in the project area are now relying on the team to formulate guidelines for rehabilitation of the Densu basin.

The guidelines will consider the problems of sewage, industrial effluent, and inappropriate landfill arrangements. To prevent siltation, agroforestry is one recommended and locally accepted means of rehabilitating deforested areas in the river basin. The idea of dredging the river at Nsawam or channelling through canals is also being explored. It is proposed to measure the improvement in the quality and flavour of water in the Weija reservoir, the reduction in chemicals used in water production, and reduced incidence of flooding in the basin as indicators of the success of the rehabilitation exercise.

The IDEA team has also identified areas for which training is necessary to enable the continued successful implementation of environmental management strategies. These include: river basin management, waste management, environmental impact assessment, urban systems management (with special reference to rapidly growing tropical townships) and environmental health. They plan to establish priorities for this training and seek assistance through the IDEA network.

The Ghana project has brought together institutions, agencies and the communities at risk through their district administrations in a broad-based network to tackle a watershed management problem. It has created environmental awareness among local communities, and, through the press and other media, has highlighted nationally the urgent need to tackle environmental degradation in this and other river basins. In addition, the experience being gained by professionals involved has widened their perspectives and improved the capability of their respective institutions. The team now faces the task of maintaining the co-ordinated relationship developed among the technical agencies on the one hand, and the eight district administrations on the other, during the next phase of implementing, monitoring and evaluating the rehabilitation programme.

The IDEA initiatives enable the project to complement institutional development, and legal and formal environmental controls, with voluntary action at the local level. In this way motivation is devolved, and local mechanisms are evolving which can maintain water quality as new development pressures arise. The main outcome of these efforts is to create a pool of personnel trained in river basin management, and a parallel network of local action. The result is a prototypical river basin management system which could be transferred to other watersheds. Based on the success achieved, the Government could recommend that the methodology be extended to other river basins in Ghana, and this possibility is being considered.

Watershed management in the Harare Region of Zimbabwe

This project arose out of concern that the rapid growth in population and industrialisation in the area of Harare is degrading water quality in Lake Chivero, the main source of drinking water for Harare, although it is downstream of the city. In particular, the rapid spread of a blanket of water hyacinth over one metre thick across more than 40 per cent of the surface of the lake, has generated much concern about the need to sustain water quality.

The overall objective of the project is to develop a well co-ordinated institutional mechanism for the management of the Harare watershed which would lead to a reduction in the amount of pollutants entering the water system. To achieve this aim the team engaged in three complementary activities: information gathering and awareness raising; water quality monitoring; and generating participation in activities to reduce the water hyacinth problem.

The project team, recognising that neither urbanisation nor industrialisation were likely to abate, decided to expand from a focus on water quality monitoring to promotion of watershed management. They identified:

- the main agencies in central and local government with potential responsibility for watershed management;
- some of the major sources of pollution – domestic and sewage waste, and industrial effluents – from both public and private companies; and
- the trends in population and industrial growth likely to result in major environmental impacts.

Among the latter, for example, major concerns include pollution caused by the main fertiliser plant for the country (partly government-owned), and discharges from sewage works of a rapidly growing and poorly planned town with low-cost housing near Harare.

The team initiated a project advisory group representing eight main agencies with relevant responsibilities in the watershed area. They also reviewed the current legal and institutional framework for watershed management, and documented gaps between adequate policy and law and inadequate implementation and enforcement. They have developed a survey questionnaire piloted to senior agency officials. The main survey was immediately followed up with face to face interviews with key people in government and industry.

The occasion of an international IDEA Programme meeting in Harare in 1990 was used by the project team as a springboard to launch a major awareness campaign, including front page newspaper coverage, and to alert senior government officials in the industrial and financial departments, to the need to reconcile industrialisation with environmental quality. The meeting helped forge new links between government officials and industrialists in the region.

The project team and advisory group are now promoting a three-pronged effort: to encourage enforcement of existing pollution control laws, to encourage the private sector to invest in pollution control and recycling technology, and to develop a co-ordinated managerial system for water quality maintenance. Having initiated direct communication between government, the research sector and the business community, the project team is now in a position to help establish some effective mode of inter-institutional collaboration.

Watershed management in the Kafue Basin of Zambia

The original concern of the National Council for Scientific Research, base of the Zambian project team, was over declining water quality in the entire Kafue River Basin, in spite of the existence of various laws for environmental protection and pollution control. The basin covers an estimated area of about 15,000 square kilometres. Although the problems of the entire watershed were well documented by the team, this proved unwieldy as a project, due to the great distances involved. With assistance from the team leaders from Ghana and Zimbabwe, the Zambian team decided to redefine the scope of their project to focus on problems on the lower Kafue River in the vicinity of Lusaka and in the mining area on the Copperbelt, where problems arise from pollution from inadequately treated raw sewage, industrial effluents and agricultural run-off, as well as poor practices in solid waste disposal.

One particular problem identified in these two areas is the failure of municipalities to maintain existing sewage treatment plants due to financial constraints and lack of skilled manpower arising from the 10-15 year economic recession in the country. This problem is exacerbated by high rates of urbanisation, currently increasing at about 6.7 per cent annually, as well as lack of resources in the private sector for investment in pollution control technology and lack of personnel in government agencies responsible for environmental monitoring.

Following detailed problem definition, the Zambian team established an initial advisory group of six relevant agencies, including government departments for Agriculture, Commerce and Industry, local government, the National Commission for Development Planning, the National Council for Scientific Research, and Zambia Consolidated Copper Mines. The first meeting identified constraints on water quality improvement, including the inability of relevant institutions to implement existing legislation on environmental protection and pollution control, and lack of monitoring of industrial and sewage effluents.

The advisory committee then proceeded to organise discussion meetings during 1991 in both the lower and upper Kafue areas. These brought together representatives of industry, local authorities and central government agencies. The discussions focused on environmental concerns and pollution risks, and a number of recommendations for action were made.

In connection with the development of mechanisms for inter-institutional co-ordination, which is the main thrust of the project, the priorities identified are:

1 Establishment of a special committee of the National Environmental Council (currently being established under the Environmental Protection and Pollution Control Act of 1990) to deal specifically with policy issues of the Basin's environment and development.
2 Encouraging and promoting the formation of community-based environmental action associations to address issues of environmental quality at the grassroots level. One such association, the Kafue Water Users Association, has been established.

3   The urgent need to generate a resources and environmental quality data base to facilitate periodic reviews of the state of the environment and environmental impact assessments of new development projects.
4   The need for huge investment in: rehabilitation and expansion of Districts' systems for water treatment and distribution, sewage and solid waste collection and disposal; training of skilled staff in local and national government; installing efficient treatment plant in industry; and promoting public awareness on environmental issues.

Waste management

Co-operative wastewater treatment in Malaysia

Since 1987, the manufacturing sector has been the leading economic sector in Malaysia, followed by the agricultural and mining sectors. The main manufactured products for export are electrical/electronic goods, textiles and rubber-based products. Small scale, or 'backyard' industries, play a major role in the industrialisation process of the national economy and account for about 90 per cent of employment in the manufacturing sector. These industries include metal finishing, textiles, and food processing.

Following recognition of the need to enforce standards for the discharge of effluents under existing environmental quality regulations, a survey in 1985 indicated that metal finishers were a major source of toxic and hazardous wastes (acids and alkalis containing metals such as chromium, nickel and aluminium). The survey identified more than a hundred small-scale operators employing less than 20 people, of which slightly more than half were located in the Klang Valley surrounding Kuala Lumpur. These metal finishers produce items such as nuts and bolts for the automotive industry, components for the electrical and electronic industries, as well as various household utensils. They play an important role in industrial development.

It was recognised early in the project that, although strict enforcement of pollution control legislation was desirable, simply putting the metal finishers out of business was not a viable option. A more sophisticated response was necessary. The IDEA team therefore redefined the problem as:

1   a pollution problem;
2   an economic problem, concerning the viability of the enterprises, their contribution to industrial growth, the costs of waste metal removal from the effluent and the cost-effectiveness of communal treatment run co-operatively;
3   a land use problem in terms of the incompatibility of industrial and residential uses; and
4   a spatial problem of whether to relocate the businesses near a waste treatment facility or to transport the waste from the industries to a central facility.

Figure 11.3 illustrates the management problems involved. Failure to comply with stipulated effluent discharge standards and to install pollution control measures was generally linked with financial, technical and spatial constraints. The government, through the IDEA project, decided on a common wastewater treatment facility, to be managed by a co-operative of metal finishers.

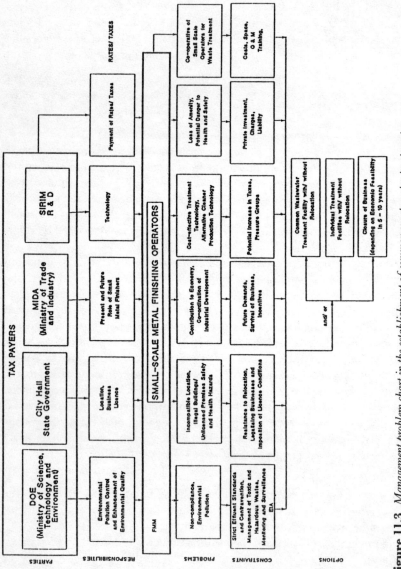

Figure 11.3 *Management problem chart in the establishment of common wastewater treatment facilities among small metal finishing industries in Malaysia*

Source: Malaysian IDEA Team, Department of Environment, Malaysia

The objectives of the country task were set out as follows:

- Short term: identification of wastewater characteristics of the industry as well as pollution load in the selected study area of the Klang Valley.
- Medium term: development of consensus over measures acceptable to the metal finishers and the various government enforcement agencies in controlling pollution, managing toxic and hazardous wastes, and preventing nuisance to adjacent areas.
- Long term: proposal on co-operative arrangements for a common wastewater treatment facility in the Klang Valley, and consequently an enforcement of environmental quality standards.

The project team established a working committee which includes relevant central and local departments, research institutes, and most importantly, representatives of the metal finishers, formed into a newly established Metal Finishing Society. However, these small businessmen were not used to any kind of co-operative activities, particularly in conjunction with the public sector, and much development work by the project team has been necessary, and continues. From this, a proposal has been developed for co-operative waste treatment facilities, with or without plant relocation.

Like the projects in watershed management, the Malaysian project has generated much interest because the problem of how to attempt to control small-scale industry is common to many countries. The project's co-operative approach, both among the industrialists and between the public and the private sector, is undoubtedly innovative. However, some of the metal finishers remain decidedly unco-operative, in keeping with their usual individualistic style. The project team has had to make delicate decisions over whether to use the carrot of incentive and dialogue, or the stick of legal enforcement of pollution control regulations. The current approach is to hold discussions with the remaining, unco-operative small-scale operators to explain to them the advantages of joining the metal finishing co-operative for mitigation of pollution. It is an open and very interesting question whether a government department in charge of pollution control can work collaboratively with backyard industrialists for both economic development and pollution control, without the assistance of a mediator from an outside party. The question of whether more formal mediation techniques would be helpful was being considered by the Malaysian team at the time of writing (January 1992).

Waste management in Lagos

Lagos, a sprawling city of around seven million people, is home to numerous domestic and multinational industrial firms. About 70 per cent of all industries in Nigeria are in Lagos, and very few have waste treatment facililties. The IDEA project focuses on the institutional arrangements for waste management in Lagos State. Research focused initially on Ikeja Municipality, one of the four main industrial areas in the state. Ikeja has a substantial resident population of some 250,000 and also contains a major landfill site of the Lagos State Waste Disposal Board (LSWDB). Ikeja provided a pilot area within which to begin to understand the complex issues of waste disposal in the wider State.

The main governmental agencies with a responsibility for waste include the Federal Ministry of Science and Technology (FMST), the new Federal Environmental Protection Agency (FEPA), and the state government, represented by the LSWDB. The complexity of evolving institutional arrangements initially caused delay in the implementation of the project. But, in 1991, a workshop was held to examine: the need for improvements to the waste management system for Lagos Metropolis; various agencies' arrangements and responsibilities in this regard; and possibilities for a new workable alliance among the agencies to tackle waste management efficiently under the auspices of IDEA.

The inter-institutional aspects of this IDEA project have been developed considerably. The participants in the workshop included a number of representatives of FEPA, FMST and LSWDB, the Federal Ministry of Industry, the Federal Ministry of Education, the Municipality of Ikeja (Department of Health and Environmental Services), the business sector (including local representatives from multinational companies), the University of Lagos, the University of Calabar, the National Institute for Oceanography and Marine Research (NIOMR), the National Centre for Genetic Research and Biotechnology, and the Commonwealth Fund for Technical Co-operation. Many of these representatives have agreed to form an advisory group. It was also agreed that the Manufacturers Association of Nigeria (MAN) would be invited to join that advisory group.

A first step of the advisory group was to identify the following requirements as critical to improved waste management for the Lagos Metropolis:

- additional landfill sites;
- a system for monitoring and controlling toxic, liquid industrial wastes in the Lagos area;
- more sewage treatment facilities, partly needed to keep up with urban population growth;
- definitions and standards for various kinds of wastes and pollutants;
- cost effective waste disposal, possibly including commercialisation, joint treatment facilities, 'user pays' charging and local sourcing of supplies and replacement parts;
- development of local managerial and technical capacity in all agencies, instead of relying on expensive outside consultants;
- the creation and/or rationalisation of laboratory facilities for Lagos State;
- the minimisation of waste production, including exploration of recycling options;
- better organisation among government agencies for factory inspection, and possibly more integrated pollution control; and
- forward planning, to deal with increasing proportions of inorganic wastes (mainly due to an increase in packaging).

In Nigeria as a whole policy and administrative systems for environmental management, and the relationship between Federal and State governments in this area, are evolving rapidly. The meeting felt that waste management arrangements in Lagos State, and funding for these, could serve as a pilot for other states, especially those with large cities. FEPA confirmed that such an analysis from the IDEA project would be very helpful to its own task in establishing an environmental management structure for the country.

Resource management

Management of coral sand exploitation in Mauritius

Accelerated economic growth in Mauritius in the 1980s was accompanied by a construction boom in offices, hotels and residential developments. More than 35 major tourist hotels now ring the island, and an 18 storey office block is one of a number of new offices under construction in the capital, Port Louis. Such developments have put enormous pressure on the supply of construction aggregates, both crushed basalt and natural coral sand. Inland coral sand deposits are virtually exhausted, resulting in an increased amount of coral sand being extracted from the lagoons inside the reefs, about 320,000 tonnes per year at present. This is having disruptive effects on the environment, including beach erosion, increased sea water turbidity, and disruption of the food chain in the lagoons. The coral sand resource cannot be managed in any sustainable fashion, as the replacement time for a few years' extraction must be measured in centuries. The objective of the project is to encourage the use of replacement materials for coral sand in construction, as a critical element in the sustainable management of coastal resources.

The environmental implications of continued use of coral sand as a construction material are becoming known in Mauritius, but when the IDEA project began there was no consensus as to the nature or extent of the problem. Indeed some members of Parliament were still urging increased exploitation of the resource as necessary for economic growth. Although replacement construction materials are technically and economically feasible, as demonstrated at the University of Mauritius, there were no appropriate institutional arrangements for mediating the need for replacement construction material with the need for continuing economic growth and development. The IDEA project also noted conflicting interests within the government, and between government and the private sector. Insofar as lagoonal mining causes beach erosion, continued extraction of coral sand will have a negative impact on the tourist industry. This, along with pollution of lagoons from hotel effluent, suggest the need to mediate conflicting uses within a systematic framework for management of the coastal zone.

The IDEA team have documented the institutional and technical aspects of the problem in great detail, and drawn together information from all relevant published and ongoing studies. A project steering committee was established including almost all the main government ministries, and representatives of important private sector firms and the academic community. The IDEA team, with the steering committee, embarked on a public awareness programme and a systematic assessment of the organisational and economic constraints on outright banning of coral sand extraction. They have also embarked on a programme to encourage the construction and aggregate industries to make use of replacements on a voluntary basis, and are assisting in the retraining of builders to adjust to using the new materials.

Of particular interest in terms of project output is a development in 1991. The Government's Ministry of Lands and Environment, which declined to join the advisory group in 1989, established a technical committee for 'Phasing out the use of coral sand by 1993', with a very similar terms of reference to that of the IDEA committee. The government Committee has invited the university to participate, and has indicated that they will use the final report of the IDEA project as a working document. The IDEA Team Leader summarises the situation:

> The (IDEA) Steering Committee is being viewed as having the task of making a study of the coral sand problem and making appropriate recommendations for alternatives, whereas the Ministry of Environment Committee will have as a major priority the implementation and enforcement of such recommendations. In any case, the setting up of the Ministry Committee is indicative of increased awareness of the coral sand problem among the relevant authorities.[3]

This institutionalisation of the environmental problem first addressed by the IDEA project in Mauritius constitutes a most satisfactory outcome, and indicates the effectiveness of the temporary 'parallel organisation' that can serve to focus action on an important environmental issue.

Resource management and environmental control in Guyana

Guyana is under great pressure to exploit natural resources, partly to meet the requirements of structural adjustment. This pressure extends to gold mining. Although a number of multinationals, mainly American and Canadian, intend to mine gold in the near future, current gold mining is mainly carried out by individuals and small, mainly family groups. There are about 10,000 miners. The main method of gold extraction involves a technology called 'missile dredges' capable of mechanically dredging river banks and cutting into the foreshore.

Tailings from missile dredging form small islands which interfere with navigation, and the missiles often change the contour of the river bank and cause serious downstream turbidity. There are severe social impacts, including disruption of traditional food fishing activities of local, mainly Amerindian, residents of the areas, and the degradation of their drinking water.

Such disruption has been documented in the Pakaraima and Upper Mazaruni Mountains, a rainforest area which is home to the Akawaio Indians. Waterways provide the main thoroughfare in the area and many of these are already blocked. Fish are unable to spawn as their breeding grounds are destroyed by the dredgers, whose operations are reported to render water undrinkable 60km downstream. Recently in Guyana there has been increasing political and public awareness of the environmental damage caused by this form of mining, and a concern to exert control over this and all other environmentally damaging forms of gold mining. The new road from the Brazilian border to tidewater at the Guyanan capital, Georgetown, brings with it the grave danger that the near anarchy of the Brazilian goldfields will spill over into Guyana.

Against this background, the project team established the following objectives:

- National: to ensure that environmental considerations are an essential and integral part of sustainable national economic development objectives.
- Immediate: to promote greater co-operation among, and strengthen the

institutional capability of, the agencies involved in the protection and development of natural resources through a study of gold mining projects.

The project team, led by the head of the government's agency for environment,
decided that the project should first tackle the absence of any environmental
legislation for Guyana which would give the government some authority for action.
This attention to the problems of gold mining, and the need for inter-agency co-
operation to address it, would then have benefits which would flow throughout the
government's approach to environmental policy. To this end, both the Geology and
Mines Commission and the Guyana Agency for Health Education, Environment
and Food Policy (GAHEF) collaborated to address the problem.

The Guyana team leader drew up a draft environmental protection bill for the
country. He then sought the assistance of the IDEA programme in refining that
legislation and in assessing the many substantial institutional and administrative
implications that flowed from it. The IDEA programme provided both general
advice on environmental policy and legislation in member countries, from members
of the network, and specialist legal advice in drafting acceptable and useful legislation
in a Commonwealth context. As a result of these activities, a Guyana Environmental
Protection Act was brought before the Guyanese Cabinet.

Having secured legislative authority for environmental protection and control, the
IDEA team is turning its attention to the difficult task of developing the necessary
conditions for the successful implementation of environmental policy. Six key needs
have been identified:

- acceptable standards of environmental quality;
- environmental monitoring staff and laboratory facilities;
- guidelines and expertise in environmental impact assessment;
- review of the institutional structure for pollution and environmental control;
- training to meet the human resource requirements; and
- winning financial resources within a severely constrained economy.

Through IDEA, the experiences of other countries in the setting of standards and in
environmental monitoring are being examined. In addition, linkages within Guyana
have been established with an agency with competence in monitoring, the
Mahaica–Mahaicony–Abary Agricultural Development Authority. This organisation has been funded for a number of years by the Inter-American Development
Bank to develop environmental monitoring expertise relevant to that agricultural
project. To this end, it has initiated, through its Environmental Monitoring and
Control Unit, on-the-job training of environmental field technicians. In this
programme, secondary school graduates in relevant science disciplines have been
trained in various aspects of monitoring: water quality, wildlife, fisheries, vegetation
and spatial monitoring. It is expected that the expertise developed through this
programme will be shared with GAHEF.

Guidelines for environmental impact assessment in gold mining have been
developed by GAHEF for discussion with the Geology and Mines Commission and
other appropriate agencies. Information obtained from a survey is intended to help
indicate the adequacy of the institutional structures for dealing with pollution control

and of the legislative framework, and the types of regulations required. Finally, training needs are being documented and priorities established prior to attempting to secure the necessary resources.

In considering the question of training and the broader issue of human resource capability in Guyana, the project is beginning to address a fundamental constraint on environmental management in that country, which is the 'brain drain' overseas of many of the country's skilled professionals and technicians. This evolution of the project's focus from the initial, specific environmental problem to a generic institutional problem (gold mining to environmental legislation to implementation capability) is typical of the achievements of a number of IDEA projects in broadening their attention to major constraints on environmental management and sustainable development. By attempting to overcome those constraints the lessons and the achievements of the specific IDEA projects become replicable for other environmental problem areas.

LESSONS FROM IDEA

IDEA is a practical effort to understand and resolve some of the complexities of environmental management in lower income countries, and to make that knowledge available for use in similar circumstances. A reasonable measure of success can be reported by the programme, in terms of both project outputs and transferable learning. In addition, the knowledge base in its environmental management network has grown substantially. Through practical environmental management, the programme has been able to validate many of the propositions about management and organisations which have lately found favour in the academic literature on both private and public sector management and environmental mediation. In this sense, IDEA has been a successful empirical effort in developing organisational capacity for improved environmental management.

Views of the team leaders

Participants in IDEA have reported that they found the methodology, which they themselves helped to develop, useful in addressing the serious environmental challenges identified at the beginning of the programmes. This is especially true of the team leaders, most of whom, although eminent scientists or administrators, had no particular background in environmental management or institutional development. In each project, tangible outputs in institutional development have resulted, and indicators of environmental improvement have been identified as objectives or measures of intended results. The view of team leaders on the achievements and lessons of the IDEA methodology are given below.

Achievements

1   The IDEA approach resulted in clear definition of environmental problems, and the identification of the main participants or stakeholders with an interest in those problems.
2   The approach also served to identify the main constraints to good management related to the particular problem.

3   The process of mutual problem definition resulted in a *shared* appreciation of the problem, as a basis for action.
4   The projects had a clear triggering effect, where inertia or unco-ordinated action had previously held sway. In other words, the projects served as catalysts for local action.
5   The project advisory groups provided a forum for the resolution of conflict, and induced a logical synthesis of views and objectives toward practical solutions.
6   As the problem was redefined, the number of relevant stakeholders grew, but at a pace which was manageable for the existing group. This process served to focus attention on wider, more diverse perspectives.
7   The projects mobilised local skills for direct action on the problem, and provided high value interventions at modest cost.
8   The projects led to the discovery of talented local people, linked them to the challenging tasks, provided an opportunity for further, mutual learning, linkage and recognition, and thus developed a pool of local skills in environmental management.
9   The projects led to new linkages between people in diverse institutions and organisations concerned with development, some of which will be long lasting.

Lessons

The process of evaluation also uncovered some other lessons, insights or 'confessions' from the participants, as follows:

1   Motivation at the grass roots is an imperative for successful environmental action.
2   Solutions to environmental problems will invariably be found in a wider context than is at first apparent.
3   The provision and discussion of reliable information and data builds up trust among participants.
4   The mass media must be involved and cultivated to serve the purposes of environmental education.
5   Solutions usually involve a multiplicity of policy instruments, ranging from participatory mechanisms to financial inducements and penalties.
6   The process of developing a project team needs to be recorded and documented to avoid misunderstandings and to generate agreement on, and commitment to, intended actions.
7   Innovatory approaches, because they often risk upsetting the status quo, require the development of emotional as well as intellectual commitment.
8   The interactions between the project teams from various countries helped to motivate and mobilise local people as part of a wider international network.

CONCLUSION

The IDEA Programme generated many tangible outputs in environmental management and institutional development, and a methodology for enhancing local capacity to address serious environmental problems through building action-centred networks. In particular, the challenge of problems of national concern, combined with the interactions of the diversely skilled professionals, administrators and community and business leaders in the interlinked international and local networks, generated more material for learning than we have been able to analyse and report here. Like the individual projects, the overall programme generated considerable value for money, and the lessons derived will continue to flow for some time.

12 Growth management through consensus in California

What's interesting about this is that the Legislature decided business as usual wasn't getting anybody the results they wanted. This is designed to take the issue out of the legislative arena and to try and come up with some type of consensus on how to proceed . . . If you have environmentalists, local government people, developers and ethnic groups coalescing on a set of recommendations, law-makers will be scrambling to support their position.

Susan Sherry, 1991[1]

Like the South-East of England, the Tokyo-Osaka region and an increasing number of intensively-developed regions throughout the world, California is a victim of its own economic success, on a grand scale. It is often noted that the GDP of California exceeds that of many countries in the world. Throughout the 1980s an economic boom and the attractions of the landscape and climate attracted record numbers of immigrants. During this decade, the state's population grew by 25 per cent, two and one-half times the national average. The rate of growth is so rapid that, in 1991, demographers substantially revised upwards their 1987 projections. They now suggest that by the year 2000 the population will reach 36 million. Newcomers to the state are arriving at the rate of more than 2000 a day – more than 774,000 in 1989.

There are substantial environmental costs attached to this growth, and Californian politics is marked by increasing dissatisfaction with a declining quality of life. This chapter explores an innovative network approach intended to help the contending interests in the state come to terms with that growth – the California Growth Management Consensus Project.[2] The project developed from the rising awareness in California of the links between environmental problems, land use, and the clash of special interest lobbies over economic development issues. It is an attempt to overcome the blockages and conflicts in the policy development process caused by the entrenched positions of diverse and powerful lobbies, and to build consensus between key constituencies in environmental management. Before considering the project in detail, however, we examine some of the environmental and social limits to traditional forms of growth that are becoming apparent in California.

THE ENVIRONMENTAL COST OF GROWTH

The current population of California is a little over 30 million, mostly concentrated in Southern California – in the Los Angeles/San Diego regional conurbation – and in central California around the San Francisco Bay area.

Sixteen million people live in Southern California. They own eight million motor vehicles, which make the air some of the most polluted in the United States. Seventy per cent of their water comes from northern California and the Colorado River, which passes through the Grand Canyon. The water from the north travels through 500 miles of aqueducts and canals. Out of the Colorado River, one billion gallons of water per day is drawn for Southern California: the river is so drained by this and other extractions that it disappears entirely before it reaches its outlet at the sea in Mexico. The entire estuarine ecosystem of the Colorado has simply disappeared.

California pioneered the car-based society, and the population continues to sprawl over vast areas, in part to escape rising land values in and near the major cities. To fill the current demand for housing by people working in Southern California and the Bay area, developers have turned their sights on some of the most productive agricultural land in the United States. This is the vast Central Valley, which accounts for two-thirds of the state's annual agricultural income of $17.5 billion. To find affordable housing, people are prepared to live hundreds of miles from their place of employment and drive two or even three hours to work. Already about 20,000 acres per year of the Valley is now being converted to residential use: 400,000 acres of new suburbs could exist by the year 2010. There is also a social dimension to these problems: it is mainly the white population that is fleeing to the distant suburbs, leaving Latinos, Asians and African-Americans isolated in the inner cities. Ethnic minority incomes are 30 per cent below the median and few people in ethnic minority communities have access to home ownership.

Some cities, such as Fresno, increased in population by more than 60 per cent in the 1980s. For this and other reasons, particularly the dispersal of retailing and leisure activities, the number of vehicle miles travelled on California roads is growing at twice the population rate, and the number of 'lane-miles' of congested highways is increasing by 15 per cent per year. Cars are California's biggest source of air pollution: 50 per cent in the cities, and more in non-industrial areas. Already a serious problem in urban regions, air pollution is now a problem in agricultural areas.

The soil is also increasingly polluted. Agricultural production in the Central Valley is entirely dependent on irrigation: large areas of farmland are in danger of becoming unproductive because of salination. In the cities, a tremendous growth in high tech industry, such as among the semiconductor and computer producers in 'Silicon Valley', has polluted water supplies with heavy metals. A shortage of treatment facilities means untreated wastewater from both domestic and industrial sources is being discharged into the natural environment. This in turn raises the cost of treatment of drinking water.

There is a serious risk of water shortages. The coastal strip of Southern California is located in semi-arid desert, receiving on average only 10–15 inches of rainfall per year. The years 1985–1990 were marked by drought, with rainfall down to the lowest levels since recording began in the late 1880s. At the best of times, natural water supplies meet less than one-third of current needs in that region, and demand is likely to grow by some twenty per cent by the year 2000. Already 40 of the state's 350 groundwater basins are overdrawn, 11 critically so. The water situation is so severe that private industry is on record as saying the situation 'threatens the economic and social fabric of the state'.[3]

LIMITS TO GOVERNANCE IN CALIFORNIA

The weight of these and other growth-related problems rests largely on local government, which is rapidly coming up against the limits to governance. Cities, towns and counties are no longer able to provide the schools, transport infrastructure, sewage treatment capacity and solid waste disposal sites necessary to match the population boom. At the same time, the ability of local government to raise tax revenues is limited by fiscal constraints. The current shortfall in expenditure on infrastructure in the state is $40–50 billion. In a desperate attempt to balance the books, many local governments are reported to be making land use and zoning decisions based primarily on the possibilities for revenue generation. The result of what in California is called the 'fiscalisation' of land use is:

> ... a growing imbalance between jobs and housing, a shortage of regional facilities to provide the services necessary for a complex society, and rising levels of air pollution, traffic congestion and social segregation. There is growing awareness among leaders throughout the state that these problems, if left unaddressed, threaten the very foundations of California as an economically powerful, democratic and socially cohesive society.[4]

Additionally, the inequitable distribution of the benefits of growth limits the ability of lower income residents to 'purchase' public goods and services. For example, to get around taxation limitations, local governments increasingly rely on user fees for services, which become unavailable to those on lower incomes. Similarly, fees on new homes pay for much of the new infrastructure supporting growth. But lower income residents are mostly priced out the home ownership market, and thus cut off from the infrastructure and services related to the new development.

The potential for innovative response to these problems within existing institutional arrangements in California is limited. Local authorities do not have the statutory authority or the institutional capacity to address many of the problems which confront them. Against this background, the mayors of the four largest cities in California convened 'growth management forums'. However, it became obvious that efforts at the city level could not unlock the solutions to what were clearly statewide problems.

At the state level, the policy apparatus is described as being 'near paralysis':

> As diverse constituencies advocate on behalf of their own growth-related agendas before the Legislature and Governor's Office, they checkmate each other. Thus develops the political gridlock that so typifies growth management policy discussions at the state level.[5]

Background papers prepared by the Growth Management Project team identify some of the reasons for that paralysis: a 'state policy muddle', lack of clarity on issues, lack of leadership and strategic planning at the state level, dysfunctional planning, agencies working at cross-purposes, and unco-ordinated implementation of policies.[6] The papers give examples:

- New infrastructure investments, such as motorways and sewer lines, or irrigation projects, which take no account of their tendency to induce growth and related problems such as urban sprawl, traffic congestion and pollution, or in the case of irrigation, salination.

- Major decisions taken, such as the location of a new university campus, without due regard for other policy considerations concerning transport, rural conservation and air quality.
- The failure of single sector agencies, such as Air Pollution Control Districts or Regional Transportation Planning Agencies, to come to grips with the multi-dimensional nature of growth management concerns.
- The failure of advisory regional co-ordination bodies, called Councils of Governments, to have any real impact on land use and development decisions.

These problems, common the world over, are the result of two broad issues addressed in this book: the failure to develop integrated, comprehensive policy in environmental management, as opposed to fragmented, sectoral vision and action; and the difficulty in achieving a balance between centralised, or strategic, decision making and decentralisation of functions. In California, and in the United States generally, there is a strong bias towards local decision making. In a sense, the US is overly decentralised, compared with say, the UK, which is overly centralised. In each case, new types of mediation and conflict resolution, and adequate and binding institutional arrangements, are required.

THE NEED FOR ENVIRONMENTAL MEDIATION

California is on the threshold of critical decisions as to the limits of sustainable growth. These decisions, or the failure to make them, will affect quality of life for decades to come. At the same time, differing perceptions of the benefits and costs of surging population and economic growth have polarised the society into 'pro' and 'anti' growth factions. The discussion is said to be framed 'almost exclusively by environmentalists on one side, developers and tax-hungry local officials on the other'.[7] The power of polarised interest groups in the legislative process has led to a situation in which elected representatives cannot make progress on environmental management. The interplay of entrenched interests creates a blockage in the legislature, and leads to stagnation in strategic policy making. Specific measures are vetoed through the pressure of one group or another on legislators, and the inability to break the legislative impasse means that higher-level policy making is stymied.

To break out of this policy paralysis and meet the challenge of growth, the Legislature of the State of California, working with the Center for California Studies at the California State University at Sacramento, has embarked on an innovative and fascinating project in growth management: one that provides a model for managing development through the fostering of consensus in an action-centred network. The Growth Management Consensus Project (GMCP) is helping to establish a basic consensus on a number of key issues and policies at the state level, and is a case study relevant to many of the exploding urban regions of the world.

The general objective of the project is to:

> ... chart out the contours of those controversies ... in an attempt to initiate dialogue, find common ground, identify solutions that require state-level

leadership, and develop policy agreements among the stakeholders that can provide a context for implementing solutions. *The project's purpose is to explore the proper role of state government in managing growth.*[8]

ORIGINS OF THE GROWTH MANAGEMENT PROJECT

In attempt to shed some light on a confused and politically contentious area of growth management, the policy research offices of the two houses of the California State Legislature decided to take joint action. These are the Senate Office of Research and the Assembly Office of Research. They approached the Center for California Studies and asked for discussions to be convened that would explore, identify and articulate what they called 'bottom-line' points of agreement or disagreement among the key stakeholders in the state on the growth management issue. The 'bottom-line' is the point where constructive discussion and formal mediation can get no further: where stakeholders agree, or agree to disagree. Where points of consensus could be reached by negotiation, they would be clearly identified in writing. This process would identify areas for action where widespread, all-party political support would be likely to emerge. Where agreement was impossible, the project's task would be to define precisely the points of contention, and to try to generate alternative options for resolving these issues.

The project's objectives were summarised by the Center for California Studies:

1 Identify the four to five key growth management issues requiring state-level leadership.
2 Identify the key interests (needs or conditions) that participating constituencies consider to be an important part of a workable solution.
3 Develop specific and explicit agreements among the participating constituencies on the main policy issues to inform and guide state policy.
4 Identify: issues where there is disagreement, and the basis for this; interests that need to be satisfied; and alternative settlement options that were discussed but not agreed.
5 Prepare a final report for the Legislature, the Governor, the press and the public.

Discussions would not attempt to suggest specific pieces of legislation, but rather provide an overall framework for the Legislature to address growth management questions. To meet the University's needs for autonomy, and to reinforce the non-partisan nature of the effort, the project would be independent of government and the legislative process. The project was to inform the legislative process, but not be influenced by it.

Four components of the projects were identified:

● Identification of relevant stakeholders from major organisations with statewide constituencies and interests, their recruitment and orientation.
● Preliminary identification of key issues for discussion.
● A series of statewide meetings of participants selected by major stakeholder organisations with the specific purpose of identifying and negotiating policy agreements in writing to inform and guide policy; the discussions are profession-ally facilitated and/or mediated.

- Publication and wide dissemination of project results.

At each stage in the process, substantive policy issues and procedural ground rules are identified, refined and clearly articulated so that participants can focus their undivided attention on central policy concerns.

IDENTIFYING STAKEHOLDERS

The first step in the development of the consensus-building work was to identify and recruit the key interest groups, or stakeholders. The University team selected organisations from four broad constituencies in California:

- environmental protection lobbies;
- local government;
- business; and
- land/infrastructure development interests.

The process of recruiting organisations from these constituencies was difficult and sensitive, as is the case whenever multi-sector partnerships or consultations are put together. The organisations in question needed careful persuasion that the initiative was worth supporting:

> ... most of these groups were cautious and protective, concerned that this endeavour could politically isolate them, weaken their strategic position vis-a-vis their legislative foes, or waste their organisational resources.[9]

Once the agreement of the four constituencies had been secured concerning the principle of participation, the task was to select a group of stakeholder organisations representative of the broad constituencies, of the main sectors in the state economy, and of the ethnic balance in California. Project workers collaborated with organisations from all constituencies, which selected their official stakeholders, to arrive at a final list of bodies to be invited to participate. This group of invitees in itself represented a major success in consensus-building, since the final list had to be 'representative of California's body politic on the issue [of growth management], manageable in terms of the numbers of participants, and not so politically volatile as to cause an early collapse of the project'.[10]

The final list of 32 invited organisations comprised an assembly of interests of unprecedented breadth. Ethnic minority communities were formally represented in the debate on environmental management for the first time; and many of the invitees had never sat around the same negotiating table before. The list included representatives of local and regional governments, labour unions, agricultural interests, environmental lobbies, water suppliers, air pollution control districts, Latino, African-American and Asian Pacific organisations, regional voluntary sector initiatives, low and moderate income housing lobbies and business/development interests. All but the water suppliers chose to attend.

The process behind the interplay of stakeholders in mediation projects such as the Growth Management Project is elaborate, designed to build up confidence and minimise breakdowns in communication. Each stakeholder organisation in turn selects a representative and an alternative. To keep the group manageable only the representative takes part in discussion. The alternative must attend all plenary sessions as an observer, and be prepared to take over in case of illness or other unforeseen event. This avoids the all too common situation where some participants always seem to be unavailable. All stakeholders taken together constitute a plenary, and all project 'ground rules', which are put out in writing, may be modified only by a full plenary session.

The list of stakeholder slots for statewide meetings (Table 13.1) gives a good idea of the range of organisations participating. Each organisation is selected as a statewide constituency with a large membership. Representatives in turn are selected according to the following criteria:

● ability to articulate and represent the interests of the stakeholder organisation;
● rapport and credibility with his or her own constituency;
● grasp of, or willingness to learn about, the technical and policy issues involved;
● ability to listen to, and openly discuss negotiation issues with, people holding diverse views; and
● willingness to participate in co-operative problem-solving procedures to resolve differences.

The Project team encouraged stakeholder organisations to appoint senior executives to the consensus-building exercise rather than send lobbyists.

Discussions are considered confidential within participating agencies, until such time as written agreements are entered into. This is to encourage participants to speak freely. Each stakeholder may also invite one or more staff to meetings as observers and advisers. One of these is to be designated formally as staff liaison officer to the Project.

IDENTIFYING ISSUES

At the beginning of the Project, it was decided that an issue-by-issue approach to the litany of problems (air pollution, shortage of affordable housing, etc) was not the most productive approach. In preparation for negotiation sessions, the Project team, working with legislative staff, produced papers that identified a broad range of state-level policy issues and options. It was made clear that these background papers do not define issues for discussion in the meetings, but that they are information and discussion papers about major policy initiatives and implementation strategies. The latter were defined as governmental structure, institutional arrangements and the authority of agencies. In the space available here we can only summarise the main issues to arise in the discussion papers.

Lack of certainty in conservation, development and social equity

The process of making land use decisions in California, as in many places, is based on unsystematic and varying criteria. In other words, there is a policy vacuum. In these circumstances, each individual major development tends to be fought out at a high level of political and legal confrontation.[11] No constituency, whether developers, low cost housing advocates, environmentalists or government, has any assurance that their interests will be represented in decisions. The overall quality of decisions is

Table 13.1 *Stakeholders identified in the California Growth Management Consensus Project*

Thirty-one participants	Selecting organisation
1 City Elected Official	League of California Cities
1 City Planner	League/American Planning Assoc.
2 County Elected Officials	County Supervisor Assn of Calif.
1 COG Representative	Calif. Councils of Governments
1 So. Coast Air Quality Man. Dist.	So. Coast Air Quality Man. Dist.
1 Other Air District	Co. Air Poll. Control Officers Assn
1 Local Transportation Agency	Selected by League/CSAC/Cal COG
1 Residential Developer	Calif. Building Industry Assn
1 Non Residential Developer	Calif. Business Properties Assoc.
1 Community Developer	Calif. Housing Council
1 Realtor	Calif. Assn of Realtors
1 Broad-Based Business	Calif. Chamber of Commerce
1 Large Employer	Calif. Manufacturers Assn
1 Utility	Council for Environ./Economic Bal.
1 Agriculture	California Farm Bureau
1 Labor	Calif. Labor Federation, AFL-CIO
5 Environmentalists	Sierra Club California
	Green Belt Alliance
	Planning & Conservation League
	Natural Resources Defense Council
	Environmental Defense Fund
2 Low Income/Affordable Housing	Western Ctr. on Law and Poverty,
	Calif. Rural Legal Assistance &
	Calif. Homeless & Housing Coalition
5 Community-Based Organisations	Mex. Amer. Legal Defense & Ed. Fd.
	Latino Issues Forum
	NAACP
	Coalition of Asian Pacific Americans
1 Bay Vision 2020	Bay Vision 2020
1 2000 Partnership	2000 Partnership

Source: Growth Management Consensus Project, California State University, Sacramento

bound to be poor in these circumstances, and the high cost of uncertainty disadvantages all parties and generates cynicism about the political process. The paper recommends that the state government establishes a more stable planning process that reconciles conflicts at the policy level rather than project-by-project.

The unsustainable pattern of urban sprawl

The paper recognises that urban sprawl is the result of powerful market and cultural forces, but argues that it is an unsustainable land use pattern, which assumes a limitless supply of land.[12] Sprawl increases demands on infrastructure, wastes financial resources, wastes valuable agricultural land, results in air pollution and disadvantages existing urban areas, financially and socially. The paper recommends the creation of three types of public policy strategies:

1 Market strategies to reflect the ultimate scarcity of land and the true cost of infrastructure and resource use.
2 Regulatory strategies to establish common outcomes of planning and zoning statewide, and performance standards to ensure environmentally acceptable development.
3 Planning policies and strategies to direct the use of supporting market and regulatory strategies and to bring greater certainty to decisions about conservation and land use.

Public finance and growth management

This paper notes that land use decisions in California became increasingly influenced by public finance considerations in the 1980s: the process of 'fiscalisation' mentioned above.[13] This is the result of three changes in policy. First, the disengagement of federal and state governments from funding public works projects, called 'fend-for-yourself-federalism'. At the local level, the result is that funds are shifted away from discretionary programmes, such as public works, and into areas of mandated expenditure.

Second, the 1980s was a period of major constraints on many areas of public expenditure in the US. The result in California, with its system of decision-by-referendum, has been voter-approved initiatives limiting local government revenues and expenditure (only one of which is the well-known proposition 13). These conditions force local officials to use development and land use decisions to raise the revenues necessary to support local government:

> Under Proposition 13 ... property tax revenues only accrue to those communities where development occurs. The situs method [of tax allocation] profoundly influences land use decisions; local officials are enticed to approve only lucrative projects, regardless of the impacts on job/housing balance, air pollution, traffic congestion, sewer capacity, water supply, or open space.[14]

The paper offers several strategies for making land use choices more fiscally neutral, and for adjusting some property assessments to reflect key land use policies. The paper also reviews ways of making more effective use of the the 'state's scarce public works dollars' through linking capital spending with land use policy.

Implementation: the role of the state

A final discussion paper looks at the direct and indirect influences the state has over land use, conservation and development, through its role in initiating projects (university campuses, water projects, etc), as a funder through public works grants, and as a regulator and source of legislation.[15]

THE METHOD OF CONSENSUS-BUILDING

There were meetings of statewide stakeholders spread over 13 days in a six month period in 1991. These involved a substantial commitment from the participants. The main stakeholder representatives were expected to attend every day of the statewide meetings. The time devoted by participants to the process represented a very substantial investment. This level of commitment also was a departure from the usual pattern of token attendance by busy senior decision makers at comparable events. The Project provided one or more professional mediators to assist the stakeholders in their plenary discussions. The Project Director also assumed the role of facilitator or mediator as appropriate. Facilitators are expected to remain neutral and impartial toward the substance of the issues under discussion. Small working groups convened meetings inbetween formal statewide stakeholder sessions, in order to discuss particularly difficult issues and carry out preliminary negotiations. The formal meetings were lengthy and could involve up to 70 participants working in a number of negotiating sessions. The structure of the discussions was shaped largely by the stakeholders themselves. Early in the process, the organisations with common interests formed 'caucuses' in order to discuss issues and formulate their own consensus before moving into 'mixed interest' sessions. The negotiations thus moved from a 'caucus' phase to a 'cross-caucus' discussion, then to attempts at plenary, project-wide agreements. The stakeholders formed seven caucuses:

- business and development;
- local government;
- environmental protection;
- affordable housing;
- air pollution district authorities;
- social equity (ethnic minority groups);
- civic organisations (voluntary sector groups).

Participants established a set of key issues for negotiation, concentrating on questions for statewide strategic thinking on environmental management rather than on specific items for legislation:

- state policies in interrelated areas of environmental, economic and social policy;
- institutional reform to facilitate better strategic policy making;
- fiscal restructuring to provide the resources needed for sustainable growth management.

The decision making process within the Project was based on consensus, not on majority voting. Consensus is defined as a settlement or solution with which all parties can agree. Consensus does not necessarily imply unanimity:

Some parties may strongly endorse a particular solution while others may accept it as a workable agreement. This instance still constitutes a consensus. Each party participates in the consensus without embracing each element of the agreement with the same fervor as the other parties, or necessarily having each of his or her constituency's interests satisfied to the fullest extent. However, given the combination of gains and trade-offs in the decision package, *a consensus is the strongest agreement that the involved parties can make at this time given current circumstances and alternative options*[16] [our emphasis].

Tentative consensus agreements reached in Plenary were referred to the stakeholders' constituent groups for discussion and final consultation, prior to final approval by the Plenary and designation as a 'final agreement'. Once issues were agreed by consensus they could not be reopened; the process must move forward.

Negotiations on many issues in this kind of process will not result in consensus. In that case, a stakeholder has a number of options:

1   to stand aside and allow the issue to be approved in the interest of overall progress;
2   to allow consensus but request a minority view be included in the Final Report; or
3   to block the consensus, in which case the reasons for this will appear in the Final Report. (The Final Report is entirely subject to the approval of the plenary).

OUTCOMES OF THE PROJECT

The results of the GMCP were made public early in 1992 in a report that received wide coverage in the Californian media.[17] The project was never seen as a process likely to lead to overall consensus on a wide range of environmental management issues, and in the event the areas of 100 per cent consensus were few. However, the process produced 'emerging agreements' – proposals enjoying majority support within each of the caucuses – on some thirty issues, although these do not necessarily reflect the official policy of the participants' organisations. On around thirty other issues, no consensus or 'emerging agreement' could be reached, but the negotiations clarified the nature and extent of the disagreements.

Consensus was achieved on the broad strategic objective of moving California towards 'compact, efficient and integrated urban development patterns' and away from the uncontrolled land use policies of recent decades. The issue of the design of urban areas was seen as fundamental in devising policies for growth management, and the consensus achieved represents a powerful boost for planning approaches based on higher density settlements with mixed housing and business and the targeting of state infrastructure policy on 'compact urban form'.[18]

Emerging agreement rather than total consensus was arrived at on the broad outline of several areas of policy, as described below:

● The need to integrate consideration of social and economic equity in policy-making on growth management: previous debates on economic development and environmental protection had unfolded with little attention being paid to the implications of policy for ethnic minority communities and low income groups.

- The need for greater clarity in the designation of land for conservation or for development – although there was no consensus on the way in which an improved designation process should work or on the means of dealing with impacts of designations on land owners.
- 'Easy' consensus was reached on the need to reduce dependence on single-occupant vehicles, but not over measures to cut vehicle miles travelled, for example through new transport pricing policies.
- Strong support was expressed for improved co-ordination between state, regional and local performance standards in relation to growth management goals; consistent implementation of planning policy across the different levels of government; preservation of local control over planning when not inconsistent with policy at the state level; and the use of new procedures including conflict resolution. Where agreement did not emerge was in relation to specific measures at the local level for deciding on development proposals; institutional reform at the state level; and mechanisms for enforcement of local plans and performance standards.
- There was emerging agreement on the necessity of more public expenditure to ensure the investments demanded by the policies and institutional reforms that most participants wished to see in pursuit of a new growth management strategy for California. Support for more public investment was made conditional upon increased cost-effectiveness in government spending and careful matching of expenditures to priority areas.

CONCLUSION

The emphasis in the California Growth Management Project on the far-reaching effects of traditional patterns of economic growth, and on the role of consensus in developing policy in environmental management, deserves close attention. In the 'hothouse' climate of a booming region, when there is money to be made from almost any kind of development in the short term, policy development for environmental protection and sustainable economic change becomes highly contentious. In this context, the achievement of consensus on long term strategic goals is extremely difficult. In California, as in much of the democratic world, the power of special interest groups contributes substantially to blocking specific measures for sustainable environmental management and discouraging political debate and consensus on long range strategy. Yet for sustainable development to be achieved, it must be possible to work out a vision and integrated policy framework for environmental management by government, and to achieve a consensus on key goals for government, business and citizens.

Like our other case study initiatives, the California Growth Management Project represents a modest beginning in the process of building up a basic, multi-sector consensus on issues in environmental management. The achievement of the venture may seem very low-key: a few areas of consensus, more of emerging agreement, and a number of areas in which no meeting of minds took place. However, the Project needs to be judged as an initial attempt at building up a sense of potential partnership in strategic policy making among a very wide range of interest groups, whose mutual antagonisms were creating a severe blockage in the policy process. In the light of its experimental character and the widespread appreciation of its contribution to the debate on growth management in California the project deserves to be seen as a success and an encouraging model for future exercises.

Much of the value of the Project lies in the fact that so many of the stakeholders involved were required to deal face to face with adversaries and to acknowledge areas in which values and policies were held in common, and where consensus appeared to be possible. Even the acknowledgement of disagreements could be seen to be of some value, since they were now set against areas of perhaps unexpected agreement and potential progress, and the parties concerned had developed a far better appreciation of each other's point of view. As the project team noted in their report on the initiative, 'A grudging respect among even the unlikeliest of foes developed'.[19] The process succeeded in establishing new contacts and working relationships between groups, within and across constituencies: in this way, the project is fostering the development of an action-centred network based on shared problems, insights and potential for collaborations.

The political neutrality of the University team as mediator and the existence of a set of ground rules that clearly specified the safeguards for the participants were crucial to the integration of so many diverse stakeholders into the process. This indicates that the mediation approach can achieve a level of participation and trust in negotiation that more traditional methods of resolving disputes cannot attain. The involvement of ethnic minority groups and low income lobbies brought a new dimension to the debate on environmental management and raised all parties' awareness of the issue of social equity in relation to development in the state.

The lesson emerging from the initiative is that mediation techniques have a potentially valuable role in forging consensus and clarifying areas of dispute in environmental management. It is vital to emphasise that the approach is by no means a substitute for the legislative process or for traditional political debate and brokering. However, it does provide a method for bringing interests together and establishing mutual confidence in a way which complements established political procedures and gives them a more productive context in which to operate. With this experience behind them, the University team has since established a full service in mediation and conflict resolution to apply the method to other areas of policy in California in which many interests have reached an impasse and blocked the legislative process.

Clearly the Growth Management Project has been a success in bringing antagonistic groups together, and in clarifying areas of agreement and dispute in environmental management. That it can also be a stimulus to action is also clear. The process has already helped to inform the legislative debate and to begin to overcome 'policy paralysis'. The knowledge that so many special interests could agree on a number of key issues was a spur to elected representatives to introduce new measures in the state legislature. By early 1992, two legislators had included several of the project's emerging agreements into growth management bills, and the project team was confident that many of the ideas generated by the exercise would find their way into state policy on growth management.

The Growth Management Project explored issues of specific relevance to California, but the underlying process can be applied to many areas of environmental management in which the interplay of interest groups threatens to block all progress towards sustainable development and cohesive thinking on long range policy options. This is an increasingly familiar situation in the advanced industrial countries, where powerful lobbies for economic development vie with the burgeoning environmental protection movement, and where the awareness of ecological and social limits to growth raise many problems of social equity. It will become more familiar in the newly industrialising world as environmental debates open up and unrestrained development comes under question. The great potential of techniques for mediation and consensus-building will surely be explored by many other states, North and South, as the conflicts of interest mount in the debate on sustainable development.

13   The Netherlands National Environmental Policy Plan*

The National Environmental Policy Plan (NEPP), published in 1989 by the government of the Netherlands, is perhaps the most striking example to date of long range policy making in environmental management at the national level. Inspired by the vision of sustainable development set out in the Brundtland Report, the NEPP analyses the challenges posed by environmental problems and sets out policy goals for the next twenty years, cutting across administrative boundaries, economic sectors and levels of activity from the local to the international. It is of considerable interest as a model of public policy development in environmental management for a densely-populated and heavily polluted industrial country. However, the process through which the Plan has been assembled and revised is also significant: the NEPP is the product of an emerging process of networking and consensus-building at the level of the nation-state. It is not the work of any one political party or ideological movement, but rather the output of a process sharing features of the network approach at the local and regional levels described in our other case studies.[1,2]

The NEPP is an example of good practice in policy integration and networking relevant to all industrialised countries, but it arises from distinctive features of Dutch political culture, and must be understood against the background of Dutch traditions in physical planning and of the ecological pressures at work in the Netherlands.

THE NETHERLANDS POLICY BACKGROUND

Land use and industrial development

The Netherlands is a small, densely populated country in which the taming and management of nature have been fundamental to the very existence of the nation. The land is almost entirely given over to intensive agriculture, industry, transport infrastructure and housing. Large areas are also, famously, the creation of environmental management: the coastal landscape has been for centuries the site of prodigious efforts at land reclamation and dike construction. The urban environment is no less striking, dominated by an enormous network of cities – including Amsterdam and Rotterdam – known as the 'Randstad' (urban ring). The industrial base of the Netherlands is centred on intensive agriculture: the country is the world's third largest exporter of farm produce.[1,2]

The institutional framework: planning and consensus-building

The need to control and reshape landscape, and the pressures on the country from population growth and industrialisation, have greatly influenced the institutional

* See also pp. 198–199.

framework of policy making in the Netherlands. The two decades after World War II saw the gradual development of a system of national physical planning as a means of managing industrialisation and post-war reconstruction and housing a growing population. The national system set out broad lines of development for land use, and more detailed planning was carried out by provincial and local government.[3]

The evolution of the planning system has reflected changes in ideas about the role of the state in economic development and social policy over recent years. The 'top-down' strategic planning approach of the immediate post-war period was modified by the 1970s, with greater efforts to consult the public, and elaborate systems for co-ordination of land use plans between different sectors.[4] By the late 1980s, when the Fourth Physical Planning Report was produced, the ascendancy of free market liberalism in the West was reflected in the further downplaying of detailed strategic planning. Emphasis shifted to a facilitating role for central government and partnership between the public and private sectors and the stimulation of voluntary action by companies and individuals:

> The more rational approach to strategic planning, based on systems thinking, was set aside in favour of an approach characterised by negotiations with important agents of economic change; an orientation towards market forces; much more open-ended and broad policies combined with safeguards for the implementation of specific elements considered to be 'of national importance'; and a strong revival of design in spreading the message of planning.[5]

The tendency to seek consensus is rooted in two other aspects of Dutch political culture. First, what Jamison et al[6] call 'the segmentation of Dutch society into various religious or political blocs, which is known in Dutch as *Verzuiling*'. This term means 'pillarisation', indicating the existence of distinct social 'pillars' on which the political order rests. This concept stems from the religious divisions that characterised Dutch society from the formation of the nation-state in the late sixteenth century, and which were modified by the process of early industrialisation. The political process was dominated by bargaining between the elites representing each religious or ideological 'pillar':

> Since the beginning of the twentieth century, these elites developed a policy of accommodation and pacification . . . This political attitude forms the basis of Dutch corporatism. Because each pillar represented a minority in Dutch society, none could make decisions without support from the others.[7]

Second, this historical tendency towards consensus-building is reinforced by the nature of Dutch political institutions. The electoral system is based on proportional representation, and coalition government is the norm, with consequent reliance for political stability on consensus-building and detailed negotiations between different political parties. The system is also characterised by considerable autonomy for ministers, who are directly responsible to Parliament rather than to the Prime Minister. As Faludi notes, in this context 'formulation of planning policy becomes a matter of interdepartmental negotiations . . . The advantage is that many planning documents are signed by all ministers responsible for policies set out therein'.[8] Finally, the emphasis on consensus is also promoted by the highly decentralised nature of the

Dutch state. There are 12 regional or provincial authorities and nearly 800 local authorities or municipalities. Although central government has a considerable amount of control over finances, the provinces and municipalities play a significant role in land use planning and implementation of environmental management laws, notably in the field of water management. The decentralised structure leads to 'interlocking of policy-making processes on all three levels of public administration' and to considerable 'bargaining and negotiation' between them over their respective roles in implementing policy.[9]

Pollution and the rise of environmental politics

The geography of the Netherlands and its success in developing intensive and highly productive agricultural industries have been the source of the country's severe environmental problems. It receives large loads of airborne pollution from neighbouring countries as well as from domestic sources. The Rhine and Meuse rivers drain large industrial areas of North-Western Europe and collect many pollutants from factories and agricultural runoff: the build-up of pollutants in the rivers damages drinking water and ultimately affects the North Sea. River pollution has also led to the accumulation of toxic chemicals in the Rhine estuary, making costly special storage necessary for sediments dredged from the delta area.[10]

The Netherlands also suffers from the effects of acid rain, to which domestic and neighbouring countries' sulphur dioxide and nitrogen oxide emissions contribute. The growth in road traffic has led to increased nitrogen oxide loads, cancelling out improvements in emission control technology; the number of cars is forecast to rise from around 5 million in 1989 to 7–8 million by 2010.[11] The first version of the NEPP envisaged an action plan on acid rain to the year 2000 that would protect only 20 per cent of the country's forests: given the scale of the problem, it was thought that only such a modest interim target was feasible.[12]

Other serious problems include loss of habitats for wildlife; subsequent loss of animal and plant species; and the disposal of household and industrial waste. But the overriding environmental problem facing the country is the pollution generated by its spectacularly productive agricultural sector. Two issues dominate this area of policy: the 'manure mountain' produced by the enormous livestock population (over 100 million animals), and the pollution of soils, groundwater and surface water by the pesticides and fertilisers hitherto essential to the great gains in agricultural productivity.[13] The quantity of manure produced by livestock is such that ammonia pollution of soils and air is a serious problem; the tonnage of manure greatly exceeds that which can be spread safely on farmland and recycled as fertiliser pellets. Moreover, leaching of pesticides and chemical fertilisers from fields into groundwater and surface water is facilitated by the network of canals and drainage ditches.

Public awareness of these problems has risen steadily since the initial stirring of environmental consciousness in the 1960s. This has been paralleled by the development of a strong and diverse environmentalist movement, and by the gradual recognition of environmental policy as a priority by political parties.[14] The 1970s saw the establishment of a Ministry of Health and Environmental Hygiene, and the passage of numerous laws to control pollution. In the 1980s there was a strong surge in support for determined action on environmental crises as awareness grew of the effects of acid rain, the problem of ozone depletion and the potential threat of global warming and sea level rises that would be disastrous for the Netherlands. This phase culminated in the publication in 1988 of a report entitled *Concern for Tomorrow* by the National Institute of Public Health and Environmental Hygiene, which publicised the scale of the emerging global environmental problems. This report produced a new sense of urgency among public and political organisations, and was an important input to the National Environmental Policy Plan.[15]

ORIGINS OF THE NEPP: TOWARDS INTEGRATED ENVIRONMENTAL POLICY

The environmental policy measures adopted in the Netherlands during the 1970s were typically 'media-oriented', with different pieces of legislation focusing on specific problems such as air pollution and soil contamination, all requiring different consultation and licensing procedures.[16] The rise of awareness of international pollution problems and of linkages between different pollution problems led to a gradual shift in the 1980s towards integrated policy making in environmental management. The move was also prompted by the need to deal with inconsistency in standard-setting and policy making between government departments.[17]

The first concrete steps towards integrated environmental management in the Netherlands came in 1984, with a workshop held in collaboration with the United States Environmental Protection Agency (EPA) in order to develop ideas for a new policy framework. The outcome was the preparation of a four-year programme for environmental policy across government departments, presented to Parliament at the end of 1984. Between 1984 and 1989 several more multi-year programmes were published. Meanwhile, an earlier administrative reorganisation had contributed to the process of integration: the General Directorate for the Environment was detached from the Health and Environment Ministry in 1982 and was merged with the Ministry for Housing and Physical Planning. The new department allowed for improved integration of environmental management into 'mainstream' policy making, and the new Minister brought environmental issues directly to Cabinet discussion for the first time – previously they had been the province of junior ministers.[18]

The key elements of the emerging integrated approach to environmental management were:[19]

- the identification of environmental themes as the basis for policy;
- the identification of target groups as partners in policy development and implementation; and
- the process of internal integration in environmental policy making.

The focus on environmental 'themes' (such as acidification or waste disposal) replaces the traditional compartmentalisation of problems on the basis of 'media' (air, soil, groundwater, sea water). Instead, policy makers are to work with cross-cutting concepts that allow all aspects of an ecological issue to be addressed. The basis for this approach is the recognition, now widespread, that a problem such as acidification is not simply a threat to air quality, but also to soil and water quality. Policy must therefore acknowledge the linkages between environmental media and analyse pollution flows 'in the round'.[20]

The need to identify and work with target groups is fundamental to the Dutch approach. The target groups include manufacturers, farmers, utilities and other constituencies whose co-operation is essential to the successful implementation of policies for reduction of emissions. The identification of these groups is carried out on the basis of the various themes: problems and proposed solutions are elaborated and the sectors of the economy involved in implementing the changes become apparent. The target groups are seen as negotiating partners to be involved in the development of environmental management plans, rather than as obstacles, or groups on which policies are to be imposed. The approach is underpinned in central government by the appointment of group managers within the Ministry of Housing, Physical Planning and the Environment, who have a dual mediating role as 'translators': conveying the demands of environmental management to the target groups; and relaying the concerns of the target groups back to central government.[21]

Finally, the process of internal integration concerns the continuing attempt to ensure that environmental management becomes a priority throughout government and industry, and among all citizens, rather than being seen as an 'external' issue to be dealt with only by the relevant ministries and specialist agencies. The 'internalisation' strategy involves:

- new lines of communication on environmental issues between public agencies and the three levels of government;
- elimination or reduction of emissions at source rather than at the end of production processes;
- emphasis on developing 'closed loop' management of industrial processes to minimise waste and emissions and reduce energy needs; and
- public education programmes to raise awareness of companies' and individuals' responsibility for cleaning up the environment – as the NEPP says, 'The private citizen is a de facto manager of the environment'.[22]

Integration is a long term development, as yet only partially complete even within government.[23] The process was accompanied by new funds for research programmes and for environmental organisations to develop public education schemes.[24]

In summary, the approach developed in the mid-1980s involved systematic analysis of pollution flows in order to develop the environmental 'themes' and set priorities and standards for reduction of emissions, and then seeking to work with target groups and convince them of the need to take greater responsibility for managing their impact on the environment. The focus on partnership with the target groups, the formation of linkages between different sectors and tiers of government, and the use of mediating target group managers all indicates the initial development of what we have called an 'action-centred network' approach at the national level.

Although the strategy of internalisation and working with target groups was seen as successful by the Ministry, there was a recognition that a more comprehensive approach to planning for long range environmental management was needed. De Jongh[25] sets out the main reasons for the decision to embark on the development of what became the NEPP:

- the need for a long term strategy based on environmental forecasts;
- the need to give a clear indication to Dutch industry of exactly what environmental policy would imply for its operations over the long term;
- the need to secure wider co-operation of other government departments with interests in aspects of environmental policy, such as the ministries of Agriculture, Transport, and Economic Affairs;
- the desire to enhance public understanding of the demands of environmental management, and in particular to emphasise the positive features of new policies rather than associate environmental planning always with analysis of ecological threats;
- the new impetus to long term environmental management provided by the publication of the Brundtland Report.[26]

The ground for the NEPP was prepared by the Dutch government report *Concern for Tomorrow*, produced in 1988 by the National Institute of Public Health and Environmental Hygiene. The report made a considerable public impact, and concluded that the sustainable development path urged by the Brundtland Report could only be reached by the Netherlands if emission and waste reductions of 70–90 per cent were made by 2010. The required reductions could only be made either through cutting the volume of emission sources or through 'structural changes' in production and consumption patterns (for example, reducing car journeys and implementing new forms of industrial process to minimise waste).

According to de Jongh, the message of the report had a profound effect on the officials working on the NEPP:

> . . . the positive element we were looking for was found: . . . to avoid volume-reduction measures, structural changes in consumption and production patterns should be prepared. But such changes . . . can be a challenge, not only for policy makers, but also for developers and technology innovators.[27]

The NEPP was to set out a vision of *opportunities* for economic development and improved quality of life, as well as to analyse problems.

KEY ELEMENTS OF THE NEPP

The Plan was submitted to Parliament in May 1989 by the Minister of Housing, Physical Planning and Environment on behalf of his department and of the Ministries of Economic Affairs, Agriculture and Fisheries, and Transport and Public Works. It is a substantial report, given the title in its English translation of *To Choose or to Lose*. The main aspects of the NEPP are outlined below.

Multiple timescales for action and policy development

The preface states that the NEPP 'contains the strategy for environmental policy in the medium term directed at the attainment of sustainable development . . . The long term objectives in this NEPP are intended to provide tentative direction to this process'. The NEPP uses distinct timescales, setting out short term policy proposals, medium term strategic goals, and long term aspirations to 2010. The intention is to produce a new NEPP every five years. This approach recognises 'lag times' in the understanding of environmental problems and the development and implementation of policies, a factor that requires policy makers to think in terms of decades for the solution of many problems.

Multi-level analysis of environmental issues

The NEPP, drawing on the report *Concern for Tomorrow*, identifies five scales on which ecological problems develop and must be tackled:

1   local: the built environment, soil contamination, local air pollution, noise pollution;
2   regional: waste disposal, eutrophication, landscape degradation, changes in soil balance;
3   fluvial: eutrophication, deforestation, soil erosion, pollution of groundwaters, rivers and coasts, accumulations of chemicals in soils;
4   continental: acidification, photochemical airborne pollution;
5   global: enhanced greenhouse effect, depletion of the ozone layer, pollution of oceans, loss of biodiversity.

The levels are not independent – problems overlap, and increasingly they are occurring at higher levels as industrialisation spreads around the planet. At the fluvial level the policies of any one country must typically be accompanied by concerted action by its neighbours; at the continental and global levels joint action by many countries is essential.

Emphasis on integrated policy

The NEPP identifies the main problems facing environmental policy makers: the externalisation or 'roll off' of problems by producers and consumers, the displacement of environmental problems by inadequate co-ordination of abatement measures, excessive energy and resource consumption, the neglect of recycling and waste minimisation, and the failure to manage feedback of damaging emissions and waste streams. The solution proposed is to focus on integrated pollution control. This is to be achieved not only through application of best available technology, the well-known Polluter Pays principle and the principle of reducing pollution at source rather than at the 'end of the pipe', but also through structural measures and the process of internalisation.

Structural measures include the radical modification of production processes to cut energy consumption, enhance quality of output, and close product life cycles as far as possible by recycling and by minimising waste. 'Internalisation', as mentioned above, involves the encouragement of producers and consumers to take on responsibilities in environmental management and the development of environmental policy as an integral part of the business of all government bodies and industrial organisations. The NEPP speaks of 'external integration' as the process through which environmental considerations enter the mainstream of policy making in all government agencies. Links are also to be developed between central and local government in order to improve enforcement of environmental regulations.

Policy development based on environmental themes

The NEPP identifies several themes for the elaboration of specific policies:

- climate change and the need for reduction of greenhouse gas emissions, especially of carbon dioxide and CFCs;
- acidification;
- eutrophication;
- diffusion of harmful chemicals;
- waste management;
- disturbance (noise pollution, odour and local air pollution);
- dehydration of soils relating to the need to reduce household and industrial consumption of water to restore a balance between consumption and ground-water and surface water sources);
- 'squandering' (relating to the need to prevent waste by developing measures that will indicate the value of environmental resources and reward behaviour compatible with sustainable development; policies include development of environmental accounts, product life cycle analyses, and corporate environmental programmes).

Co-operation with target groups

A further continuation from the programmes of the mid-1980s is the identification of several target groups for consultation and co-operation in the development and implementation of policies flowing from the various themes listed above. The NEPP makes it clear that the long term goals will only be reached if there is extensive and intensive collaboration between government and the different interests represented by the target groups.[28] The following target groups are specified:

- agricultural producers;
- transport sector;
- manufacturers, especially chemical producers, and refineries;
- gas and electricity suppliers;
- construction industry;
- consumers and retailers;
- environmental protection industry;
- research and educational establishments;
- environmental organisations, trade unions, voluntary bodies.

For each group the NEPP indicates the implications of the measures required under each of the environmental themes, the contributions required of organisations and individuals over the period 1990–94, and longer term, and what role the government expects to play in helping to meet the objectives. The measures envisaged place major demands on the target groups and mean radical change in existing patterns of consumption and production. Some of the main objectives for various target groups are noted below.

- Agriculture: a 70 per cent reduction in ammonia emissions from 1980 levels by the year 2000; a 50 per cent cut in the use of pesticides, with elimination of harmful substances; construction of manure processing plants with an overall capacity of 20 million tonnes by 2000 (current capacity is around 500,000 tonnes).

- Transport sector: exhaust pollution from passenger cars to be cut by 75 per cent from 1980 levels by 2000; 10 per cent reduction in carbon dioxide emissions from vehicles by 2010; use of cleaner technologies for vehicles; structural measures such as increased taxes on fuel, road-pricing and new public transport investment to reduce single-passenger car journeys in favour of public transport, cycling and shared car transport; structural measures in land use planning to reduce the need for travel.
- Manufacturers and refineries: integration of environmental concern into mainstream business and development of internal environmental audits and controls; sulphur dioxide emissions to be cut by 80 per cent by 2000; estimated environmental costs for industry as a whole to rise from 1.8 billion guilders in 1988 to 3–3.5 billion by 1994; complete life-cycle analyses for new products and replacement of harmful chemicals.
- Consumers: energy consumption in 2000 to be at 1985 levels; limited growth only in passenger miles per car, and more use of transport modes other than private cars; by 2000, all used batteries, small chemical waste, tin, glass and paper to be collected separately for disposal and recycling.
- Environmental protection sector: waste processing companies to ensure the improvement of the disposal system to minimise landfill site dumping, incinerate more waste and use the heat generated, and promote recycling; drinking water suppliers to develop a role as all-round 'environmental firms', signalling problems and improving public information; environmental technology producers are given a key role in developing clean integrated processes and helping to introduce the major policy changes in industry.
- Environmental organisations, trade unions, voluntary bodies: special emphasis is laid on the 'indispensable' role of environmental interest groups and campaigners in highlighting environmental problems, raising public awareness, disseminating information and promoting environmental consciousness among all of the various target groups.

EVOLUTION OF THE NEPP SINCE 1989

The NEPP thus represents an ambitious statement of governmental intent, and presents a remarkable challenge to the different sectors of Dutch society and economy. However, in the short time since its publication it has become more ambitious still in its goals, as described below.

Ironically, given its origins in a process of consensus-building and mediation, the NEPP has attracted much attention abroad for apparently causing the fall of the then Dutch coalition government in 1989 – the first time a government had been toppled by an environmental issue, according to many commentators. In fact, the political developments in question demonstrate the remarkable level of consensus across party lines achieved in the evolution of the Plan. The coalition government that prepared the NEPP comprised the centrist conservative Christian Democrats and the centre-right free market Liberals. The radical nature of the NEPP is all the more striking for being the product of an administration essentially fiscally conservative and pro-business in character. The coalition was an uneasy one, and in the debates over the NEPP the Liberals seized on a single proposal – for abolition of tax relief for commuters – and opposed it to the point of bringing down the coalition. While the fall of the government was seen abroad as the first case of an environmental issue bringing down an administration, this was a simplistic view of the situation. The dispute over the commuter tax relief was more a pretext for the eruption of long standing personal rivalries within the Liberal party and the coalition: the NEPP was by contrast a matter of near-total cross-party consensus, and in the subsequent elections all of the main parties espoused variations on the NEPP.[29]

The outcome of the 1989 elections was the formation of a new coalition, this time between the Christian Democrats under the Prime Minister Ruud Lubbers, and the social democratic Labour Party. The change of government led to changes in the NEPP. A revised version appeared in June 1990, known as the National Environmental Policy Plan Plus (NEPP-Plus). The remarkable degree of consensus on environmental issues ensured continuity of policy on sustainable development. The NEPP-Plus differed from its precursor mainly in calling for more rapid implementation of many policies and more ambitious targets for reduction of emissions over the 1990–94 period, and to the end of the century. Environmental spending by government, industry and agriculture and households is set to rise still further, reaching 16 billion guilders in 1994. Some of the key points of the NEPP-Plus are:

- higher targets for reduction of carbon dioxide emissions, involving absolute reductions of 3–5 per cent by 2000 from 1989 levels (a special carbon tax on fossil fuels will partly meet the costs of this policy, raising 150 million guilders by 1994);
- an Energy Conservation Plan calls for a 20 per cent cut in energy consumption from 1990 levels by 2000; and the energy utilities have developed a plan to promote conservation in households, industry and government;[30]
- the target of a 10 per cent cut in the quantity of waste generated by 2000, with further measures to promote recycling and waste prevention;
- increased investment in public transport, tougher financial measures to discourage the use of private cars, and changes in land use planning policy to encourage public transport access to housing and business developments;
- increased attention to the development of new regulatory mechanisms and financial incentives to promote sustainable development;
- improved efforts to achieve integration between the NEPP-Plus and its successors after 1994 and the strategic plans produced by other Ministries, for example on agriculture, physical planning and nature conservation (the Nature Policy Plan of 1990 sets out policy goals for the next 30 years).

The NEPP-Plus retains all the key features of the original NEPP in relation to environmental themes and the principle of dialogue and partnership with target groups. It slightly reduces the extra costs to be borne by agriculture and households, while increasing the contributions to be made by manufacturers (up by 16 per cent from the level set out in the NEPP) and by government (up by nearly 50 per cent).

It thus represents a strengthening of many of the NEPP's proposals. It received parliamentary approval in 1990 and is being implemented. The NEPP-Plus came in for considerable criticism from environmental campaigners and politicians on the grounds that the revision of the first Plan had meant a year lost in the struggle against pollution;[31] and the revision of the NEPP unleashed controversy over the timescale for stabilising carbon dioxide emissions.[32] Despite the arguments that greeted the new government, the principle of regular updating of the NEPP and the consensus on the need to make radical 'structural change' in pursuit of sustainable development seem to have become firmly established, among not only political parties, but also industry and the general public. This is the result of substantial efforts to develop consultative networks and mediating systems to assist in policy formation.

THE PROCESS BEHIND THE NEPP: NETWORKING, MEDIATION, ITERATION

The acceptance of environmental issues as top priorities for policy by the main political parties was accompanied by a new openness towards the environmentalist movement. Increasingly, government agencies sought the opinions and advice of lobby groups, and the latter gained in professionalism and scientific expertise.[33] A 'new pragmatism' developed among many environmentalists about collaboration with the political and industrial establishment in pursuit of environmental goals, and despite tensions among some campaigning groups over the danger of 'incorporation' in the mainstream political culture, the lines of communication between environmental organisations, business and public agencies are clear.

The spirit of consensus-building and co-operation between different interest groups is basic to the development of the NEPP. De Jongh[34] notes that:

The process of preparation of the NEPP was founded on the idea of 'open planning': industry and interest-groups should be involved in the process of preparation and should not be confronted with final decisions.

The development of the NEPP took place in an atmosphere of heightened urgency over ecological threats and intense public discussion:

. . . a substantial part of the Dutch population was confronted repeatedly with drafts of the NEPP . . . The battles among the various ministries – tiresome enough even when fought behind closed doors – came out into the open. For more than a year environmental policy was one of the major topics being handled by the media.[35]

De Jongh[36] describes the process of compiling the original NEPP. The development of the NEPP began in 1986 with a workshop involving representatives of industry, local and provincial authorities, environmental organisations and the Ministry of Housing, Physical Planning and Environment. This meeting established an agenda of key issues and concepts for policy development. This was followed in 1987 by the creation of an inter-ministerial group to elaborate the Plan. In addition a high-level steering group was established, along with 'circles' of officials focusing on specific themes and concepts. 'Theme co-ordinators' were required to provide reports on the quality standards to be aimed for in the long term and the measures needed to achieve them. Consultations went on meanwhile with industry and environmental organisations.

In the autumn of 1988 a further, wider round of consultation was carried out to assess the response of representatives of the target groups and of local and provincial government to the analysis of the report *Concern for Tomorrow* and its proposed targets for emission reduction. This set of discussions was managed by professional facilitators and sought to answer the question, 'What can your target group contribute to meeting the challenge of the required reductions in emissions?' De Jongh notes that the outcome of the consultation was important not so much for its effect on the content of the NEPP draft as for its effect on the target groups: minds were concentrated on the urgency of the demands of environmental management, and a major contribution was made to 'agenda-building' within the target groups as well as within government. The final phase of drafting was largely confined to government, with the debate focusing on short term implications for expenditure.

The process thus involved the creation of networks designed to produce improvements in the draft of the Plan, changes to the internal agendas of government agencies and target groups, and qualitative responses to the concepts and objectives set out in the Plan. The process was relatively open, and de Jongh stresses the importance in strategic planning for environmental management of bringing in ideas from interest groups, and in particular of people not 'heavily involved in day-to-day policy making on one aspect' of environmental policy. The process of consultation with target groups will be repeated in the development of the next NEPP, thus setting up a long term process designed to produce continual improvement of the Plan in the light of environmental, technological and economic change. As successive versions of the NEPP are prepared, the networks linking public agencies, governmental tiers and target groups will be strengthened.

The implementation of the NEPP also involves an extensive process of networking and mediation in relation to the technical means of implementation and the timimg of specific measures. The NEPP proposes the establishment of a NEPP Steering Committee for Industry, with representatives of industrial sectors and of government agencies, to co-ordinate consultations and to monitor and evaluate implementation of policies affecting industry. For other target groups, separate programmes of consultations are envisaged on implementation of NEPP policies.

The NEPP also proposes the use of voluntary agreements or 'covenants' that may be a substitute for government regulation where they can achieve effective results. An example of the approach is the plan to use covenants between government and industrial sectors on energy saving: agreements can be signed after joint investigation of the scope for investments in pursuit of NEPP objectives, and this arrangement allows a 'customised' setting of targets for industries instead of top-down regulation.[37]

CONCLUSION

The NEPP Plus is only a first step towards a sustainable development path, and will be modified after 1994. New policies at European Community level, economic and technical change, and new information on ecological problems from the local to the global level will all need to be taken into account as medium and long term goals are set. The NEPP approach is too new to be judged: the degree of success of the Dutch move to integrated planning for sustainable development will only become clear later in the 1990s.

Notable uncertainties and constraints remain despite the general success of the consultative process to date. First, as the NEPP-Plus says, there is a need for still better integration and co-ordination within government. The Dutch system has generated large numbers of plans and memoranda since the mid-1980s, and it is important that coherent linkages should be established between long range plans in areas such as land use and nature conservation and the NEPP-Plus and its successors.

Second, achieving the goals set out in the NEPP-Plus requires prodigious efforts at monitoring and evaluation, especially in measuring effects, and this alone will place massive demands on the networks built up within government, and between government and the target groups. The targets set out in the Plan may need to be revised in the light of improved scientific information about pollution loads and the impact of specific measures; and the mechanisms for implementing the Plan have yet to be developed fully.

Third, the remarkable consensus on environmental priorities and the need for structural change in pursuit of sustainable development is sure to be put under strain. The initial response of leading environmental bodies to the NEPP-Plus was highly critical,[38] and the large costs involved in meeting the short range goals will provoke opposition from business as the economy is strained by recession and by intensified competition in the post-1992 European market. Moreover, the Government has yet to take action on limiting greenhouse gas emissions that will significantly affect motorists' habits. Road pricing measures have not been introduced, and the NEPP's recommendations on personal transport and restricting traffic growth are the issues that have generated most controversy and least consensus.[39] As in California's debate on growth management (see Chapter 12), it is relatively easy to agree on the need to reduce car dependence, but specific measures produce 'marked nervousness on the part of the politicians about putting these into practice'.[40] The importance of the car in consumer culture poses major challenges to consensus-building on environmental policy in the Netherlands as it does in other industrial countries.

Fourthly, and crucially, support for the Plan will certainly be put under pressure if the Dutch government's commitment to sustainable development is not matched by its partners in the European Community and the OECD.[41] Many of the problems analysed in the Plan are continental in nature and require co-ordinated policies in several countries. If the Netherlands' European Community partners do not join in a cohesive and ambitious strategy for moving towards sustainable development, and if the Plan's environmental measures do prove to be disadvantageous for Dutch industry, especially for agricultural producers, there will be clamour for a slowdown in the implementation of the Plan or modification of targets.

Despite these constraints, there is clearly a deep-seated consensus within the political system and industry on the inescapability of radical policies for managing sustainable development. Moreover, it is unlikely that the Netherlands' European Community partners will be able to argue for long against adoption of similar objectives given the build-up of common problems of emission reduction, energy inefficiency and waste disposal.

Although it would be foolish to imagine that the NEPP approach could be exported without problems to countries with different traditions and institutional frameworks, it surely has lessons for other countries. These relate to the implications for environmental management of the recognition of the linkages between environmental problems traditionally dealt with on a fragmented basis, and between different levels of geographical scale. The Dutch approach recognises that multi-level, long-lasting and multi-dimensional environmental problems demand long range, holistic solutions. This implies the need to reorganise policy responses on the basis of environmental themes, the analysis of which in turn indicates the need to involve key target groups in designing and implementing solutions. The target groups must also be mobilised over the long term, in an iterative process of mediation, consultation, and evaluation, in order to keep up with dynamic changes in the environment. Finally, the need for long term continuity demands top-level commitment to the overall goals of sustainable environmental management among political parties and target groups, even if opinions differ widely on specific measures. The Dutch experience provides a model of action-centred networking and mediation at the level of the nation-state that cannot be ignored by other democracies facing the demands that the imperative of sustainable development will place on their institutions and capacity for consensus-building in the 1990s and beyond.

14   Conclusions

Our hope is that by concentrating on the generation of trust through careful experimentation with different structures and procedures, humanity at least stands a chance of coping with the challenges of global environmental change.

S Rayner and T O'Riordan[1]

This book has developed ideas about the forms of organisation for environmental management most suited to the challenges posed by sustainable development. The claim has been made that organisational innovation is critical to the task of managing sustainable industrial development. A key innovation is the development of the action-centred network, a flexible non-hierarchical partnership between different interests. This model can be implemented both in developed and in industrialising countries, and at all levels of environmental management from the local to the national. It is an appropriate organisational 'technology' in the face of the challenges posed by the need for sustainable development. Like the problems it addresses, it cuts across policy compartments. It fosters the policy integration and consensus that are demanded if structural change in industrial and industrialising societies is to be achieved. This chapter sums up the argument.

INDUSTRIALISM BECOMES A GLOBAL SYSTEM

The post-war period has seen a spectacular development in international trade and production. Industrialism is becoming a global system. The low income countries aspire to industrialisation; the ex-communist states aspire to achieve Western-style modernisation; the reach of telecommunications and transport is now global, taking the messages of consumer culture to every country. It is practically impossible to 'opt out' of the industrial system.[2] In the wake of industrialisation comes environmental disruption on a hitherto unimagined scale.

The rapid development of new industrial economies and the acceleration of technological change in the West generate complex and dynamic forces in the international economy. Great structural inequalities divide the high income world from the poor South; the pressure of new competition generates tensions within the West; and the collapse of communist economies has unleashed a wave of free market capitalism in the former Soviet bloc and in the Third World. These forces intensify global stresses on the environment. The interactions between the global economy and ecosystems are only dimly understood, but are known to be of vast complexity and dynamism. The world of global modernity is thus immensely turbulent.

LIMITS TO MODERNITY

As modernity becomes a global condition, it is becoming clear that there are limits to industrial development as the West has known it and as the rest of the world would like to know it. Industrialism has conquered the globe, bringing for billions undeniable material benefits and advances in understanding. But it is increasingly clear that industrialism as we have known it is unsustainable. Limits to modernity are becoming evident in a number of areas.

Political culture and environmental management

In Parts I and II it was argued that the challenges posed by environmental crises place severe constraints on long-established elements of political culture in industrial societies. The two great models of industrialism – socialist centralised planning and liberal capitalism – are both inadequate. The removal of the communist model from much of the world demonstrates the *failure* of centralised planning rather than the ultimate *success* of liberal capitalism. The latter system, especially in its laissez-faire conservative form, also cannot deal adequately with emerging regional, continental and global environmental problems through its favoured mechanism, the decentralised free market. Environmental management for sustainability is an intensely political process, involving continuous mediation between environmental values and socio-economic goals. It is inescapably bound up with trade-offs between competing interests, and between decentralised and centralised action. It calls for new forms of consensus-building between the state, market institutions and the groupings of 'civil society'.

Science and sustainability

In Part II it was argued that the emergence of global environmental problems poses profound challenges to the rationality that has dominated Western science and technology since the Enlightenment. Key features of this model of scientific understanding include a split between human observers/actors and 'nature', and between facts and values; and a view that systems can best be understood through analysing their components. We have gained vast knowledge through the application of this model, but its limitations are revealed by global environmental change. The environment is not separate from humanity: rather, human activity is a fundamental feature of ecosystems in the new global environment. The need to achieve sustainability means that the technologies generated from scientific understanding cannot be seen as value-free, but must be assessed on the basis of social goals and values affecting the environment. Finally, the immense complexity of ecosystems and global systems such as the atmosphere defeats the traditional analytic approach: the science of global environmental change is marked by uncertainty and the need for holistic understanding of dynamic systems. The science of global environmental problems is bound up with political issues, the need for action in the face of uncertainty, and the fact that traditional scientific analysis is not sufficient to provide solutions.[3]

Social and ecological limits

While many physical limits to growth may be distant, social and ecological limits apply to the growth of consumerism in industrial societies. The ecological limits are set by the emergence of global environmental threats. The social limits derive from the inherently self-defeating character of much 'positional' consumption[4] and the element of pointlessness in what Ernest Gellner calls the 'perpetual potlatch' culture of consumerism: 'Affluent society simply chases its own tail'.[5] Global environmental threats also draw attention to the unsustainable inequalities between the rich industrial countries and the poor South: in particular, the gross disparities between energy consumption and resource use by the West and the low income countries in which the mass of the world's population lives. Ecological threats are exacerbated by key features of the global economic order such as the debt burden on the Third World. There has been a failure to integrate environmental sustainability as a basic concern in the global policy making bodies – the IMF, World Bank, GATT and transnational corporations.

The implications of these limits are as yet unclear. There is no prospect of a renunciation of industrialism, even if that were desirable; and there can be no denying the aspirations of the lower income countries to improved standards of living and a greater share of the world's energy consumption. Given these constraints, we must try to reconcile industrialism with the maintenance of the global commons: in short, to aim for a sustainable 'eco-industrial' society. The nature of a sustainable system is poorly understood, and we are unlikely to arrive soon at a conception of sustainability as an 'end product'. Rather, we need to manage in ways that will bring closer the various goals we can associate with sustainability – in other words, consider sustainable development as a *process* that we can improve by continuous learning and adaptation of organisational forms and policies.

MANAGING IN TURBULENT ENVIRONMENTS: THE ACTION-CENTRED NETWORK

In Part III we examined the main institutional constraints on managing for sustainable development: the fragmented nature of policy making in key institutions; failure to promote organisational learning; the lack of policy integration in economic management; the massive complexity of environmental problems; the difficulty in balancing 'top-down' and 'bottom-up' initiatives in environmental management and planning; and the great turbulence of the world as industrialism becomes a global condition.

Part IV argued for innovative organisational forms for environmental manage-ment – action-centred networks. These are designed to overcome the constraints afflicting traditional systems and methods, and to fit the nature of the problems of environmental change. In the face of dynamic, complex, interconnected problems, we need flexible, experimental organisations spanning disciplines, bridging policy compartments and social sectors. These organisational forms are capable of rapid learning, using all available knowledge (including 'local' skills and knowledge, not just those deemed 'scientific'). They are based on equal partnership between different sectors, and foster consensus wherever possible, since environmental change causes major conflicts of interest between environmental, economic and social goals. They seek to develop flexible initiatives, with a continual process of problem specification, action, feedback and revision of policy.

Action-centred networks are developing the world over, at various scales of activity from the local to the national. They reflect an emerging consensus among environmental campaigners and international bodies for environmental protection on the organisational mechanisms for promoting sustainable development.[6] In Part V we considered examples ranging from the local Groundwork Trusts in the UK, to the IDEA project in lower income countries at the regional/fluvial level, the California Growth Management Consensus Project at the state government level, and the Netherlands National Environment Policy Plan. These diverse initiatives are all affected by various constraints and weaknesses, and all must be regarded as a modest beginning rather than a definitive achievement. But they represent striking examples of good practice and fruitful experimentation, and deserve attention from decision makers.

At the local level, the Groundwork Trusts in the UK demonstrate how the action-centred network approach can be used to encourage business to enter partnerships with government, public agencies and community organisations to carry out environmental regeneration in urban areas. The Groundwork initiative offers business a way in to deeper commitment to environmental management and wider partnership with local communities.

At the fluvial, regional level the IDEA programme shows the benefits of action-centred networks for analysing and tackling problems of environmental management in low income countries. IDEA allows stakeholders from different sectors to work together and learn from each other in identifying problems, developing ways of overcoming conflicts, and mobilising local skills in areas such as watershed management and waste disposal. In California, the Growth Management Project has initiated a similar process among often antagonistic interest groups in order to help stakeholders identify areas of actual and emerging consensus.

Finally, at the national level the Netherlands National Environmental Policy Plan (NEPP) represents the most ambitious attempt to date by an industrial country to devise a strategy for movement towards sustainable development. The NEPP is a dynamic process: a set of goals subject to revision in the light of new circumstances and evaluation of achievements. The creation of a consultative network of 'target groups' is fundamental to this: the NEPP and its successors are to be developed on the basis of discussion and consensus throughout Dutch society. As the NEPP notes, we are all *de facto* environmental managers: progress towards sustainable development depends on understanding and acceptance of responsibility by all groups and by individual citizens. For this to be developed, the policy process cannot be wholly 'top-down' in design – instead, it must be based on mediation, partnership and the fostering of consensus where possible.

CONCLUSION: THE FUTURE OF THE NETWORK MODEL

What is missing in this account are examples of the multi-sector action-centred network at the international level. It is hard to see what other form of organisation could begin to make real progress in forging and then implementing agreements between nation-states, international agencies and transnational corporations on the threats to the global environment. Global warming, appropriate technology transfer and the loss of biodiversity are matters of intense controversy between nation states, and rapid progress toward meaningful international treaties is unlikely, even the time is not on our side in coping with ecological degradation.

In such a context, the worldwide promotion of multi-sector partnerships for environmental management at all levels would be a powerful innovation in the cause of sustainable development. Already there are extensive networks linking NGOs around the world, and the UNCED Conference in Rio de Janeiro in 1992 stimulated more networking among campaigning bodies. Forty-eight TNCs have formed a powerful Business Council for Sustainable Development, with a national sub-grouping in Malaysia, to promote debate in business on environmental issues.[7] There are myriad multinational governmental bodies in need of improved co-ordination and better integration of environmental policy.[8]

How can these international networks be brought into co-operative ventures? How could the values and techniques of the action-centred network approach be diffused? One initiative often mentioned in the context of global environmental change is the Marshall Plan. Many argue that only a Marshall-scale transfer of money and technology from the West to the ex-communist countries and Third World can hope to make a reality of sustainable development in countries seeking to emulate Western forms of industrialism.[9] Massive transfers of financial and technological resources are crucial, but organisational skills and institutional design are also fundamental to realising sustainable development. The action-centred network is a necessary feature of the organisational basis for sustainable environmental management, and its techniques need to be diffused (in the West as well as the rest of the world) as much as do clean technologies.

The rich Western powers, so far reluctant to contemplate a massive transfer of money and technology, could well afford to finance a 'Marshall Plan' for environmental management. This would take the form of a programme of diverse initiatives to build up international multi-sector networks for action on key problems. For example, it could empower NGOs to work closely on project assessment with international business groups and bodies such as the World Bank, IMF and GATT, in pursuit of better integration of environmental concerns into mainstream policy. The initiative would also seek to transfer skills in environmental management and mediation; to generate new ideas for environmental management at all levels from the local to the global; and to allow mutual learning between organisations of all kinds. An international network drawing on the experience of Groundwork in the UK could disseminate the techniques of local partnerships in urban environmental improvement; an international Growth Management Project could spread techniques of environmental dispute resolution and mediation; and the IDEA system, already an international network in the Commonwealth, is well placed for wider dissemination in the Third World.

Such a programme would seek to transfer best practice in environmental management, including the expertise of voluntary agencies and local communities, not only from the West to the ex-communist world and the Third World, but also between Third World countries, within the industrialised world, and from low income countries to the West. Such a programme is far from Utopian and would be relatively inexpensive; would stimulate innovations; and would provide the essential managerial underpinning for effective transfers of resources and technology.

The action-centred network for environmental management is no panacea. The approach will not always succeed. Not all problems are amenable to consensus-building. The approach is not a substitute for campaigning, regulation, market-based incentives or technological innovation, and other means through which environmental problems are addressed and resolved. But it is an essential comple-ment to them. On an industrial planet, faced with mounting ecological problems and massive political and economic turbulence, the old institutional forms and manage-ment approaches can no longer analyse environmental challenges adequately, devise solutions that fit the multi-faceted and complex problems, and mobilise diverse social groups in a democratic framework to implement them. The action-centred network offers a solution that fits the nature of our new problems. It can make a key contribution to managing the process of sustainable development.

Notes and references

CHAPTER 1

1   Swanson, T and Barbier, E, 'The end of wildlands and wildlife?', in Swanson, T and Barbier, E (eds), *Economics for the Wilds: Wildlife, Wildlands, Diversity and Development*, Earthscan, London, 1992.

2   See for example: Mannion, A M, *Global Environmental Change: A Natural and Cultural Environmental History*, Longman Scientific and Technical, London, 1991 (co-published in the US with John Wiley and Sons, New York); Myers, N, *The Gaia Atlas of Planet Management*, Pan Books, London and Sydney, 1986; Schnelling, T C, 'Global environmental forces', *Technological Forecasting and Social Change*, Vol. 38, pp. 257-64, 1990; Holdgate, M, *The Environment of Tomorrow's World*, The David Davies Memorial Institute of International Studies, London, 1991; Defries, R S and Malone, T (eds) *Global Environmental Change and Our Common Future: Papers from a Forum*, National Academy of Sciences, Washington, 1989; Turner, B L, Clark, W C, Kates, R W, Richards, J F, Mathews, J T and Mayer, W B (eds), *The Earth as Transformed by Human Action*, Cambridge University Press, Cambridge, 1990; Arthur, W, *The Green Machine: Ecology and the Balance of Nature*, Basil Blackwell, Oxford, 1990; Calder, N, *Spaceship Earth*, Penguin, London, 1991.

3   For detailed arguments in favour of the 'technocentric' view of global environmental change, see Simon J and Kahn, H (eds), *The Resourceful Earth*, Basil Blackwell, Oxford, 1984. See also Repetto, R (ed.), *The Global Possible*, Yale University Press, 1985.

4   Carley, M, 'Land use and the crisis of automobility', *Futures*, April, 1992.

5   Mannion, op cit, p. 326.

6   Singh, A and Tabatabai, H, 'Facing the crisis: Third World agriculture in the 1980s', *International Labour Review*, vol. 129, pp. 479-500, 1990.

7   *The Economist*, 'The green counter-revolution', 20 April, 1991, pp. 107-8.

8   *The Economist*, 'Aid to Africa: after the market', 8 December, 1990, pp. 92-3.

9   Tickell, C, 'Environmental refugees: the human impact of global climate change', *NERC News*, July, 1989, pp. 14-20.

10   Postel, S and Ryan, J C, 'Reforming forestry', in Brown, L, et al, *State of the World 1991*, World Resources Institute, Washington.

11   Mannion, op cit, pp. 237-41.

12   Edberg, R, *Vart Hotade Hem*, Bra Bocker, Hoganas, 1982.

13   Tickell, C, 'Timber and Destruction', *New Scientist*, 31 August, 1991, pp. 47-8.

14   Martin, C, *The Rainforests of West Africa*, Birkhauser Verlag, 1991.

15   Mannion, op cit, p. 238.

16   Simons, P, 'Politics beneath the tree line', *New Scientist*, 2 February, 1991.

17   Prance, G, 'Future of the Amazonian Rainforest', *Futures*, pp. 891-903, November, 1990.

18 Repetto, R, *The Forest for the Trees? Government Policies and the Misuse of Forest Resources*, World Resources Institute, Washington, 1988.

19 European Parliament Session Documents, *Report drawn up on behalf of the Committee on the Environment, Public Health and Consumer Protection on the Environmental Problems in the Amazon Region*, Muntingh, H (rapporteur), Series A, document A3-182-90.

20 Ibid, p. 10.

21 Daniel, J, 'The unkindest cut of all', *Nature Canada*, vol. 18, pp. 37–44, 1989.

22 See OECD, *Market and Government Failures in Environment Management*, OECD, Paris, 1992; Jones, T and Wibe, S (eds), *Forests: Market and Intervention Failures*, Earthscan, London, 1992.

23 Calder, op cit, p. 119.

24 Mannion, op cit, pp. 224–6.

25 Myers, op cit, pp. 46–7.

25 Mannion, op cit, p. 229.

26 Mannion, op cit, pp. 206–10.

27 Brown, op cit, p. 15.

28 Carley, P M, 'The price of the plan: perceptions of cotton and health in Uzbekistan and Turkmenistan', *Central Asian Survey*, vol. 8, pp. 1–38, 1989. Carley reports that poisonous chemicals are applied to the cotton crop in Uzbekistan at the rate of 54.5 kg per hectare compared to the average of 1 kg per hectare in the former USSR.

29 Carley, ibid, pp. 14–15.

30 Turner, K and Jones, T (eds), *Wetlands: Market and Intervention Failures*, Earthscan, London, 1991.

31 *The Virginian Pilot*, 'Environmentalists raise the red flags', 27 August, 1991; Dalyell, T, 'Wetlands caught in the tourist trap', *New Scientist*, 22/29 December, 1990.

32 Pearce, F, 'A dammed fine mess', *New Scientist*, 4 May, pp. 36–9, 1991.

33 Pearce, F, 'Power of the Himalayas', *The Independent on Sunday*, 1 December, 1991.

34 Pearce, op cit.

35 Pearce, op cit.

36 Forestier, K, 'China puts world's largest dam back on the agenda', *New Scientist*, 28 September, 1991.

37 Theys, J, '21st century: environment and resources', *European Environment Review*, vol. 1, pp. 2–7, 1987.

38 Hall, D, 'An enabling and decentralising strategy for the Third World', *Town and Country Planning*, January 1991, pp. 8–11.

39 Margolis, S, 'Bombay ducks growing crisis of urban poverty', *Planning*, no. 850, 1990, pp. 30–31.

40 Anton, D, *Urban Environments and Water in Latin America With Particular Emphasis on Groundwater*, Ottawa: IDRC-MR266e, 1990.

41 Park, P, 'Great Lakes pollution linked to infertility', *New Scientist*, 28 September, 1991.

42 Hordoy, J and Satterthwaite, D, *Environmental Problems in Third World Cities:*

A Global Problem Ignored? IIED Publications, London, 1990.

43 Mannion, op cit, p. 240.

44 McGee, T G, 'Asia's Growing Urban Rings', *Work in Progress*, vol. 13, p. 9, United Nations University, Tokyo.

45 Orski, C K, 'Managing suburban traffic congestion: a strategy for suburban mobility', *Transportation Quarterly*, vol. 41(4), pp. 457–76, 1987.

46 Orski, op cit, p. 463.

47 See for example Barde, J-P, and Button, K (eds), *Transport Policy and the Environment*, Earthscan, London, 1990.

48 Orski, op cit, p. 464.

49 Robertson, J T, 'Assessing our second(hand) America', *American Planning Association Journal*, pp. 271–6, Spring, 1987.

50 The World Vehicle Strategic Review and Forecast Data Book, Report no. 006, Euromotor Reports Ltd, London.

51 Estimated by the Rijksinstituut voor Volksgezondheid en Milieuhygiene (RIVM), Bilthoven, The Netherlands.

52 See for example, Tengstrom, E, *Automobility – Is It Approaching a Global Crisis?*, paper presented to the conference *Human Responsibility and Global Change*, University of Goteborg, Sweden, 1991.

53 Girardet, H, 'Closing the circle', *Town and Country Planning*, December, 1991, pp. 336–9.

54 Grubb, M, *The Greenhouse Effect: Negotiating Targets*, The Royal Institute of International Affairs, Energy and Environmental Programme, London, 1989.

55 On the scientific analysis of global warming, see IPCC, *The Scientific Assessment of Climate Change: Policymakers' Summary*, Cambridge University Press, Cambridge, 1990; Leggett, J (ed), *Global Warming: the Greenpeace Report*, Oxford University Press, Oxford, 1990; Schnieder, S H, *Global Warming*, Sierra Club, San Francisco, 1989.

56 Tickell, op cit, p. 15.

57 Schnelling, op cit, p. 257.

58 Grubb, op cit, p. 22.

59 Ibid. See also Christie, I, 'Social and political aspects of global warming', *Futures*, January/February, 1992.

60 Arizpe, L, 'The Global Cube', *International Social Science Journal*, no. 130, pp. 599–608, 1991.

61 Robinson, J B, 'Modelling the interactions between human and natural systems', *International Social Science Journal*, no. 130, pp. 629–48, 1991. See also International Federation of Institutes of Advanced Study, *The Human Dimensions of Global Change: An International Programme on Human Interactions with the Earth. Report of a Symposium, Tokyo, 1988*, IFIAS, Toronto; 1989.

62 Theys, op cit, p. 7.

63 See Turner, R K, Kelly, M and Kay, R, *Cities at Risk*, BNA International, London, 1990; McCulloch, J (ed.), *Cities and Global Change*, Climate Institute, Washington DC, 1991.

64 See Pearce, D W (ed.), *Blueprint 2: Greening the World Economy*, Earthscan, London, 1991.

65   See Schramm, G and Warford, J (eds), *Environmental Management and Economic Development*, World Bank/Johns Hopkins University Press, Baltimore, 1989.

CHAPTER 2

1   Sen, A, 'What did you learn in the world today?', *American Behavioral Scientist*, vol. 34, pp. 530–48, 1991.

2   Rahman, M A, 'Towards an alternative development paradigm', *ifda dossier*, no. 81, pp. 7–28, 1991.

3   Korton, D, *Getting to the 21st Century: Voluntary Action and the Global Agenda*, Kumarian Press, West Hartford, CT, 1990.

4   IUCN, *World Conservation Strategy: Living Resource Conservation for Sustainable Development*, IUCN-UNEP-WWF, Gland, Switzerland, 1980.

5   World Commission on Environment and Development, *Our Common Future*, Oxford University Press, Oxford, 1987, p. 89.

6   Ibid, p. 213.

7   Mathews, J T, 'Environment, development and security', *Bulletin of the American Academy of Arts and Sciences*, vol. xliii, pp. 10–26, 1990.

8   Rees, W T, 'The Ecology of Sustainable Development' in Daysh, Z, Carley, M, Ekehorn, E, Phillips-Howard, K and Waller, R (eds), *Human Ecology, Environmental Education and Sustainable Development*, CHEC and Centre for Human Ecology, University of Edinburgh, 1991. See also Rees, W T, 'Atmospheric change: human ecology in disequilibrium', *International Journal of Environmental Studies*, vol. 36, pp. 103–24, 1990.

9   Rees, op cit.

10   On the concept of sustainability and its operationalisation, see: Daly, H E, 'Towards some operational principles of sustainable development', *Ecological Economics*, vol. 2, pp. 1–6, 1990; Daly, H E and Commoner, J B, *For the Common Good: Redirecting the Economy toward Community, the Environment and a Sustainable Future*, Green Print, London, 1990; Pearce, D W, 'Economics, equity and sustainable development', *Futures*, vol. 20, pp. 598–605, 1988; Pearce, D W and Turner, R K, *Economics of Natural Resources and the Environment*, Harvester Wheatsheaf, Hemel Hempstead, 1990; Jacobs, M, The Green Economy: Environment, Sustainable Development and the Politics of the Future, Pluto Press, London, 1991.

11   On market and intervention failures in transport see Barde, J-P and Button, K (eds), *Transport and the Environment*, Earthscan, London, 1990.

12   See Pearce, D W et al, *Blueprint for a Green Economy*, Earthscan, London 1989; Pearce, D W and Turner, R K, 1990, op cit.

13   See Pearce, D W (ed), *Blueprint 2: Greening the World Economy*, Earthscan, London, 1991.

14   See for example Swanson, T and Barbier, E (eds), *Economics for the Wilds*, Earthscan, London, 1992; Turner, R K and Jones, T (eds), *Wetlands: Market and Intervention Failures*, Earthscan, London, 1991.

15   See Pearce et al, 1989, op cit; Pearce (ed), 1991, op cit.

16   Anderson, V, *Alternative Economic Indicators*, New Economics Foundation,

London, 1990. Anderson notes that GNP is similar to GDP but includes income (such as profits and dividends) resulting from property located in other countries, and excludes property income flowing overseas. In the case of the UK for example, there is little difference between the two figures.

17 Sartari, G, 'Rethinking democracy: bad polity and bad politics', *International Social Science Journal*, vol. 129, pp. 437–50, 1990.

18 On discounting, see Pearce and Turner, 1990, op cit, chapter 14. See also Jacobs, 1991, op cit.

19 Agarwal, A and Narain, S, *Towards Green Villages*, Centre for Science and Environment, New Delhi, 1990. See also the UN Development Programme's Human Development Index, presented in UNDP's annual reports.

20 See Pearce (ed.), 1991, op cit.

21 Daly, 1990, op cit.

22 Rees, 1991, op cit.

23 Daly, 1990, op cit.

24 Thring, M, personal communication.

25 Georgescu-Roegen, N, *Energy and Economic Myths: Institutional and Analytical Economic Essays*, Pergamon, Oxford, 1976.

26 Daly, 1990, op cit. See also Daly, H E, *Steady-State Economics*, second edition, Earthscan, London, 1992.

27 Alexander, W, 'A Sustainable Human Ecology', paper delivered to the *Conference on Human Responsibility and Global Change*, Goteborg, 1991.

28 This is a modification of a definition in Rees, W T, *Defining Sustainable Development*, Research Bulletin, UBC Centre for Human Settlements, Vancouver, May 1989.

29 Dator, J, 'It's only a paper moon', *Futures*, pp. 1084–102, December, 1990; see also Swanson and Barbier 1992, op cit.

30 Anderson, W T, *To Govern Evolution*, Harcourt Brace Jovanovich, Dallas, 1987, cited in Dator, ibid.

31 UN Development Programme, *Human Development Report 1992*, Oxford University Press, Oxford, 1992.

32 Vandergeest, P, 'Peasant strategies in a world context: contingencies in the transformation of rice and sugar palm economies in Thailand', *Human Organization*, vol. 48, p. 117, 1989.

33 Ablin, R, 'The shrinking realm of laissez-faire', *Challenge*, March/April, p. 24, 1989.

34 Sen, op cit, pp. 532–4.

35 Alexander, 1991, op cit.

36 Prairo, R, in *Far Eastern Economic Review*, May 22, 1990.

37 Egero, B, 'No longer North and South — the New Challenges of Demographic-Economic Interrelations', paper presented at the *International Conference on Human Ecology*, Goteborg, 1991.

38 Tabah, L, 1990, 'The world's population: a look ahead', paper presented to a DAC meeting on population and development, Paris, cited in Egero, 1991, op cit.

39 Fukuyama, F, 'The end of history', *The Independent*, 20/21 September, 1989,

reprinted from *The National Interest*.

40   Heilbroner, R L, *The Nature and Logic of Capitalism*, W W Norton, New York, 1985.

41   Fukuyama, op cit. See also Fukuyama's elaboration of his thesis, in *The End of History and the Last Man*, Hamish Hamilton, London, 1992.

42   Sacks, J, 'The environment of faith', *The Listener*, 15 November, 1990.

43   Hirst, P, 'New ideals that follow "the end of history"', *The Independent*, 25 September, 1989.

44   Sacks, 1990, op cit.

45   Leiss, W, *The Limits to Satisfaction*, University of Toronto Press, Toronto, 1986.

46   *ifda dossier*, 'Indonesia: the Institute for Philosophy and the future of humanity', no. 81, p. 113, 1991.

47   Egero, 1991, op cit, p. 5.

48   Bell, D, 'American exceptionalism revisited: the role of civil society', *The Public Interest*, no. 95, pp. 38–58, 1989.

49   Sen, A, 'The moral standing of the market', *Social Philosophy and Policy*, vol. 2(2), 1985.

50   Weale, A, 'The end of society?', *The Times Higher Education Supplement*, December, 1988.

51   Ibid. The quotation is in part from Marquand, D, *The Unprincipled Society*, Jonathan Cape, London, 1988.

52   Bell, 1989, op cit.

CHAPTER 3

1   Inayutullah, S, 'Rethinking science: P R Sarkar's reconstruction of science and society', *ifda dossier*, no. 81, pp. 5–16, 1991.

2   Collingwood, R G, *The Idea of Nature*, Clarendon Press, Oxford, 1945.

3   Yearly, S, 'Greens and science: a doomed affair?', *New Scientist*, 13 July, pp. 37–40, 1991.

4   Cited in Yearly, op cit.

5   Dwivedi, O P, 'Political science and the environment', *International Social Science Journal*, no. 109, pp. 377–90, 1986.

6   Putnam, C, 'Do it again, Sam', *New Scientist*, 14 April, 1988.

7   Pearce, F, 'A dammed fine mess', *New Scientist*, 4 May, 1991.

8   Keller, K H, 'Science and technology', *Sea-Changes: American Foreign Policy in a World Transformed*, Council on Foreign Relations, Washington, 1989.

9   Grove-White, R, 'Mysteries in the Global Laboratory', *The Times Higher Educational Supplement*, 26 October, p. 15, 1990.

10   Grove-White, op cit.

11   Robertson, J T 'Assessing our second(hand) America', *American Planning Association Journal*, Spring, pp. 271–6, 1987.

12   Hillman, M, Adams, J and Whitelegg, J, *One False Step: a Study of Children's Independent Mobility*, Policy Studies Institute, London, 1991.

13   Collingwood, op cit, p. 9.

14   Cited in Collingwood, op cit, p. 102.

15 Jones, A, 'From fragmentation to wholeness: a green approach to science and society', *The Ecologist*, vol. 17, pp. 236-40, 1987.

16 Jones, op cit, p. 236.

17 Capra, F, *The Turning Point*, Wildwood House, London, 1982, p. 50.

18 Capra, op cit, p. 66.

19 Jones, op cit, p. 240.

20 Cited in Jones, ibid; see also Bohm, D, *Wholeness and the Implicate Order*, Routledge and Kegan Paul, London, 1980.

21 Jones, op cit, p. 237.

22 Oltneau, J, 'Between globalism and fragmentation', *Institute for the Humanities Newsletter*, vol. 3(2), Simon Fraser University, Vancouver, 1990.

23 van Steenbergen, B, 'Potential influence of the holistic paradigm on the social sciences', *Futures*, December, 1071-83, 1990.

24 Giddens, A, *Modernity and Self-Identity*, Cambridge University Press, Cambridge, 1991.

25 Held, D, 'Central perspectives on the modern state', Held, D et al (eds), *States and Societies*, Martin Robertson, Oxford, 1984, p. 33.

26 Held, op cit, p. 42.

27 Wallerstein, I, 'Marxism as utopias: evolving ideologies', *American Journal of Sociology*, vol. 91, pp. 1295-308, 1986.

28 Benton, T, *Philosophical Foundations of the Three Sociologies*, Routledge and Kegan Paul, London, 1977.

29 Giddens, A, *Studies in Social and Political Theory*, Hutchinson, London, 1977, p. 29.

30 Goldberg, M A, 'The irrationality of rational planning', Breheny, M and Hooper, A (eds), *Rationality in Planning*, Pion, London, 1985.

31 Carley, M, *Rational Techniques in Policy Analysis*, Heinemann Educational Books, London, 1980.

32 Simey, T S, *Social Science and Social Purpose*, Constable, London, 1968.

33 Lanza, R, 'The past needs its people', *New Scientist*, 12 January, 1991.

34 See Gleick, J, *Chaos: Making a New Science*, Cardinal, London, 1988; *The New Scientist Guide to Chaos*, Penguin, London, 1992.

35 See for example Davies, P, *The Cosmic Blueprint*, Touchstone Press, New York, 1988.

36 Inayatullah, op cit.

37 van Steenbergen, op cit.

38 Ibid.

39 See Goldstein, W and Mohnen, V V, 'Global warming debate in the USA: the clash between scientists on policy projections', *Futures*, vol. 24(1), January/February 1992.

40 See Funtowicz, S and Ravetz, J, *Global Environmental Issues and the Emergence of Second Order Science*, Council for Science and Society Occasional Paper no. 1, London, 1990; in the same series, see also Rayner, S and O'Riordan, T, *Chasing a Spectre: Risk Management for Global Environmental Change*, Council for Science and Society, London, 1990.

41 Derived from O'Riordan, T and Turner, R K, *An Annotated Reader in Environmental Planning and Management*, Pergamon Press, Oxford, 1983. See also

Pearce, D W and Turner, R K, *Economics of Natural Resources and the Environment*, Harvester Wheatsheaf, Hemel Hempstead, 1990, pp. 13–15 and chapter 15. On concepts in environmental ethics, see Hargrove, E C, *Foundations of Environmental Ethics*, Prentice-Hall, New Jersey, 1989.

42 Pearce and Turner, 1990, op cit, p. 234.

43 Ibid, chapter 15.

CHAPTER 4

1 Lijphart, A, 'Majority rule in theory and practice: the tenacity of a flawed paradigm', *International Journal of Social Science*, no. 129, pp. 483–94, 1991.

2 Jacobs, M, *The Green Economy*, Pluto Press, London, 1991, pp. 128–129.

3 Heilbroner, R L, *The Nature and Logic of Capitalism*, W W Norton, New York, 1985.

4 Held, D, 'Central perspectives on the modern state' and 'Future directions for the state' in Held et al (eds), *States and Societies*, Martin Robertson, Oxford, 1984.

5 Spragins, T A, *Understanding Political Theory*, St Martin's Press, New York, 1976.

6 Lane, L M, 'Individualism, civic virtue and public administration', *Administration and Society*, vol. 20, pp. 30–45, 1988.

7 Chandler, W U, *The Changing Role of the Market in National Economies*, Paper 72, Worldwatch, WEashington, 1986.

8 Lane, op cit, p. 32.

9 Lane, op cit, p. 36.

10 Hobbes, T, *Leviathan or the Matter, Forme and Power of a Commonwealth Ecclesiastical and Civil*, Millan, New York, 1977.

11 Hobbes, op cit, p. 132.

12 Held, op cit, p. 41.

13 Spragins, op cit, p. 34.

14 Held, op cit.

15 Held, op cit.

16 Rousseau, J L, *The Social Contract and Discourses*, Everyman, London, 1927.

17 Rousseau, J L, *Social Contract*, Book 4, chapter 2, cited in Dahl, R A, *Democracy and its Critics*, Yale University Press, New Haven, 1989, p. 355.

18 Chandler, op cit, p. 7.

19 Moss, L S, 'Power and value relationships in "The Wealth of Nations"', O'Driscoll, G P (ed), *Adam Smith and Modern Political Economy*, Iowa State University Press, Ames, 1979.

20 Mill, J S, *On Liberty*, Dent, London, 1931.

21 Moss, op cit.

22 Held, op cit, p. 62.

23 Schapiro, J S, *Movements of Social Dissent in Modern Europe*, Princeton: D Van Nostrand, 1962.

24 Badie, B, 'Democracy and religion: logics of culture and logics of action', *International Social Science Journal*, no. 129, pp. 511–22, 1991.

25 Kleiman, M A R, 'Liberalism and vice control', *Journal of Policy Analysis and Management*, vol. 6, pp. 87–98, 1987.

26 Hayek, F A, *The Road to Serfdom*, Routledge and Kegan Paul, London, 1976 (originally 1944).

27 Ablin, R, 'The shrinking realm of laissez-faire', *Challenge*, March/April, 23–5, 1989.

28 Scully, G W, 'The institutional framework and economic development', *Journal of Political Economy*, vol. 96, pp. 652–64, 1988.

29 Skolimowski, H, *Eco-Philosophy*, Marion Boyars, Boston and London, 1981.

30 Bell, D, 'American exceptionalism revisited: the role of civil society', *The Public Interest*, no. 95, pp. 38–56, 1989.

31 Gellner, E, 'Civil society in historical context', *International Social Science Journal*, no. 129, pp. 495–510, 1991.

32 Keane, J, 'Democracy and the media', *International Social Science Journal*, no. 129, pp. 523–540.

CHAPTER 5

1 Suess, Dr, *The Lorax*, Collins, London, 1972.

2 Helleiner, G K, *The New Global Economy and the Developing Countries*, Edward Elgar, Aldershot, 1990.

3 Brown, L, 'The new world order', in Brown, L, et al, *State of the World 1991*, Earthscan, London, 1991, p. 6.

4 Giddens, Anthony, *The Consequences of Modernity*, Polity Press, Cambridge, 1990.

5 'Sisters in the wood: a survey of the IMF and the World Bank', *The Economist*, 12 October, 1991.

6 OECD, *Trade, Investment and Technology in the 1990s*, OECD, Paris, 1991.

7 World Bank, *The Challenge of Development: World Development Report 1991*, Oxford University Press, Oxford, 1991, pp. 107–8.

8 United Nations, *Global Outlook 2000*, New York, 1990, chapters 2 and 8.

9 Ibid; Beeman, William and Frank, Isaiah, *New Dynamics in the Global Economy*, Committee for Economic Development, New York, 1988.

10 World Bank, 1991, op cit, p. 17.

11 OECD, *The Newly Industrialising Countries*, OECD: Paris, 1988.

12 Beeman and Frank, 1988, op cit, p. 11.

13 World Bank, 1991, op cit, p. 12.

14 United Nations, 1990, op cit, chapters 3 and 8.

15 Ibid, p. 53.

16 Ibid; Brown et al, 1991, op cit.

17 See Chase-Dunn, Christopher, *Global Formation*, Blackwell, Oxford, 1989.

18 World Bank, 1991, op cit.

19 French, H F, 'Restoring the East European and Soviet environments' in Brown et al, 1991, op cit, chapter 6.

20 *The Guardian*, 16 October, 1991.

21 OECD, 1988, op cit.

22 *Economist*, 12 October, 1991, op cit.

23 See Dahrendorf, Ralf, *Reflections on the Revolution in Europe*, Chatto and Windus, London, 1990; Glenny, Misha, *The Rebirth of History: Eastern Europe in the Age of*

Democracy, Penguin, Harmondsworth, 1990.

24   George, Susan, *A Fate Worse than Debt*, Penguin, Harmondsworth, 1988.

25   Durning, A, 'Asking how much is enough', in Brown et al, 1991, op cit, chapter 9.

26   Ibid, p. 154.

27   UNDP, *Human Development Report 1992*, Oxford University Press, 1992.

28   Durning, 1991, op cit, p. 162.

29   Ibid, p. 163.

30   Meadows, D H et al, *The Limits to Growth*, Universe Books, New York, 1972.

31   Durning, 1991, op cit, p. 162.

32   See Giddens, Anthony, *Modernity and Self-Identity: self and society in the late modern age*, Polity Press, Cambridge, 1991, chapter 6.

33   DeLillo, Don, *Mao II*, Jonathan Cape, London, 1991.

34   Hirsch, Fred, *Social Limits to Growth*, Routledge and Kegan Paul, London, 1977.

35   Ibid, p. 109.

36   Lowe, M D, 'Rethinking urban transport', in Brown et al, 1991, op cit, chapter 4.

37   Pucher, John, 'Capitalism, socialism and urban transportation: policies and travel behaviour in the East and West', in: *APA Journal*, Summer 1990.

38   Nicholson-Lord, David, 'Death by tourism', in: *The Independent on Sunday*, 5 August, 1990.

39   French, 1991, op cit.

40   World Bank, 1991, op cit, p. 105.

41   Ibid.

42   Jackson, Ben, *Poverty and the Planet*, Penguin, Harmondsworth, 1990.

43   Ibid, p. 63.

44   Ibid, chapters 3 and 4.

45   See WCED, *Our Common Future*, Oxford University Press: Oxford, 1987; IUCN/UNEP/WWF, *Caring for the Earth: A Strategy for Sustainable Living*, Gland, Switzerland; published in UK by Earthscan, London, 1991.

46   See Barbier (ed), 'Tropical deforestation', and Swanson, Tim, 'Conserving biological diversity', both in Pearce, D W (ed.), *Blueprint 2: Greening the World Economy*, Earthscan, London, 1991.

47   Bown, William, 'Trade deals a blow to the environment', *New Scientist*, 10 November, 1990.

48   Shrybman, Stephen, 'International trade and the environment', in: *Alternatives*, vol. 17(2), 1990.

49   Ritchie, Mark, 'GATT, agriculture and the environment', *The Ecologist*, vol. 20(6), November/December, 1990.

50   Shrybman, 1990, op cit.

51   CEC Task Force, *1992: The Environmental Dimension*, Commission of the European Communities, Brussels, 1990.

52   Shrybman, 1990, op cit.

53   World Bank, 1990, op cit, p. 11.

54   *The Pocket World in Figures*, Economist Publications, London, 1991.

55   George, 1988, op cit.

56 Ibid; Adams, Patricia, *Odious Debts*, Earthscan, London, 1991.
57 Postel, S and Flavin, C, 'Reshaping the global economy', in Brown et al, 1991, op cit, chapter 10, p. 171.
58 Bourgignon, Francois and Morrisson, Christian, *Adjustment and Equity in Developing Countries*, OECD, Paris, 1991.
59 Adams, 1991, op cit.
60 Jackson, 1990, op cit; *Economist*, 12 October, 1991, op cit.
61 Postel and Flavin, 1991, op cit.
62 World Bank, 1991, op cit, p. 24.
63 George, 1988, op cit, chapter 7.
64 World Bank, 1991, op cit, p. 92; see also Adams, W H, *Green Development*, Routledge, London, 1990, chapter 7.
65 Sagasti, F, 'Cooperation in a fractured global order', *New Scientist*, 14 July, 1990.
66 World Bank, 1991, op cit.
67 Ibid, p. 140.
68 Jackson, 1990, op cit, pp. 51–3; Adams, W H, 1990, op cit, chapter 8.
69 Sarre, Philip and Smith, Paul with Morris, Eleanor, *One World, One Earth*, Earthscan, London 1991, pp. 159–62.
70 Mackenzie, Debora, 'The West pays up for Third World seeds', *New Scientist*, 11 May, 1991; see also WCED, 1987, op cit..
71 See World Bank, *Development and the Environment: World Development Report 1992*, World Bank, Washington, 1992.
72 Helleiner, 1990, op cit.
73 UN Centre on Transnational Corporations, *Benchmark Corporate Environmental Survey*, UN, New York, 1991.
74 See Schmidheiny, S/Business Council for Sustainable Development, *Changing Course*, MIT Press, Boston MA, 1992.

CHAPTER 6

1 Friedmann, J, 'Policy, planning and the environment', *Journal of the American Planning Association*, vol. 56, pp. 334–46, 1989.
2 Agarwal, A and Narain, S, *Towards Green Villages: A Strategy for Environmentally Sound and Participatory Rural Development*, Centre for Science and Environment, New Delhi, 1991.
3 Mill, J S, *On Liberty*, Dent, London, 1931.
4 Smith, B C, 'The justification of local government' in Feldman, L D and Goldrick, M D (eds), *Politics and Government of Urban Canada*, Methuen, Toronto, 1969.
5 Giddens, A, *Modernity and Self-Identity*, Cambridge University Press, Cambridge, 1991.
6 Miles, I, *Social Indicators for Human Development*, Francis Pinter, London, 1985.
7 Rhodes, R A W, *The National World of Local Government*, George Allen and Unwin, London, 1985.
8 Jenkins, P, 'Squeezing democracy in liberty's name', *The Independent*, 7 May, 1987.

9   Eversley, D, *Regional Devolution and Social Policy*, Methuen, London, 1975.

10 Sharpe, L J, 'Central co-ordination and the policy network', *Political Studies*, vol. 28, pp. 27-46, 1985.

11 Smith, B C, *Decentralisation: The Territorial Dimension of the State*, George Allen and Unwin, London, 1985.

12 Frenkel, M, 'The distribution of legal powers in pluricentral systems' in Morgan, R, (ed), *Regionalism in European Politics*, Policy Studies Institute, London, 1986.

13 Bogdanor, V, 'Federalism and devolution: some juridical and political problems' in Morgan, ibid.

14 Rondinelli, D A and Nellis, J R, 'Assessing decentralisation policies in developing countries', *Development Policy Review*, vol. 4, pp. 3-23, 1986.

15 Ibid, p. 5.

16 Frenkel, op cit.

17 Frenkel, op cit.

18 Bedi, R, 'The imperial island' in *Indian Express*, 17 April, 1988.

19 'Deadly effects of Delhi's power' in *The Independent*, 25 May, 1991.

20 *The Independent on Sunday*, 1 September, 1991.

21 Agarwal, op cit.

22 Sattaur, O, 'The green solution for India's poor', *New Scientist*, 15 September, 1990.

23 Laitin, D, 'Political culture and political preferences', *American Political Science Review*, vol. 82, pp. 589-97, 1988.

24 Peeters, Y J D, 'Constitutional remedies for government overload', *Government and Policy*, vol. 5, pp. 219-24, 1987.

25 Weaver, C, *Regional Development and the Local Community*, John Wiley, Chichester, 1984.

26 Gottman, J (ed), *Centre and Periphery: Spatial Variation in Politics*, Sage, Beverly Hills, 1980; Wellhofer, E S, 'Core and periphery: territorial dimensions', *Urban Studies*, vol. 26, pp. 340-55, 1989; Wallerstein, I, 'Semi-peripheral countries and the contemporary world crisis', *Theory and Society*, vol. 3, pp. 461-83, 1976; Wallerstein, I, *The Capitalist World Economy*, Cambridge University Press, Cambridge, 1980.

27 Hebbert, M, 'The new decentralism — a critique of the territorial approach', in Healey, P. et al (eds), *Planning Theory: Prospects for the 1980s*, Pergamon, Oxford, 1982.

28 Friedmann, J, 1989, op cit.

29 Lewis, D, 'The rape of the rainforest', *The Guardian*, 1 November, 1991.

30 Friedmann, op cit.

31 Friedmann, J, *Retracking America: A Theory of Transactive Planning*, Doubleday Anchor, Garden City, NJ, 1973; Friedmann, J and Arbonyi, G, 'Social learning: a model for policy research', *Environment and Planning*, A, vol. 8, pp. 927-940, 1976.

32 Friedmann, J and Weaver, C, *Territory and Function*, Edward Arnold, London, 1979; see also Friedmann, J, *Basic Needs, Agropolitan Development and Planning from Below: the Construction of Political Communities*, University of California, Los

Angeles, Urban Planning Program Paper, 1978; 'Development from above or below?', *Journal of the American Institute of Planners*, vol. 48, pp.249-60, 1982; 'Regional development in industrialized countries: endogenous or self-reliant?' in *Selected Writings*, University of California Academic Publishing, Los Angeles, pp. 237-60, 1984; 'Political and technical movements in development: agropolitan development revisited', *Environment and Planning D: Society and Space*, vol. 8, pp. 927-40, 1985.

33 Friedmann, 1989, op cit.

34 Kohr, L, *The Breakdown of Nations*, Dutton, New York, 1978 (second edition).

35 Mawhood, P (ed.), *Local Government in the Third World: the Experience of Tropical Africa*, Wiley, New York, 1983.

36 Bogdanor, op cit.

37 Frankel, op cit, p. 21.

INTRODUCTION TO PART IV

1 Self, P, 'What's wrong with public administration?', *Public Administration and Development*, vol. 6, pp. 329-38, 1986.

2 Kerrigan, J E and Luke, J S, *Management Training Strategies for Developing Countries*, Rienner, Boulder and London, 1987.

CHAPTER 7

1 Gow, D D and Morss, E R, 'The notorious nine: critical problems in project implementation', *World Development*, vol. 16, pp. 1399-418, 1988.

2 King, A and Schneider, B, *The First Global Revolution*, Simon and Schuster, London, 1991.

3 Dassah, A L, 'Man and the River Densu and its Basin', *Institutional Development for Environmental Action – the Accra Workshop Report*, Carley, M and Smith, M (eds), Commonwealth Consultative Group on Technology Management, London, 1991. Figure 7.1 appears in the *Institute of Aquatic Biology, 1990 Annual Report*, CSIR Ghana, Accra.

4 Jreisat, J E, 'Administrative reform in developing countries: a comparative perspective', *Public Administration and Development*, vol. 8, pp. 85-97, 1988.

5 Ibid.

6 Regan, D, 'British administrative reform: the need for incentives', *Public Administration Review*, vol. 44, pp. 545-50, 1984.

7 Dichter, S F, 'The organisation of the '90s', *The McKinsey Quarterly*, no. 1, pp. 145-55, 1991.

8 Coulson, A, 'Feasible planning in a poor country: a utopian postscript to a country case study', *World Development*, vol. 18, pp. 13-19, 1990.

9 Tampoe, M, 'Driving organisational change through the effective use of multi-disciplinary project teams', *European Management Journal*, vol. 8, pp. 346-54, 1990.

10 Honadle, G and Cooper, L, 'Beyond coordination and control: an interorganizational approach to structural adjustment, service delivery and natural resource management', *World Development*, vol. 17, pp. 1531-41, 1989.

11   Knowles, H P and Saxberg, B O, 'Organisational leadership of planned and unplanned change: a systems approach to organisational viability', *Futures*, vol. 20, pp. 252–65, 1988.

12   Haas, P M, 'Intergovernmental institutions', paper presented to the *Annual Meeting of the American Association for the Advancement of Science*, 1991.

13   Knowles and Saxberg, op cit.

14   Zand, D E, 'Collateral organization: a new strategy', *Journal of Applied Behavioural Science*, vol. 10, pp. 63–9, 1974.

15   Knowles and Saxberg, op cit.

16   Sagasti, F R, 'National development planning in turbulent times: new approaches and criteria for institutional design', *World Development*, p. 16, pp. 431–48, 1988.

17   Rahmin, A, 'The interaction between science, technology and society', *International Social Science Journal*, vol. 33, pp. 508–21, 1981.

18   Baker, R, 'Institutional innovation, development and environmental management: an administrative trap revisited. Part I', *Public Administration and Development*, vol. 9, pp. 29–47, 1989. 'Part II', vol. 9, pp. 159–67, 1989.

19   American Consortium for International Public Administration, *Institutional Development: Improving Management in Developing Countries*, Washington, 1986.

20   Whittington, D and Calhoun, C, 'Who really wants donor co-ordination?', *Development Policy Review*, vol. 6. pp. 295–309, 1988.

21   Montgomery, J D, 'Environmental management as a Third World problem', *Policy Sciences*, vol. 23, pp. 163–76, 1990.

22   Cited in Carley and Smith (eds), op cit.

23   Brandl, J, 'On politics and policy analysis as the design and assessment of institutions', *Journal of Policy Analysis and Management*, vol. 7, pp. 419–24, 1988.

24   Baker, op cit.

25   Hulme, D, 'Learning and not learning from experience in rural project planning', *Public Administration and Development*, vol. 9. pp. 1–16.

26   Baker, op cit.

27   Cited in Carley and Smith (eds), op cit.

28   Brenner, C, *Technological Change, Structural Adjustment and Liberalisation in Developing Country Agriculture*, OECD Development Centre paper, 1990.

CHAPTER 8

1   Miller, R B, 'Human dimensions of global environmental change' in DeFries and Malone, T (eds), *Global Change and Our Common Future*, National Academy Press, Washington, 1989.

2   Godet, M, 'Effective strategic management: the prospective approach', *Technology Analysis and Strategic Management*, vol. 1, pp. 45–5, 1989.

3   Rittel, H W J and Webber, M M, 'Dilemmas in a general theory of planning', *Policy Sciences*, vol. 4, pp. 325–33, 1973.

4   Emery, F E and Trist, E L, 'The causal texture of organizational environments', *Human Relations*, vol. 18, pp. 21–32, 1965; and *Towards a Social Ecology*, Plenum Press, New York, 1973.

5   Ramirez, R, 'Action learning: a strategic approach for organizations facing turbulent conditions', *Human Relations*, vol. 36, pp. 725-42, 1983.

6   Trist, E, 'Collaboration in work settings: a personal perspective', *Journal of Applied Behavioural Science*, vol. 13, p. 271, 1977.

7   Gallopin, G C, 'Human dimensions of global change: linking the global and local processes', *International Social Science Journal*, no. 130, pp. 707-18, 1991.

8   Trist, E, 'The environment and systems response capability: a futures perspective', *Futures*, vol. 12, pp. 113-27, 1980.

9   Schon, D A, *Beyond the Stable State*, W W Norton, New York, 1971.

10 Hoggart, P, 'A new management in the public sector?', *Policy and Politics*, vol. 19, pp. 243-56, 1991.

11 Robins, J A, 'Ecology and society: a lesson for organisation theory from the logic of economics', *Organization Studies*, vol. 6, pp. 335-48, 1985.

12 Bateson, G, *Steps to an Ecology of Mind*, Chandler, San Francisco, 1972.

13 von Bertalanffy, L, *General System Theory*, Penguin, Harmondsworth, 1968.

14 Kirby, M, 'Complexity, democracy and governance', *United Nations University Newsletter*, vol. 8, p. 9, 1985.

15 Robins, op cit, pp. 339-40.

16 Miles, I, *The Poverty of Prediction*, D C Heath, Farnborough, 1975.

17 Robins, op cit, p. 336.

18 Rhodes, R A W, *Control and Power in Central-Local Government Relations*, Gower, Farnborough, 1981.

19 Rhodes, R A W, *Public Administration and Policy Analysis*, Saxon House, Farnborough, 1979.

20 DiMaggio, P, 'State expansion and organizational fields', Hall, R H and Quinn, R E (eds), *Organizational Theory and Public Policy*, Sage, Beverly Hills and London, 1983.

21 Trist, E, 'Referent organizations and the development of inter-organizational domains', *Human Relations*, vol. 36, pp. 269-84, 1983.

22 Rhodes, R A W, 'Power dependence, policy communities, and inter-governmental networks', *Public Administration Bulletin*, no. 49, pp. 4-31, 1985.

23 Rhodes, op cit, p. 15.

24 Dunlevy, P, 'Professions and policy changes', *Public Administration Bulletin*, no. 36, 1981; 'The architecture of the British central state', *Public Administration*, vol. 67, pp. 391-417, 1989.

25 Wilkie, T, 'Ministers barred Sellafield inquiry', *The Independent on Sunday*, 1 December, 1991.

26 Vickers, G, *The Art of Judgment: a Study of Policy Making*, Basic Books, New York, 1965.

27 Rhodes, R A W, *The National World of Local Government*, George Allen and Unwin, London, 1985, p. 39.

28 Trist, 1983, op cit.

29 Aldrich, H, *Organizations and Environments*, Prentice Hall, Englewood Cliffs, 1979.

30 Assael, H, 'Constructive role for interorganizational conflict', *Administrative Science Quarterly*, vol. 14, pp. 573-81, 1979.

31 Barrett, S and Hill, M, 'Policy, bargaining and structure in implementation theory', Goldsmith, M (ed), *New Research in Central–Local Relations*, Gower, Aldershot, 1986.

32 Dacks, G, *A Choice of Futures: Politics in the Canadian North*, Methuen, Toronto, 1981.

33 Godet, M, *Crises are Opportunities*, Gamma Institute Press, Montreal, 1985.

34 Gemmill, G and Smith, C, 'A dissipative structure model of organization transformation', *Human Relations*, vol. 38, pp. 295–316, 1985.

35 CDR Associates, *Decision Making and Conflict Management: An Overview*, Boulder, Colorado, 1989.

36 Young, K, 'Economic development in Britain', *Environment and Planning C*, vol. 4, pp. 439–50, 1986.

37 Hoggart, op cit.

38 Hoggart, op cit. It has long been recognised that organisations, like societies, have distinctive cultures, or patterns of basic assumptions, and this concept has been much studied by sociologists, anthropologists and organisation theorists. Ouchi and Wilkins provide an overview of the sociological literature, and Allaire and Firsirotu of the anthropological approaches. Franks analyses the relationship between organizational culture and development. Ouchi, W G and Wilkins, A L, 'Organizational culture', *Annual Review of Sociology*, 457–83, 1985; Allaire, Y and Firsirotu, M, 'Theories of organizational culture', *Organisation Studies*, vol. 5: 194–226, 1984; Franks, T, 'Bureaucracy, organization culture and development', *Public Administration and Development*, vol. 9: 357–68, 1989.

39 Merritt, R L and Merritt, A J, *Innovation in the Public Sector*, Sage, Beverly Hills, London, New Delhi, 1985.

40 Bateson, op cit, p. 18.

41 Argyris, C and Schon, D, *Organizational Learning*, Addison-Wesley, Reading, Mass, 1978.

42 Morgan, G, 'Cybernetics and organization theory', *Human Relations*, vol. 35, pp. 521–37, 1982.

43 Ramirez, op cit, pp. 738–9.

44 Rogers, E and Kim, P, 'Diffusion of innovations' in Merritt and Merritt, op cit, p. 102.

45 Godet, op cit (no. 2).

46 Winter, R, *Action Research and the Nature of Social Inquiry*, Avebury, Aldershot, 1987, p. viii.

47 Brown, L, 'Action research' in *Action Research for Professional Development*, Elliot, J and Whitehead, D (eds), Institute of Education, Cambridge, 1982.

48 Schon, D A, *The Reflective Practitioner: How Professionals Think in Action*, Maurice Temple Smith, London, 1983.

49 Kirby, op cit.

50 Whalen, H, 'Ideology, democracy and the foundations of local self-government', in Feldman and Goldrick, op cit.

51 Webber, M, 'A difference paradigm for planning' in Burchell, R W and Sternlieb, G (eds), *Planning Theory in the 1980s*, Center for Urban Policy Research, New Brunswick, NJ, 1978.

CHAPTER 9

1 Stewart, J D, 'The environment — no respecter of organisational boundaries', *Town and Country Planning*, pp. 170-2, June, 1991.

2 Knowles, H P and Saxberg, B O, 'Organisational leadership of planned and unplanned change', *Futures*, pp. 252-65, June, 1988.

3 Sagasti, F R, 'National development planning in turbulent times; new approaches and criteria for institutional design', *World Development*, vol. 16, pp. 431-48, 1988.

4 See for example Peters, T J and Waterman, R H, *In Search of Excellence*, Harper and Collins, New York, 1982.

5 Comfort, L, 'Action research: a model for organisational learning', *Journal of Policy Analysis and Management*, vol. 5, pp. 100-18, 1985.

6 Hirschman, A O, 'The case against one thing at a time', *World Development*, vol. 18, pp. 1119-22, 1990.

7 American Consortium for Public Administration, *Institutional Development in Developing Countries*, report of a series of seminars, 1986, p. 108.

8 McGrath, J E, 'Groups and the innovation process' in Merritt, R L and Merritt, A J (eds), *Innovation in the Public Sector*, Sage Publications, Beverly Hills, London and New Delhi, 1985.

9 Healey, P, 'The future of local planning and development control', *Planning Outlook*, vol. 30, pp. 30-40, 1987.

10 Coulson, A, 'Feasible planning in a poor country: a utopian postscript to a country case study', *World Development*, vol. 18: 143-19, 1990.

11 Cernea, M M, *Nongovernmental Organizations and Local Development*, Discussion Papers No. 40, World Bank, Washington, 1988.

12 See, for example, International Exposition of Rural Development, *Approaches That Work*, Institute of Cultural Affairs, Brussels, 1988.

13 Cernea, op cit.

14 Carley, M, *Housing and Neighbourhood Renewal*, Policy Studies Institute, London, 1990; Christie, I, et al, *Profitable Partnerships: a Report on Business Investment in the Community*, Policy Studies Institute, London, 1991.

15 Rowe, J S, 'Implementing Sustainable Development', unpublished paper, Department of Crop Science and Plant Ecology, University of Saskatchewan, 1990.

16 Fairclough, T, 'The environmental reflex: policies, procedures and people', *The Courier* (ACP European Community) no. 118, pp. 88-91, 1989.

17 Stewart, op cit.

18 Webb, A, 'Coordination: A problem in public sector management', *Policy and Politics*, vol. 19, pp. 229-41, 1991.

19 Webb, op cit, p. 238.

20 Webb, op cit, p. 239.

21 Chapman, M, 'Building consensus on environmental policy: a new approach', *Policy Studies*, vol. 12, pp. 1-10, 1991; see also Susskind, L and Cruickshank, J, *Breaking the Impasse: Consensual Approaches to Resolving Public Disputes*, Basic Books, New York, 1987.

22   Castellano, M, 'Collective wisdom: participatory research and Canada's native people', *IDRC Reports*, vol. 15, pp. 24–5, 1986.

23   CDR Associates, *Decision Making and Conflict Management: An Overview*, Colorado, Boulder, CDR, 1989.

24   Chapman, op cit, p. 5–6.

25   Ibid.

26   Holdgate, M, 'Practical targets for sustainability and development', *Maintenance of the Biosphere*, Polunin, N and Burnett, J H (eds), Edinburgh University Press, Edinburgh, 1990.

27   King, A and Schneider, B, *The First Global Revolution*, Simon and Schuster, London, 1991.

28   American Consortium for Public Administration, op cit.

29   Ministry of Housing, Physical Planning and the Environment, *A Clean Environment: Choose It or Lose It. Highlights of the National Environmental Policy Plan*, Den Haag, no date.

CHAPTER 10

1   Quoted in Sarre, P, Smith, P and Morris E, *One World for One Earth*, Earthscan/Open University, London, 1991.

2   Davidson, J, 'Groundwork — a partnership veteran', in *Partnership Review*, Nature Conservancy Council, Peterborough, September, 1989.

3   See Forrester, Susan, *Business and Environmental Groups — a natural partnership?*, Directory of Social Change, London, 1990.

4   See Elkin, T, Mclaren, D and Hillman, M, *Reviving the City: towards sustainable urban development*, Friends of the Earth/Policy Studies Institute, London, 1991, chapter 4.

5   See Forrester, 1990, op cit.

6   See English Nature, *Partnership Review*, Peterborough, February, 1991.

CHAPTER 11

1   American Consortium for International Public Administration, *Institutional Development: Improving Management in Developing Countries*, Washington, 1986.

2   See for example, Carley, M, Smith, M and Odei, M, 'Production, human resources and environmental management: resolving conflicts in the process of integration' forthcoming in *Humankind in Global Change*, Proceedings of the Symposium of the 1991 Annual Meeting of the American Association for the Advancement of Science, Washington; Carley, M and Smith, M (eds), *Institutional Development for Environmental Action: Kuala Lumpur Report* (1989), *Harare Report* (1990), *Georgetown Report* (1991), *Accra Report* (1991), Commonwealth Consultative Group for Technology Management, London; Carley, M, Smith, M and Varadarajan, S, 'A network approach to enhanced environmental management', *Project Appraisal*, vol. 6, pp. 66–74, 1991.

3   Personal communication.

CHAPTER 12

1 Quotation from Inman, B, 'California trends', *San Francisco Examiner*, 3 March, 1991; and Delsohn, G, 'Is consensus on growth possible?', *The Sacramento Bee*, 21 July, 1991. Dr Susan Sherry is the Director of the Growth Management Consensus Project (GMCP).

2 In preparing this chapter we have drawn on unpublished and published material provided by the Growth Management Consensus Project, Centre for California Studies, California State University, Sacramento; and on material prepared by CDR Associates, Boulder, Colorado, the professional mediators to the Project. We are very grateful for their assistance.

3 GMCP, *Project Summary*, unpublished, no date.

4 GMCP, *Overview to Policy Background Papers*, January, 1991.

5 GMCP, *Project Summary*, op cit.

6 GMCP, *The Role of the State in Managing Growth*, no date.

7 Delsohn, op cit.

8 GMCP, *Project Summary*, op cit.

9 Susan Sherry, 'Growth Management Consensus Project', *The Land Use Forum: a Journal of Law*, February 1992, published by California State Bar Association.

10 Ibid.

11 GMCP, *Achieving Certainty for Conservation, Development, and Social Equity*, no date.

12 GMCP, *Achieving Compactness in Land Use*, no date.

13 GMCP, *Growth Management and Public Finance*, no date.

14 Ibid.

15 GMCP, *The Implementation Role of the State*, no date.

16 GMCP, *Ground Rules*, draft, 14 January, 1991; parts of this document are cited as based on *Procedural Guidelines for Principled Negotiation and Cooperative Problem Solving for use in Contract Negotiations and Public Policy Dialogues*, developed by CDR Associates, Boulder; and Carpenter, S and Kennedy, W J D, *Managing Public Disputes*, Jossey-Bass, San Francisco and London, 1988.

17 Growth Management Consensus Project, *Summary of Findings*, Center for California Studies, California State University, Sacramento, January, 1992.

18 Ibid.

19 Ibid.

CHAPTER 13

1 Financial Times, *Survey of the Netherlands*, 10 December 1991.

2 Ministry of Housing, Physical Planning and Environment, 'What future for agriculture?', in *Environmental News from the Netherlands*, no. 1, November 1990.

3 Mastop, H, Postuma, R, 'Key notions underlying Dutch strategic planning', *Built Environment*, vol. 17(1), 1991.

4 Faludi, A, 'Fifty years of Dutch national physical planning: introduction', *Built Environment*, vol. 17(1), 1991.

5 Ibid, p. 57.

6 Jamison, A, Eyerman, R, Cramer, J, *The Making of the New Environmental Consciousness*, Edinburgh University Press: Edinburgh, 1990.

7   Ibid, p. 123.

8   Faludi, 1991, op cit, p. 8.

9   Gijswijt, A J, 'The Kingdom of the Netherlands', in Enyedi, G, Gijswijt, A J and Rhode, B (eds), *Environmental Policies in East and West*, Taylor Graham, London, 1987.

10   Stigliani, W M, Anderberg, S, 'Industrial metabolism and the Rhine Basin', *Options*, September 1991, published by International Institute for Applied Systems Analysis (IIASA), Laxenberg, Austria.

11   National Environmental Policy Plan (NEPP), *To Choose or to Lose*, SDU Uitgeverij, 's Gravenage, Netherlands, 1989, p. 194.

12   Ibid, p. 133.

13   Ibid.

14   Jamison et al, 1990, op cit.

15   Ibid.

16   Gijswijt, 1987, op cit.

17   de Jongh, P E, 1989a, *A Short History of Integrated Environmental Policy in the Netherlands*, paper prepared for Centre for Environmental and Economic Development workshop, London, 12 October 1989.

18   Gijswijt, 1987, op cit.

19   de Jongh, 1989a, op cit.

20   See Weale, A, O'Riordan, T and Kramme, L, *Controlling Pollution in the Round*, Anglo-German Foundation, London, 1991.

21   de Jongh, 1989a, op cit.

22   NEPP, 1989, op cit, p. 115.

23   de Jongh, 1989a, op cit.

24   Jamison et al, 1990, op cit.

25   de Jongh, 1989a, op cit.

26   World Commission on Environment and Development (WCED), *Our Common Future*, Oxford University Press, Oxford, 1987.

27   de Jongh, 1989a, op cit.

28   NEPP, 1989, op cit, p. 179.

29   Rogaly, J, 'Voters can take a lot more greening', *Financial Times*, 25 August 1989; see also Lenstra, W J, 'The role of the Netherlands National Environmental Policy Plan (NEPP) in energy policy', in Barker, T (ed.), *Green Futures for Economic Growth*, Cambridge Econometrics, 1991.

30   Association for the Conservation of Energy (ACE), *Lessons from the Netherlands*, ACE, London, 1991.

31   See *Environmental News from the Netherlands*, no. 1, November 1990, pp. 5-7.

32   Lenstra, 1991, op cit.

33   Jamison et al, op cit.

34   de Jongh, P E, 1989b, *The Process of Preparation of the National Environmental Policy Plan in the Netherlands*, paper prepared for Centre for Environmental and Economic Development workshop, London, 12 October 1989.

35   Lenstra, 1991, op cit.

36   de Jongh, 1989b, op cit.

37   Lenstra, 1991, op cit.

38 See *Environmental News from the Netherlands*, no. 1, Nov. 1990, pp. 6–7.
39 Gossop, C, 'Choose it or lose it — lessons from the Netherlands NEPP', *Town and Country Planning*, June, 1990.
40 Ibid.
41 Lander, R, Mass, R, 'The economics of sustainability', *Town and Country Planning*, June, 1990.

CHAPTER 14

1 Rayner, S, O'Riordan, T, *Chasing A Spectre: Risk Management for Global Environmental Change*, Occasional Paper no. 2, Council for Science and Society, London, April, 1990.
2 Giddens, A, *The Consequences of Modernity*, Polity Press, Cambridge, 1990.
3 Rayner and O'Riordan, op cit.
4 Hirsch, F, *Social Limits to Growth*, Routledge and Kegan Paul, London, 1977.
5 Gellner, E, *Plough, Sword and Book*, Collins Harvill, London, 1988.
6 See IUCN/UNEP/WWF, *Caring for the Earth. A Strategy for Sustainable Living*, Gland, Switzerland, 1991.
7 See Schmidheiny, S/Business Council for Sustainable Development, *Changing Course*, MIT Press, London, 1992; 'The business end of UNCED', *IIED Perspectives*, no. 8, Spring 1992, International Institute for Environment and Development, London.
8 See French, H F, 'Strengthening environmental governance' in Brown, L et al, *State of the World 1992*, Earthscan, London, 1992.
9 See Gore, A, *Earth in the Balance: Forging a New Common Purpose*, Earthscan, London, 1992.

Index

UNIVERSITY OF GREENWICH LIBRARY